Leisure and Recreation Studies
Series Editors: Stanley Parker and Sarah Gregory

3   Youth and Leisure

Leisure and Recreation Studies

1 LEISURE IDENTITIES AND INTERACTIONS
    by John R. Kelly
2 LEISURE AND WORK
    by Stanley Parker

Youth and Leisure

Kenneth Roberts
Senior Lecturer in Sociology, University of Liverpool

London
GEORGE ALLEN & UNWIN
Boston   Sydney

George Allen & Unwin (Publishers) Ltd,
40 Museum Street, London WC1A 1LU, UK

George Allen & Unwin (Publishers) Ltd,
Park Lane, Hemel Hempstead, Herts HP2 4TE, UK

Allen & Unwin, Inc.,
9 Winchester Terrace, Winchester, Mass. 01890, USA

George Allen & Unwin Australia Pty Ltd,
8 Napier Street, North Sydney, NSW 2060, Australia

First published in 1983

British Library Cataloguing in Publication Data

Roberts, Kenneth
   Youth and leisure.—(Leisure and recreation studies; 3)
1. Leisure—Social aspects—Great Britain
I. Title   II. Series
306'.48'0944   GV75
ISBN 0-04-301165-9

Library of Congress Cataloging in Publication Data

Roberts, Kenneth, 1940–
   Youth and leisure
(Leisure and recreation studies; 3)
Bibliography: p.
Includes index.
1. Young adults—Great Britain. 2. Leisure—Great Britain. 3. Social
classes—Great Britain. 4. Young adults—Great Britain—Recreation.
I. Title. II. Series.
HQ799.8.G7R62   1983   305.2'35   83-11770
ISBN 0-04-301165-9

Set in 10 on 11 point Bembo by Computape (Pickering) Ltd
and printed in Great Britain by Billing and Sons Ltd,
London and Worcester

Contents

		page	
	Preface		ix
1	Introduction		1
2	Youth and Leisure in Britain since the Second World War		9
3	Theories of Youth and Leisure		32
4	Engendered Leisure		60
5	The Adolescent Procession		72
6	Breaking Out		88
7	The Traditional Sociology of Youth and Social Class		102
8	The Reappraisal of Working-Class Youth Cultures		116
9	Youth Unemployment		131
10	Ethnic Minorities		145
11	Middle-Class Youth Cultures		158
12	Leisure Services for Young People		176
	Bibliography		193
	Index		207

Preface

Age disqualifies this book's author from first-hand, up-to-the-minute experience of adolescent leisure. I doubt whether this is a handicap. We all know how misleading personal impressions can be. I left school aged 16 in 1957, the era of Bill Haley and Elvis Presley, and affluent young workers. My starting salary was £260 per annum, but with an assurance of yearly increments until age 30, and a non-contributory pension at 65. These were the rewards for a grammar-school education, O-levels and A-levels. Elders said they envied our opportunities, then accused us of misusing our wealth and freedom. Teenage crime, marriages and illegitimate births were soaring. Many of us wondered why we were missing the action. By 1961 my salary was £415 per annum. This was for office work; better money could be earned labouring – £11 basic and £13 with bonuses and overtime, as I discovered before 'retiring' to college. Politicians told us that we had never had it so good. They were right, from their position. Our parents had never been able to adorn their youth with second-hand scooters, annual made-to-measure suits, holidays at Butlins and on the Norfolk Broads. But how could we 1950s' teenagers feel affluent when the bosses in our offices and factories were spending more on annual holidays than we earned in a year?

My standard of living did not decline upon forfeiting young-worker status and becoming a full-time student. University meant greater freedom – from parents, work schedules and the thought-control that accompanies the prospect of a secure and progressive career, plus a non-contributory pension. Many students are drawn to sociology because their own experience of society discords with 'realities' portrayed in the media, then amplified in domestic and peer-group interaction. I had always found it difficult to understand contemporaries who appeared happy to accept a lifetime of climbing incremental salary scales, the eight-to-five factory grind, who regarded their earnings as good money, and believed that adolescent leisure was a great time. By 1966, five years and two degrees after I withdrew from the workforce, sociology had transformed these earlier personal uncertainties into professional problems, and I completed my first research into how and why so many young people were and remain so deluded.

I now realise that many young people (and adults) have deep misgivings about their predicaments and futures, which they are unable to act upon, or even articulate. Many imagine that their own discontents are abnormal, and best concealed lest they be construed as personal defects. This is how the façade of the 'good life' is preserved. The reason why sociology must desert common sense for abstract concepts and 'jargon' is to penetrate life's everyday appearances, and analyse the structures that shape people's lives in ways that the subjects can rarely understand, let alone control. This is why no excuse is necessary for this book being essentially a sociological analysis rather than a participant's account of youth at leisure. The author has seen both sides: sociology wins.

The sociology of leisure has been one of my major professional interests for over a decade. Another has been the entry into employment, and, in recent years, the predicaments of school-leavers facing labour markets offering an inadequate supply of jobs. The following chapters draw extensively from, and attempt to cross-fertilise, evidence and theories from youth research and leisure studies. I accept sole responsibility for the product, while gratefully acknowledging the assistance of Tricia McMillan, who typed the manuscript, and Deborah Chambers for commenting upon, and provoking an extensive revision of, an earlier draft.

K. ROBERTS

1

Introduction

Youth, Leisure and Social Change
Since the Second World War, our leisure industries have been youth-oriented. Public-sector professionals – youth workers and, more recently, managers of sports and leisure centres – have been urged to occupy potential delinquents, and any other young people with too much spare time or money for their own and the wider society's good. Self-interest has set the commercial sector in pursuit of the teenage consumer. The postwar 'bulge', then a rising birth-rate between 1955 and 1965, made young people a growing market. The gap between adolescent and adult earnings narrowed. Teenage marriage became increasingly common during the 1950s and 1960s, but most 'affluent' young workers delayed matrimony, handed their parents nominal sums for 'board', and retained sufficient cash for discretionary spending to become the commercial leisure industries' prime targets.

This is changing. The birth-rate fell between 1965 and 1977. From the mid 1980s until the end of the century, the number of teenage consumers will decline, and the spending power of those remaining will shrink, unless they have prosperous and generous parents. In any event, youth's economic and cultural independence will be eroded. Youth unemployment mounted in the late 1970s, and government measures – the Youth Opportunities Programme, the Young Workers Scheme and the Youth Training Scheme – reinforced labour-market pressures towards lowering beginning workers' wage levels and expectations.

Industry's need for young people as producers is diminishing. How will the economy adjust to the demise of the teenage consumer with sufficient spending power to lead rapidly changing tastes in fashion and entertainment? How will young people react to their loss of wage-earning status? Since 1945, the compensation for educational failure and exclusion from progressive careers has been an early entry into well-paid employment. What will happen as this consolation is withdrawn? How can the leisure services assist? Will the young people seize opportunities for fun and games in youth clubs, or cheap day-time sessions at squash, swimming, five-a-side football and arts centres? Or do the leisure services need to devise radical alternatives to our now orthodox forms of recreation that were originally developed alongside the rhythm of industrial life, to be enjoyed at the end of the working day or week, and during annual vacations?

At the time of writing, in 1982, young people have still to develop typical responses to their new labour-market conditions, and full impact of other changes is also awaited. For instance, youth cultures have yet to respond to educational trends in process since the 1960s. Over 80 per cent of secondary-age children are now in comprehensives. The statutory school-leaving age was raised to 16 in 1972–3. More young people than ever are continuing in education beyond this minimum. If state grants for all 16-plus students are introduced, their levels are likely to affirm rather than relieve parents' financial responsibilities. These educational trends are complementing the erosion of young people's employment prospects to undermine their former financial independence. However, in other respects, educational and labour-market trends are on contradictory courses. The spread of 'permissiveness' and the 'decline in standards' have been criticised, but in terms of exam passes, educational standards have risen, and today's young people are as keen to work and more ambitious than any previous generations. Teachers have been assisting more young people to gain the qualifications necessary for 'success', while job prospects have deteriorated. How will youth cultures respond to these contradictions? Will young people be more defiant? Or will they become more easily controlled, and 'responsible'?

The 'feminist revolution' is a third time-bomb that has still to explode on most youth scenes. Later chapters will explain how surveys of early leavers and secondary-school pupils continue to reveal the familiar gender differences in leisure habits. Playing and watching sport are still predominantly male activities. Girls are more interested in dancing and discos, and spend more time than boys baby-sitting, shopping and visiting relatives. Will these differences persist? Or will the feminist movement spread beyond 'the literature' and the lives of a highly educated minority? In secondary schools, it is becoming unacceptable to track girls into domestic science and commercial subjects while boys are introduced to workshops and technical skills. Efforts are being made to rectify girls' reluctance to succeed in maths and science. According to the letter of the law, careers guidance and placement can no longer discriminate between the sexes. Women's groups have embarked on consciousness-raising missions throughout the country. It would be foolhardy to rule out eventual mass changes in young women's leisure habits, though unemployment could force teenage girls and older women back into the traditional domestic role.

Race is another source of change. Britain's ethnic minorities still account for less than 5 per cent of the population, but they are more numerous in most major cities' inner areas, and since the 1960s 'second-generation' blacks and Asians, educated and increasingly born in Britain, have been progressing through and beyond the secondary schools. They face discriminatory labour markets. Their rates of unemployment have been spectacular. White and black youth are not being assimilated in mixed peer groups and clubs. Blacks have begun to develop their own sub-cultural solutions. Rastafarianism is a particularly visible example. We are likely to learn about others during the 1980s.

There appears to be a time lag of a decade or more before young people at leisure respond to wider social changes. The next chapter will explain how the post-Second World War 'new deal' created the conditions for commercialised youth cultures, but rock 'n' roll swept the generation only in the late 1950s, and another decade passed before student movements made the headlines. Must we anticipate equally spectacular developments during the 1980s and 1990s? Youth cultures are not static, and this book will face the implications of continuing changes in young people's circumstances, but the only material we can analyse thoroughly is from youth cultures of the recent past – Teddy Boy, beatnik, punk and others. The following chapters explain how and why these youth cultures have arisen, and identify the consequences for young people and the wider society. This is our best – indeed, the only basis – from which to assess the likely effects of current trends.

Youth and Leisure Studies: A Case for Cross-Fertilisation
This is not the first book about youth and leisure. It is obviously more up to date than predecessors, but the main claim to originality is the cross-fertilisation of theories and findings from youth research and leisure studies. Youth and leisure research have ploughed an overlapping terrain: inevitably in so far as youth cultures are constructed during leisure time, through leisure activities. However, each set of scholars has been preoccupied with its own specialist problems. Youth researchers have recognised that youth cultures have risen with a broader growth of leisure, but have concentrated on tracing connections between peer-group relationships and activities, and the status of young people in the wider society, as defined by their families, education and labour-market experiences.

Leisure researchers have not overlooked young people. How could they? The young have been principal recipients of time released from work and, during postwar decades, were responsible for much of the growth in recreational spending. They are strongly represented among purchasers of cinema and theatre tickets, occasional foods, records, sports equipment and, indeed, most leisure goods and services. Leisure researchers have also noted the importance of youth as a period of recreational taste and habit formation. If a person is ever going to pursue a recreational interest, the chances are that he or she will first acquire the taste when young. However, leisure researchers have rarely tangled with youth theories. They have addressed leisure issues. Does the growth of leisure enlarge opportunities for satisfying life-styles? Which recreational facilities will match people's needs? Does leisure obliterate or reflect broader social divisions? Meanwhile, youth researchers have developed and tested contending theories of adolescence. Is it a period of strain, turmoil and intergenerational conflict, or a process of socialisation into adult roles? This book attempts a closer amalgamation of youth and leisure theories than previous interpretations of youth cultures. It will show that to understand youth cultures we must draw upon theories about leisure's properties and role in modern societies, and that introducing leisure theories allows us to put rival interpretations of adolescence to compatible and more effective uses.

Drawing together the evidence and arguments from youth and leisure research will draw attention to some gaps. We know more about boys than girls, and more about working-class, particularly delinquent youth, than middle-class or even 'ordinary' working-class young people. An exception arose in the late 1960s, the period of student unrest, when the perpetrators briefly became the most researched members of their age-group. Other lacunae will be noted in the following chapters. One reason for taking stock of what is already known is to identify gaps. This book's conclusions include questions for further research to pursue and answer about past and present young people's leisure, in addition to future developments that wider social trends have already set in store.

There are many possible ways of handling the existing material on youth and leisure. The best method must depend on the objectives. Successive youth styles – Teds, then mods, then skinheads and so on – could be examined in successive chapters. Types of leisure activity such as sports, the arts and drug use would supply an alternative organising scheme. This book proceeds differently because its main purpose is to analyse and explain rather than simply describe. Chapter 2 reviews the development of youth cultures since the Second World War. It describes when and how different groups of young people have adopted discos, spectator sport, denim and marijuana – the raw material for analysis in the remainder of the book. Why not let this material, the historical record, speak for itself?

First, we need to improve upon, not simply reinforce, everyday common sense. Focusing upon different youth styles and leisure activities would 'feel' authentic only because these are the terms in which we are accustomed to hearing youth and leisure discussed in the media, and by young people. Treating fads, fashions and leisure activities one by one obscures important features of the youth scene, such as common tendencies and long-term trends. Much of the flux and heterogeneity is superficial. The next chapter emphasises the massive continuities since the 1950s.

Secondly, instead of just adding new material to previous analyses of youth cultures, we must advance theoretically. Chapter 2's survey of postwar youth cultures identifies the main features to be explained –particularly the persistence of social class and gender divisions. Contemplating the historical record defines these issues, but does not supply answers. Chapter 3 outlines, notes correspondences and points of disagreement in existing theories of adolescence, then the role of leisure, and distinguishes different interpretations of youth cultures' sources and consequences. Which interpretations best fit the leisure patterns of different groups of young people is best determined through a detailed analysis of the role of sex and gender within youth cultures (Chapters 4 to 6), and the latter's relationships with the wider system of social stratification (Chapters 7 to 11).

This book's organisation is geared to building a convincing account of how and why different types of youth culture emerge, their consequences for different groups of young people, and the wider society. To date, neither leisure scholars nor youth researchers have offered entirely satisfactory answers. Hence our uncertainty of the most appropriate responses to current trends in education, employment, gender roles and ethnic relations.

On Culture

Theories and definitions of youth and leisure are fully discussed in Chapter 3, but the term 'culture' requires prior treatment. It is scattered throughout the preceding and following pages. Their interest in youth 'culture' is a main overlap between youth and leisure research. What does the word mean? Virtually all sociology and anthropology students learn E. B. Tylor's (1871) definition: '...that complex whole which includes knowledge, belief, art, morals, law, custom and any other capabilities and habits acquired by man as a member of society'. Sometimes the phrasing is shortened to 'all learned behaviour which has been socially acquired' (Firth, 1951). The key point is that cultures are heritages, transmitted not genetically but socially.

This concept may appear too all-embracing to possess any analytical value, but its breadth is the term's strength. It rivets attention on how we inherit not only 'things' – houses, tools and factories – but also ideas about how artefacts should be used. The concept also captures the dialectic of the individual–society relationship. A society's culture precedes individuals. It awaits newcomers as an external reality. But culture only exists in individuals' minds and actions. Culture is 'absorbed' through socialisation, but can also be 'used' to respond to novel predicaments. Individuals and generations add to, modify and sometimes lose aspects of their societies' cultures. Young people's ways of life are not constructed solely from their own ingenuity. They use materials and ideas derived from families, schools, workplaces and media. But young people do not become replicas of their parents. They can use the cultures they inherit to respond to new opportunities, like the growth of leisure time, and to solve their own problems, like escaping from childhood restrictions. All leisure behaviour is cultural. This is why individuals can 'freely' choose and even design novel recreations in ways that clearly reflect their statuses within their societies.

An additional merit lies in the concept's attention to the inter-relatedness of all aspects of a culture. Social anthropologists have emphasised how the beliefs and practices of simple societies amount to total, meaningful ways of life. Modern societies are more complex. People's lives may be objectively fragmented between work, education, family and recreation, but their experiences within these domains are not compartmentalised within individuals' minds. Reactions to work can depend upon family and educational back-grounds. Youth cultures are constructed from all young people's experiences, which is why their analyses differ from other youth studies. They are not another tedious specialism, examining another fragment of young people's lives, but trying to understand how young people make sense of and respond to their total situations.

In the following chapters, 'culture' will sometimes be prefixed. *Sub-cultures* are derived from parent cultures. All parents are also children, and it is pointless to try to distinguish self-sustaining cultures from derived sub-sets. A case could be made for always prefixing 'culture' with 'sub', but this would be unnecessarily clumsy. The following chapters therefore refer to sub-cultures only when parentage is at issue. As will be explained, the source of youth sub-cultures is controversial. Are the parents wider youth cultures, national cultures or class cultures?

Various types of culture can be distinguished. *Dominant cultures*, sometimes held to be produced by economically or politically dominant strata, are generally accepted throughout a society as common knowledge, good taste, proper conduct and so on. *Sub-ordinate cultures* do not challenge but 'negotiate' dominant values to fit the realities of life for subordinate groups. In contemporary Britain, educational success is generally valued. Those who fail may not dispute the desirability of educational achievement, but sometimes negotiate this value to insist that it is only worthwhile for the 'brainy'. *Oppositional cultures*, in contrast, contest everyday, taken-for-granted realities. Deschoolers dispute the value of formal education. Members of 'gay' cultures insist that homosexuality is neither perverse, bent nor queer. Opposition can be expressed in negativistic *contra-cultures* which do not seek to replace, but simply contest dominant values. According to some writers, certain youth cultures are contra-cultures in so far as, among peers, status is earned by successful truanting rather than educational achievement, and by vandalising instead of accumulating property. *Counter-cultures* go beyond defiance and seek to change society by promoting novel values and life-styles, maybe through play rather than work, love rather than war, and in communes rather than conventional families.

All these types of culture feature in the following chapters. Which youth cultures are subordinate, negativistic and counter-cultures? The ideas conveyed by the all-embracing concept are important, and culture is also useful when subdivided to distinguish the values and ways of life of various groups.

Theory and Practice
This discussion of 'culture' may be confirming the prejudices of practitioners at the 'coalface' in youth clubs and sports centres, who deal with 'real' young people who present 'real' problems that need immediate attention. Some practitioners do not conceal their contempt for academics who inflict steady streams of questionnaires, then withdraw into esoteric foreign languages, practise their disciplines in private among consenting adults, and refuse to compile 'banks' of useful knowledge to apply to real clients' real problems, to recommend policies and make decisions.

This war between theorists and practitioners is ill-founded. Useless theories are usually theoretically unsound. Practitioners are sometimes ineffective, not only because they lack answers but also because they are not addressing the right problems. Everyone is a social theorist, including hard-nosed practitioners. Everyone working in 'the field' subscribes to views on the character and problems of young people in this day and age, and these 'theories' are used all the time to diagnose predicaments and prescribe solutions for individuals, and for young people in general, by providing youth clubs or other recreational facilities. If the following chapters appear short of advice on 'What to do on Monday', this is only because they are challenging orthodox definitions of the 'youth and leisure problem'. Practitioners who want to be told only how to run youth clubs, or how to attract more young customers into sports centres, may find much that follows useless, but this is not because the arguments are devoid of practical implications. The following chapters are an attempt to rethink the entire issue of youth and leisure. Conventional answers often fail to work because they are designed in response to misleading questions. There may be no way of attracting all young people into youth clubs. The mistake could be imagining that this is the problem.

Education for leisure in schools and the Youth Service are discussed, but do not feature prominently in the following chapters. This is because the schools and Youth Service do not account for the greater part of young people's leisure time and activities. Whether these public agencies could become more influential, and thereby enhance the quality of life for adolescents, and throughout their future lives, is considered in Chapter 12, which synthesises the book's conclusions about the sources and consequences of young people's leisure styles, and the likely effects of current changes in their situations.

We need to understand how, why and with what effects youth cultures are constructed in order to determine the opportunities that must be offered if present-day young people are to reap maximum benefit from the greater quantities of leisure time they are likely to find at their disposal, not only during adolescence, but throughout the life-span. There are practical in addition to theoretically convincing reasons for refusing to look for ready-made answers among existing provisions. The latter may be 'missing the point'. This book does not ignore policy issues and practitioners' problems. It concentrates on how young people's leisure styles are constructed in order to assist, eventually, in formulating policies and designing provisions that will have the laudable consequences that youth and leisure practitioners have always intended.

2

Youth and Leisure in Britain Since the Second World War

Youth between the Wars

Before 1939 the majority of Britain's youth left school aged 14. Their risks of unemployment were considerable, especially in the older industrial regions. School-leavers with relatives to 'put in a word' and luck on their side obtained apprenticeships and other forms of training. The remainder competed for juvenile jobs in factories and offices, running errands, handling the post, brewing tea, sweeping floors, filling ink wells and generally assisting older workers. Adolescent employment was insecure. Apprentices were sometimes used as cheap labour, then dismissed once they had served their time. Unskilled youth were liable to lose their jobs upon growing 'too old' and eligible for adult rates. Until 18 or 21, young workers normally remained outside the trade unions, and were paid boy and girl wages for their juvenile contributions. During the 1950s and 1960s, we believed that this treatment of young workers had been consigned to history. Since the mid 1970s, young workers have once more become marginal members of the labour force – their normal status since the Industrial Revolution – but contemporary youth have not reverted to a 1930s situation. We now realise that young people's economic gains were precarious, but the cultural achievements of the postwar growth decades are less easily erased.

Until the Second World War, approximately a third of all working-class families lived around or beneath the subsistence level, and poverty was a normal condition during the child-rearing phase. Malnutrition was widespread. Boys' employment prospects were enhanced if they had acquired 'sturdy builds'. It was also an asset when working-class girls could impress employers with the stamina to cope with factory jobs. Families usually needed working children's modest earnings to supplement household budgets. The youngest were sometimes cosseted while their families enjoyed a brief period of relative affluence with fathers plus older siblings in employment, if jobs were available. School children's pocket money was usually counted in coppers, not shillings. Custom and financial sense required young workers to hand wage packets to their mothers, and receive pocket money in return. Young people only went 'on board' on becoming engaged, when they needed to save, or when they achieved adult rates at 18 or 21.

Commercial leisure, for those who could afford it, usually meant evenings at the cinema, Saturday afternoons on football terraces and/or Saturday nights at the palais. 'Modern' dancing swept the country between the world wars. Billiard halls were popular among young men with time on their hands, but this clientele made them 'out of bounds' for respectable youth. Public houses neither sought nor attracted mass teenage custom. Young men were more likely to be introduced to drink by workmates than as participants in a youth culture. Homes were places to practise crafts and hobbies: needlework, collecting coins, stamps or whatever, and, above all, for listening to the radio. By the 1930s the 'wireless' was becoming standard domestic equipment and, in some homes, provided almost constant background noise between the popular programmes which would be given the full attention of their audiences. Serious reading appealed only to the educated. Pianos were status symbols as well as musical instruments: ownership was confined to the affluent. Other families sufficed with gramophones. Adults and children could use their homes to entertain kin, neighbours and friends. As today, however, young people, especially males, were expected to 'go out' with their companions. Outside school there were opportunities for males to participate in team sports organised by churches, other voluntary bodies and work-based clubs. Rambling and hiking became popular weekend and holiday activities. Teenage labour was cheap, but so was public transport. Cycling also became a mass recreation. A decent machine was a status symbol, a position it has retained only among children.

As today, the street was a favourite meeting place for groups of young people who otherwise had nothing to do. Parents and other concerned adults were aware of the temptations and opportunities for mischief. Boys were at risk of delinquency. Girls had to avoid a different kind of trouble. The youth movements that were founded in the late nineteenth and early twentieth centuries, including the Boy Scouts, the Boys' Brigade and various federations of boys' and girls' clubs, saw their mission as rescuing young people at risk, spreading sweetness and light, religion and morality, filling time with innocuous or, better still, 'worthwhile' activities. Sports and hobbies were encouraged. Martial arts – marching, uniforms and brass bands – were also favoured as means of instilling industriousness, discipline, team spirit and related virtues.

Britain's working class has never been economically or culturally homogeneous. It has always contained its own status hierarchy, and distinguished the 'rough' from the 'respectable'. In prewar times, respectable families were usually headed by skilled or at least sober breadwinners, who held down regular jobs when employment was available and placed wage packets at their families' disposal. Their wives were good managers who kept their homes spick and span, polished front doorsteps, generally maintained standards and kept out of debt, even in times of financial hardship. In periods of relative prosperity, they would put enough by to treat their families to Christmas presents, day excursions on spring and summer Bank Holidays, and holidays away from home during Wakes Weeks, at Blackpool or other (usually local) resorts. The 'English Riviera' (the south-west coast) was beyond the means of most working-class families from the industrial north and midlands. Respectable families kept their children out of trouble – at home or otherwise in 'decent' company at Sunday schools and other approved organisations.

Youth clubs catered mainly for boys; they posed the overt problems. In any case, the prevailing view was that a girl's proper place was in the home, performing domestic duties on men's behalf in alliance with their mothers – a form of child labour which continues today. Mixed clubs, particularly the 'social' variety, where members were allowed just to sit and talk, often with music in the background, were regarded as experimental during the 1920s, and remained controversial until the Second World War. They were accused not only of tempting girls from their proper place, but also of encouraging promiscuity. The youth movements and clubs were nearly all voluntary enterprises, often attached to churches or Sunday schools. They were usually run by middle-class adults for working-class (male) youth – those 'in need', who were 'at risk', from families that lacked the material resources or moral character to keep their own out of trouble. The voluntary bodies never possessed sufficient staff or cash to reach out and organise all the young people who were considered needy.

It is only in retrospect that the prewar era has been identified as the youth movements' golden age, when they possessed a clear sense of purpose, attracted thousands of committed voluntary workers, and reached as high a proportion of young people as were ever to become attached. After 1921 local authorities were permitted though not required to establish their own clubs or to support voluntary bodies, but public spending was under restraint throughout the interwar period, and nation-wide public provision had to await the outbreak of war in 1939. The welfare of the entire 14–20 age-group was then made a Local Education Authority (LEA) responsibility, and this position was confirmed in the 1944 Education Act.

There was another kind of growing up in prewar Britain. Less is known about upper- and middle-class youth from government reports and social surveys: they were not considered 'a problem'. But there is plenty of information in novels and autobiographies about the Oxbridge Set and the life-styles of Britain's 'bright young things'. The post-1945 expansion of secondary and higher education, and the growth of traditional professions, plus new science and technology based managerial and executive occupations, has now brought us to the threshold of a middle-class society, in which manual employees will be a minority, not the mass of the workforce. The prewar middle classes, in contrast, were a relatively small and privileged minority, albeit one which felt threatened by progressive taxation, the shortage of domestic servants and the rising costs of a decent education.

Middle-class children were sent to 'public' or secondary schools of some description that offered a 'grammar-school education', as it had become generally known. Access was normally by payment. Some scholarship places were available. Working-class children who failed this hurdle continued at elementary school, but one hallmark of middle-class status was that children could claim a secondary education as a birthright. Fee-paying places were available at independent and LEA grammar schools. Before the Second World War, only a small minority of middle-class youth proceeded to higher education. Upon completing secondary school, usually at 16, the majority entered family businesses, the professions or other secure and progressive careers, assisted by parents who could use influence or pay premiums. Professional training was offered on the assumption that trainees would be supported by their families. Secondary education beyond the statutory leaving age is still offered on this same assumption. In the 1930s, many middle-class girls were still being educated primarily for marriage rather than occupational careers. For some, 'coming out' was the goal of their education and subsequent occupation. Others were placed in respectable professions, including teaching and nursing, that, by the end of the nineteenth century, the middle classes had colonised for 'ladies in waiting' and those who 'failed' to marry.

Middle-class youth from sufficiently prosperous families were able to join the 'smart sets' in their areas. Entry was confined to individuals with good backgrounds, who could obtain introductions and invitations, and who could afford the clothing and other expenses associated with house parties and society restaurants. Between the wars, motoring and flying joined country sports as prestigious and exciting leisure activities (Howkins and Lowerson, 1979). There were 'black sheep' and others who occasionally overstepped the limits, but in general the behaviour of middle-class youth was never defined as a problem requiring attention from the police, courts or youth organisations. Middle-class lads did not join the Boys' Brigade, and the latter never sought such recruits, except as leaders. Middle-class families did not leave their children at risk, and had no desire to expose their young to possible corruption.

Like the working class, only more so, the middle classes contained a series of levels. Families on the fringe scraped and saved to offer their children a decent education. Did the young people from such homes enjoy any leisure? Their predicaments did not lead to government inquiries. Nor did they draw attention to their own problems. But where parents lacked the means to finance out-of-home middle-class life-styles, yet were nevertheless determined not to risk the children's prospects by allowing them to associate with the working class, young people's leisure opportunities must have been very limited. In postwar Britain, social-class differences have never disappeared, but former divisions have been blurred, and young people from 'middling' families have probably been principal beneficiaries.

Postwar Britain's New Deal for Youth

In many respects the Second World War was a watershed. There was little redistribution of private wealth benefiting the mass of the people. The gap between the highest and lowest incomes remained virtually as wide as ever. But Britain's wartime babies grew towards maturity in what was then regarded as the world's most advanced welfare state. By the end of the 1940s, over 90 per cent of the population was being cared for by the same National Health Service, and over 90 per cent of children were being wholly educated by the state. The 1944 Education Act decreed secondary education for all, and abolished fee-paying in local-authority schools. Subsequently only a limited number of direct-grant establishments qualified for public support for the education of fee-paying and scholarship pupils. In 1947 the school-leaving age was raised to 15, and by then the majority of middle- and working-class children were attending LEA primary schools and facing the 11-plus, and in most parts of the country were subsequently tracked into grammar and secondary modern schools.

It became apparent during the 1950s that inequalities of opportunity had survived these changes. Middle-class children were over-represented in the grammar schools, but half of the pupils in these schools were from working-class homes (Halsey, Heath and Ridge, 1980). The growth of white-collar employment increased the demand for qualified school-leavers, and reinforced demands for social justice. After 1949 (means-tested) grants became a right of all young people (and adults) who were offered university places. Trainees in the professions were rewarded with (usually modest) salaries, and the practice of charging premiums gradually lapsed.

The mainly working-class school-leavers who entered the labour force at 15 benefited from the postwar labour-market conditions. Full employment was achieved in most parts of the country. Firms began to complain of labour shortages. Employers' associations and trade unions joined the government in encouraging a revival of the apprenticeship system. As a result of these changes, 'juvenile' jobs and wages were swept from the youth labour market. Employers wishing to compete were obliged to offer either genuine training or decent pay with opportunities to advance rapidly towards full adult wage levels. Affluent teenage workers enjoyed an elevated status at home. Many went 'on board' early in their working lives, sometimes from the outset. Having paid their board, they were left with considerably greater spending power than their prewar counterparts. Parents who benefited directly from full employment and higher wage levels found themselves able to 'spoil' out-of-school youngsters, and school-children as well, whose pocket money was boosted by their families' affluence.

The above developments had rather different implications for boys and girls. Boys took advantage of the expansion of higher education, especially in science and technology. Girls were recruited into the expanding white-collar proletariat as secretaries, typists and operators of other office machines. Apprentices were overwhelmingly male, except in a handful of traditionally female trades, like hairdressing. Working-class girls from the secondary-modern schools were recruited as assemblers, packers and operatives in light manufacturing industry. Secondary and further education anticipated, or helped to determine, boys' and girls' futures. Boys were encouraged to study technical subjects, while girls went into domestic science and commercial courses – usually typing.

Britain entered the postwar era with a statutory local authority Youth Service, responsible for the welfare of 14- to 20-year-olds. As we shall see, this Youth Service has never discovered a generally accepted role. It has never achieved contact with more than a third of its age-group at any single point in time. Youth work's heyday was before it became a nation-wide statutory service. But the postwar leaders were unaware that their greatest glories lay in the past when they set out to discover and respond to young people's needs.

During the first postwar decade there were national surveys of uses of leisure among secondary schoolchildren (Ward, 1948) and out-of-school youth (Wilkins, 1955), plus many local studies. These investigations have left a detailed and reasonably comprehensive portrait of young people at leisure in the immediate postwar years. The new Youth Service, composed of voluntary organisations recognised and assisted by local authorities, plus the latter's own clubs, proved successful in recruiting approximately three-quarters of school-age youth. It was discovered, however, that when they left school young people also usually relinquished membership of youth clubs. Young workers considered clubs childish. The postwar investigators also discovered a trend, with age, away from the older uniformed organisations towards membership of social clubs, whether run by churches or local authorities. This developmental pattern, and the tendency for school-leavers to drift out of contact, have reappeared in all subsequent inquiries. Despite the postwar optimism, the Youth Service has never established a viable role with the majority of out-of-school teenagers.

The postwar investigators also noted, but did not make an issue of, the sharp differences between boys' and girls' leisure habits. Women had been emancipated, or so it was believed. The remaining gender differences were considered natural, or socially necessary. Boys went out the more frequently, and had the higher participation rates in sport. Girls had less to spend, partly because parents treated boys more generously with cash in hand if not presents in kind, and also because they earned less. (This still holds today: female teenagers' earnings average only 80 per cent of male wages.) It was found that the girls stayed in for more evenings, rarely practised sports, and named 'dancing' as their preferred activity on nights out. Some commentators suggested recognising dancing as a sport: it made a more widespread contribution to physical fitness among out-of-school youth, especially girls, than traditional team games, and improving health, fitness and character rather than mere enjoyment had always been the main goals of the physical training/ recreation movements. Boys' and girls' uses of their evenings out have subsequently changed, but all later inquiries have confirmed the main gender differences that emerged in the early postwar studies. Girls' lives are still the more home centred, and sport appeals mainly to boys. Later chapters will emphasise the extent to which girls' leisure remains unidimensional. Whether they stay in or go out, girls tend to be preparing for courtship or marriage. Boys develop broader tastes, and are offered multidimensional opportunities.

The second cleavage, evident throughout the country, that attracted comment from Welfare State youth's initial investigators, followed social-class lines. The prewar division between elementary- and secondary-school youth had not disappeared, but simply been displaced. Grammar-school education made the greater demands upon pupils' time; they had homework and longer journeys to school than those attending secondary moderns. Despite this, the grammar-school pupils were found to be the more active in a wide range of approved recreations: more likely to participate in sport, attend church, practise hobbies and attend youth clubs of all types – uniformed and social. The postwar Youth Service has never aimed to cater mainly for the privileged, but all subsequent inquiries have confirmed young people's behaviour as creating this social imbalance in clientele (Douglas, 1968; Prosser, 1981).

Secondary-modern pupils, and subsequently early leavers from comprehensives, have been the commercial leisure industries' main teenage customers. In the immediate postwar years, this meant being the more frequent cinema-goers, football spectators (if male) and dancers (especially girls). In the late 1940s, before the age of mass televiewing, the cinema was far and away the most common destination when young people 'went out'. Saturday night was the main occasion for leisure, as it was before 1939 and remains today. Adolescents 'go out' on other evenings, but for generations virtually all young people have recognised Saturday night as a time for out-of-home recreation. Throughout the 1950s grammar-school pupils remained protected, or they were marooned by families, schools and youth organisations, while other young people were entering employment, then using their wages to sample commercial recreation. But until the latter part of the decade, commercial provision was limited. There were cinemas and dances – to live bands at the major palais, and to records (Victor Sylvester and his competitors) at less flashy venues. Working-class girls often caught the 'dancing bug' immediately on leaving school, whereas boys were slower to acquire the habit.

There were no references to public houses in the early postwar studies of young people at leisure. Even coffee bars had still to establish themselves on the youth scene. 'What to do?' emerged as a major leisure problem among working-class early school-leavers. They could not afford to dance or visit the cinema every evening. Youth clubs did not appeal. Staying in was considered dull. 'Boredom' has proved another persistent problem, discussed in nearly every subsequent report on working-class youth's leisure.

The 1950s: The Rise of the Teenage Consumer
The 1950s saw the birth of commercialised youth cultures. Working-class teenagers possessed the necessary spending power. Financial independence led to cultural independence, and the leisure industries began to recognise youth as a distinct market. Purveyors of additional leisure goods and services joined the cinema chains, and became aware of the teenage consumer who earned 'good money', bore minimal domestic responsibilities and therefore possessed considerable disposable income (Abrams, 1961). Earlier generations of young people had dressed up to go out in adult fashions. Teddy Boys

set a new trend with their drainpipe trousers, drape jackets, velvet collars, bootlace ties, crêpe-soled shoes and greased hair (Rock and Cohen, 1970), and seemingly endless sartorial styles have subsequently been aimed, initially, at the teenage market.

The music industries learnt to profit from teenage affluence during the 1950s. Music had already become a mass-marketed commodity, initially in sheet form, then on discs for domestic gramophones. The importance of radio plugging to create hits was also firmly established. The new development in the 1950s was designing the commodity for a specifically teenage market. Part of the technique is to allow young people to identify with 'their' performers, sounds and lyrics, disguising how all artists must 'sell out' in order to become stars (Harker, 1978). When artists and songs won popularity face to face, performances had to be tailored to the varied tastes of many publics. Mass-marketed hits are manufactured to a different formula that seeks common denominators, which usually requires lyrics to be stripped of political and other controversial meanings. Christmas themes are useful. Everyone is supposed to enjoy Christmas, and it is the period of peak record sales. Hence the success of 'White Christmas' and 'Rudolph' as all-time best-sellers. How many individuals, old or young, would name these as their favourite songs?

All pop styles and stars are products of the industry rather than authentic statements of young people's feelings and interests, but their success depends upon the audiences being allowed to attach their own, sometimes disparate meanings, and to make their own uses of the products, as when Bill Haley and His Comets first introduced rock 'n' roll to Britain in the film *Rock around the clock* and inspired riots in cinemas. Elvis Presley and his numerous rivals and imitators led to a steady rise in record sales. During the 1960s, 'groups', notably the Beatles, replaced solo artists at the top of the charts. Styles and stars have proved ephemeral, but 'pop music' remains targeted at youth – they buy records. Their 'own' music has become part of virtually all environments where young people congregate. Dancing to hit records at discos has become 'in', not second best. The older palais with their live bands have all but disappeared. Those that remain have been deserted by the young. Pop festivals and concerts have filled the gap left by the music hall which was obliterated by radio, then television.

During the 1950s cosmetic manufacturers began to appeal specifically to teenage spenders, as did a branch of the catering industry. Cafés became trendy by installing juke boxes, and the coffee-bar society was born. However, at the end of the decade, public houses and manufacturers of alcoholic drink had still to begin trying to tempt teenage consumers.

Researchers and government committees (Crowther Report, 1959) drew attention to how young people's leisure was becoming more independent and less controlled. The end of National Service was seen as accentuating this trend. The case for and against conscription has never been debated solely on defence grounds, but also in terms of whether young people, and the wider society, need the 'discipline'. During the 1950s sociologists began drawing attention to the 'eclipse of community'. Working-class families were being rehoused from 'traditional' inner-city areas with their poor housing but often rich social textures of neighbourliness and kinship networks built over generations, into soulless high-rise flats and facility-bare suburban estates. The decline of traditional industries and occupations, such as dockwork and ship-building, was making it increasingly difficult for son to follow father. These trends were seen as accelerating young people's release from adult controls, setting them free to decide how to use their leisure time and money (Cohen, 1976).

Surveys showed that young people were spending less time 'at home' than formerly. The 14- to 16-year-old boys in Willmott's (1966) survey in Bethnal Green 'went out' five nights a week, on average. The life-styles of these youngsters may have been unusually outgoing. A 1960 survey among 471 Cardiff 15- to 18-year-olds reported 50 per cent of evenings still being spent at home (Crichton et al., 1962). But the trend was unmistakable. Books appeared castigating parents and teachers for abdicating their responsibilities and subjecting the wider society to a 'teenage tyranny' (Hechinger and Hechinger, 1964) as young people filled the vacuum with their own allegedly anti-social values and practices. During the 1960s, London became internationally renowned for its swinging scene, with young people leading the action. By then they had become the undisputed pioneers in fashion. Their tastes dictated general trends in dress, coiffure and music. Young people set the pace, and adults followed. A series of former teenage idols have subsequently been repackaged for family entertainment.

By the end of the 1950s, two further trends were attracting comment: the beginnings of the 'transport revolution', and the advent of television. Transport was discussed from two separate perspectives, depending upon which young people were studied. Sometimes the inadequacy of public transport was seen as the problem. Young people on outlying estates, and in small towns and villages, complained of their isolation from the 'bright lights' (Leigh, 1971). Public transport was becoming expensive, and less frequent. The bicycle was no longer a solution. Young people on outlying estates had longer distances to travel to leisure, on more congested roads, and, in any case, the bicycle had the wrong image for a fashion-conscious generation. During the 1970s the bike enjoyed a revival – mainly as a children's toy, and by then motor cycles, scooters and the family car had accelerated pedal power's decline as a means of transport.

At the end of the 1950s other commentators were debating what we now recognise as the complementary aspect of the transport revolution. They were discussing the implications of young people acquiring their own motors. A suitably decorated scooter became a 'mod' fashion in the early 1960s, while 'traditional' young people, the 'rockers' who dressed in black leather and colonised transport cafés, made the motor bike into a cult object. Investigators noted that, for young people, motor transport meant liberation – still greater freedom from adult controls. Representatives of older generations began to define this liberation as a problem when their favoured seaside and inland resorts were invaded. However, Britain's motor-cycle industry failed to read and exploit these trends. Domestic manufacturers continued to produce sports bikes and machines for the working-class family man, in diminishing quantities. It was left to European and subsequently Japanese manufacturers to style machines for the ascendant youth market.

In the United States, by the end of the 1950s, two-thirds of 19-year-old males and a half of all females were licensed drivers with vehicles at their disposal – usually their parents' (McFarland and Moore, 1961). For young people a car is more than a means of transport. It is a status symbol and offers privacy – a mobile lounge that can be transported far from adult supervision. Two-car families are still much less common in Britain than North America. Most British 17- and 18-year-olds are neither licensed drivers nor encouraged to use family vehicles as private leisure centres, but the motor car has become another common 'liberating' possession among older adolescents.

At the beginning of the 1960s over 90 per cent of British households possessed televisions, and the first inquiries had probed the effects on family life and, in particular, on children. There were fears that sex and violence on the small screen would corrupt the young. Subsequently this concern has escalated rather than subsided, elevating Mary Whitehouse into a national figure. We now know that films and television programmes can affect viewers' behaviour (Eysenck and Nias, 1978), but the effects depend upon personality. Individuals with violent predispositions are the more likely to be influenced by relevant screen models. Viewers' reactions also depend upon how screen sex and violence are placed in a context. 'Ritual' violence in horror films and Westerns makes less impression than when the action occurs in 'real-life' settings. In the 1950s there were additional worries: that television would make children passive and distract them from homework. These fears were quickly laid to rest. It was discovered that, in homes with sets, television accounted for approximately a third of children's leisure time, but mainly at the expense of radio and the cinema. 'Serious' reading, sports participation, membership of clubs and educational performances were unaffected (Himmelweit *et al.*, 1958).

Throughout the 1950s television closed down during the early evening from 6.00 to 7.30 p.m. The subsequent extension of broadcasting hours has drawn schoolchildren into the ranks of the nation's heavy viewers. Primary-age children now equal the national average of approximately nineteen hours a week (British Broadcasting Corporation, 1974). Out-of-school youth, in contrast, view less than any other age-group, apart from infants. Before the end of the 1950s, the networks were attempting to win the youth audience with *Oh Boy* and *The Six-Five Special*, forerunners of *Top of the Pops*. Specific programmes have captured teenagers' imaginations. Within some peer groups, these programmes become almost compulsory viewing and staple topics for conversation. Young people often model their own behaviour on television performers – not the violent characters, but those who demonstrate the arts of handling interpersonal, heterosexual relationships (Noble, 1975). Television is often young people's normal, sometimes their sole domestic leisure activity. They 'use' television, but 'the box' has never counteracted young people's desire to 'go out'. To the relief of some and the disappointment of others, television has never pacified the younger generation.

Television, scooters and rock 'n' roll left some 'traditional' features of adolescent leisure unscathed, including gender differences. In 1960, on average, boys still commanded more spending power than girls of the same age, whether received from parents or earned in employment (Carter, 1962), and girls were still spending the greater number of evenings at home (Crichton *et al.*, 1962). Within the youth culture's motorised sectors, the girls were placed on pillion and passenger seats. The new commercialised youth cultures reflected rather than challenged the traditional sex balance. Girls' leisure remained relatively unidimensional. They were invited to use cosmetics and clothing to make themselves attractive appendages to male peer groups, and objects for boys' leisure.

Class differences also persisted. If there was any change, the contrasts were sharpened. Throughout the 1950s, commercialised youth culture was a predominantly working-class affair. It was working-class kids from secondary-modern schools, the unqualified early school-leavers, destined for manual working lives, who became Teddy Boys and spent most evenings out, getting into new musical and other scenes. Middle-class youth attending grammar schools were cocooned from these influences by school work, caring parents and youth clubs. When grammar-school pupils took an interest in the new youth cultures, it was often from safe distances, by tuning to Radio Luxemburg, or jiving to pop records during intervals at school, church and youth-club dances.

The 'youth problem' of the 1950s - the commercialised youth culture that became associated, in press reports and public opinion, with rising levels of criminal and sexual 'delinquency' – was overwhelmingly a working-class phenomenon. It was not grammar-school pupils who instigated the property crime wave, or the park and street fights between rival gangs of Teds. Were the 1950s' teenagers really more delinquent than earlier generations? There were more goods to steal. Community controls were being eroded by rehousing and young people's own spending power. Society appeared less tolerant of violent 'games' in streets and playgrounds. The central role that pop music built in teenage social life probably helped to counteract criminal tendencies by dissolving monosexual male peer groups, according status to 'romantics' rather than 'belligerents', and isolating hardened criminals (Fletcher, 1966). Nevertheless, press analyses linked the spread of commercialised youth cultures with the rise in recorded delinquency. By 1960 indictable offences committed by 14-to 19-year-old boys had risen to twice the prewar level. All 'on-scene' teenagers came to be regarded as potential if not actual juvenile delinquents. 'African' rhythms and dances were condemned for encouraging promiscuity or, at least, precociousness and 'experimentation'. In 1962 there were 13,929 illegitimate births to 15- to 19-year-old girls, compared with 2,221 in 1938. The ascendant youth culture was held responsible for amplifying the risks of teenage pregnancy and shotgun marriage. The entire commercialised youth culture came to be defined as 'a problem'. It was claimed that young people with more money than sense were being exploited by commercial providers who offered trivia in sufficiently glossy packages to tempt teenage spenders, but failed to supply a basis for satisfying life-styles. Tried and tested values and community-based life-styles appeared threatened by a new candy-floss world of instant, brief thrills and soap operas (Hoggart, 1957). The youth culture's critics noted that some young people turned to crime 'for kicks' (Fyvel, 1963). During the 1960s a series of researchers endorsed this pessimism, arguing that, beneath the superficial gloss, boredom remained a major feature of working-class teenage leisure (Morse, 1965; Jephcott, 1967; Leigh, 1971).

By the late 1950s, the Youth Service had lost its postwar confidence; its clients were voting for 'trivia'. Moral crusaders, who regarded the commercialised youth culture as a problem to be treated, demanded action. Why were youth leaders so ineffective? The 1960 Albermarle

Report offered an answer: the Youth Service was still run on a shoe-string and its draughty church halls were unable to compete with the commercial sector. Subsequently the Youth Service was strengthened with cash and more trained leaders. The service widened its reper-toire. Uniformed organisations and social clubs were joined by detached workers seeking 'the unattached' on their own ground. Adventure training and community service were developed, most conspicuously under the Duke of Edinburgh's Award Scheme.

By the end of the 1960s, however, it was apparent that the service was not widening its appeal. Only 29 per cent of the age-group was attached – slightly less than in the 1950s (Youth Service Development Council, 1969). Most of the young people the service managed to enlist were still detaching themselves upon leaving school. In 1969, 46 per cent of 14-year-olds were attached, but only 9 per cent at the age of 20. These 'facts of life' led the Youth Service Development Council to recommend accepting that older and younger teenagers failed to mix. It proposed leaving a 'rump' Youth Service to cater for school-age adolescents, while out-of-school youth would be served by edu-cational and community organisations open to all age-groups.

These proposals have never been implemented. The 'failure' of the Youth Service has ceased to be a public issue. Some have despaired of any youth service becoming the saviour of the nation's young. Others have pointed out that, although the majority of young people are unattached at any point in time, over 90 per cent belong to some organisation at one time or another (Willmott, 1966; Douglas, 1968; Bone, 1972). If former clients can manage independently, maybe the Youth Service should consider itself successful. Is there any reason why it should aim to 'hold' young people up to 20, or any other arbitrary age?

The 1960s: Youth Cultures Surmount Class Barriers
Today proclamations of teenage tyranny and the arrival of Generation X (Hamblett and Deverson, 1964) would be dismissed as ridiculously alarmist. The 'youth problem' has been defused, and there is corres-pondingly less interest in whether the Youth Service is winning its age-group's minds and bodies. This is partly a consequence of famil-iarity. Skinheads, punks and even soccer hooligans are greeted with a sense of déjà vu. Teddy Boys and beatlemaniacs have become parents of later teenagers, and take it for granted that young people will embrace the latest crazes in dress and music. Delinquency and teenage sexual activity may be no more welcome than in the 1950s, but they are better understood. Short sharp shocks and psychotherapy are still recommended, but with less confidence that either prescription con-tains a cure.

Another development encouraging its acceptance has been youth culture transcending class divisions. During the 1960s middle-class youth attending grammar schools, comprehensives, even public schools, and certainly in the universities, ceased dressing and behaving like mini-middle-class adults. Sit-ins and demonstrations superseded rags. Blue jeans replaced suits, blazers and sports jackets. Pop ousted high culture from student unions. Teachers followed this tide, adopted denim and, in the colleges, joined the discos. Some took part in demonstrations instead of hosting sherry parties. Bright young people from impeccable backgrounds became beatniks, flower people and even rock stars. Instant reactions to hippies in lecture halls included forecasts of a generation gap superseding class conflict, and of classless youth offering a glimpse of society's future (Wilson, 1970).

We now realise that youth cultures have not grown entirely class-less. Early school-leavers and university students participate in different youth cultures. But whereas the 1950s' commercialised youth cultures were essentially working-class phenomena, since the 1960s educationally successful youth have been embracing comparable age-bounded styles, and working- and middle-class youth have been able to draw from each other's cultures. Marijuana and other soft drugs have spread from campuses to become part of most youth scenes. Students have drawn upon music and other pop industries. As a result, class divisions have been blurred, but never eradicated.

The 1960s' beatniks were not the first middle-class dropouts. Earlier generations had colonised Paris's Left Bank, New York's Greenwich Village and London's Bloomsbury, cross-fertilising radical politics with their eras' artistic and intellectual fashions, including jazz, existentialism and psychoanalysis. The angry young men of the 1950s left their mark in the theatre, cinema and novels, and on the New Left. From 1958 the Campaign for Nuclear Disarmament was organising massive marches, and the participants were mainly young, middle class and highly educated (Parkin, 1968). Then, during the 1960s, nonconformist styles spread throughout the student population, upwards among young adults, and downwards into the secondary schools. '

By the beginning of the 1970s the National Union of School Students was emulating its senior's militancy. New 'bohemian' quarters were established – Haight-Ashbury in San Francisco and St Ives in Cornwall – but the new 'hippie' settlements were not confined to these fringes. Squatters carried their culture into up-market neighbourhoods and council estates. Entire campuses became centres for cultural and political radicalism. American students led the fight for civil rights, and against the war in South-East Asia. In Britain, demonstrations against American involvement in Vietnam superseded campaigns against nuclear arsenals. By the end of the decade, students were at the forefront of world-wide struggles to liberate women and gays, and had cultivated marijuana as a major leisure drug.

There were numerous, often conflicting cultural and political tendencies within the 1960s' student movements. The Left divided into a series of perpetually warring factions. Other students were more interested in art, music and, in some cases, Indian mysticism. But as in earlier bohemian cultures, the 1960s' students fused politics, art, intellectual fashions and sexual ethics into novel life-styles and value systems. The new development during the 1960s was the extent to which these cultures were embraced by 'normal' middle-class youth rather than just a small fringe or progressive minority. College professors who explained how psychedelic drugs could heighten social and political awareness, and who blended Marxism with psychoanalysis to explore the interconnections between political radicalism and sexual liberation, became lecture-circuit celebrities, and whipping boys for 'straight' politicians and media.

Their inclusion in an account of youth cultures and their discussion alongside other leisure activities might appear tantamount to refusing to take student movements and politics seriously. This depends entirely on how working-class youth cultures are regarded. It was never possible to 'explain away' student radicalism as a symptom of sexual hang-ups and other adolescent frustrations. One instant diagnosis accused the entertainment industries of creating an aimless and superficial youth culture, then blamed the universities for succumbing to expansionist pressures, admitting students and hiring staff with no commitment to traditional university values, thereby opening their gates to mindless louts (Wilson, 1970). However, no one who actually investigated the 1960s' students concluded that the demonstrators were aimless, or their ideas superficial. The students' arguments deserved to be treated on their merits, and college authorities plus politicians learnt quickly to treat them in just this manner. Whatever the misgivings of head teachers, college principals, politicians and newspaper editors, intelligent and articulate middle-class nonconformists had to be taken seriously.

By the end of the 1960s the public was accustomed to listening while long-haired, denim-clad student militants unwound their philosophies. And this respect has slowly been extended to working-class youth. Youth cultures have become accepted parts of life in the advanced industrial societies. Teenagers can now crop their scalps, grow shoulder-length hair and/or dye it pink without being branded as requiring attention from police, courts, psychiatrists or even social workers. The spread of youth cultures into the middle classes has led to recognition that young people's ideas, tastes and activities cannot be dismissed merely because the actors are young. The case for decriminalising soft drugs has not yet been recognised in legislation, but it is taken seriously. Would it have been granted even this recognition if the pioneers had been working class? Was the pop culture of the 1950s really as vacuous, and were the Teddy Boys and rock 'n' rollers really as mindless as the media and even academic commentators once suggested? Could the young people have been trying to broadcast socially and politically significant messages? Since the 1970s working-class youth's styles in dress and music have been taken seriously, at least by a new generation of sociologists: the 1960s' students who then had to struggle to gain themselves a fair hearing (Hall and Jefferson (eds.), 1976).

Student cultures can be intellectually and politically credible, while remaining youth cultures. Students are a youth group. They have left childhood. Entry to full adult status remains in prospect, but is deferred. For economic sustenance, students depend upon parents and grants. In social terms, even mature students occupy an adolescent status. Students' life-styles are specific to their age-group, not their entire social classes of origin or destiny. During the 1960s middle-class youth started to exercise the independence that working-class teenagers had begun exploring a decade earlier. Middle-class youth's independence was based partly on the spending power bestowed by parents, maintenance grants and part-time jobs. Among students it was accentuated by living away from home, beyond parental supervision, and by the status students were accorded during the 1960s. Educationally successful youth were told by successive politicians and government committees that their abilities, qualifications and knowledge were in demand.

In expressing their independence, middle-class youth were able to draw upon the pop industries and cultures that had already been developed, mainly for and by working-class teenage consumers, but the 1960s' students were not passive receptacles; they used the available resources to pioneer their own styles, adding marijuana and other drugs, political philosophies and intellectual genres, in communes, squats, demos and sit-ins. The students were not merely supplying further evidence of adolescent turbulence. Their demonstrations were not mere 'proving offences' – means of asserting independence. Explaining student unrest required attention to the actors' political beliefs, educational and class circumstances. But was the social psychology of adolescence completely irrelevant? Keniston (1972) has advocated a psychohistorical perspective. It never diminished their politics to argue that the manner in which students expressed their convictions owed something to the psychodynamics of adolescence, and to the spread of leisure.

In certain senses, students are the new leisure class *par excellence* – free from parental supervision, usually without domestic responsibilities, at colleges where they can articulate discontents without damaging their longer-term career prospects, often with their tutors' sympathy, and sometimes encouragement. Students can drop out temporarily; a long-standing privilege for middle-class youth. Nowadays they are supported by student grants and welfare payments rather than families, and rely upon qualifications rather than kinship as passports back in. Of course, students are serious about their politics. But they are not pulling real political levers. They are not even taking irrevocable personal decisions. As Musgrove (1974) argues, student cultures are products of openness, freedom and lack of restraint – in other words, of leisure.

Before, during and since the 1960s, many students have been uninterested in politics and, indeed, all intellectual movements. Throughout the years of student unrest, the radical activists were a minority. Since the 1960s, campuses have been less turbulent. Fiercer competition for jobs has discouraged dropping out; ways back in are less assured. But students and other middle-class youth are still weaving the same mixtures of political convictions, intellectual fashions and pop materials into styles of life whose adherents become distinct 'types of people', defined by the youth cultures with which they align. Students are still the pioneers, and models for other aspiring young people in secondary schools and further education. Their styles have continued to spread into adult age-groups. Some 1960s' flower people are still wearing beards and denim, and smoking pot.

In addition to age divisions, there is now another cultural schism, moving up the age range year by year, between cohorts that grew to maturity before and since young people began doing their 'own things'. The latter have the greater understanding and tolerance of successive younger generations, of their own social class backgrounds. They have always shared some common resources with working-class teenagers, but student styles have remained distinctly middle class. It is working-class youth who have become skinheads with cropped hair, rolled-up jeans and industrial boots, expressing a perpetual interest in locating aggro and inviting trouble. Students wear denim in styles that give the clothing an entirely different meaning.

The 1970s and Beyond

It is difficult to keep abreast with teenage tastes in dress, music and hair artistry. The youth scene appears in constant flux – incomprehensible to adults. It puzzles young people as well, which is why so many spend so much time following the charts, noting the latest idols' coiffure and costumes. One way of demystifying young people's leisure is to distinguish and date the successive fads that have swept the charts and boutiques. A drawback is that such accounts inevitably grow out of date before reaching print. Another is that the attention to detail obscures massive continuities. An alternative strategy, adopted in this book, is to search behind the fads, and relate their common features to the predicaments and opportunities of the young people involved, as defined by wider social trends in education, employment and leisure.

The purpose of this survey of postwar youth and leisure is, therefore, not to distinguish a host of styles for detailed analysis in later chapters, but to reveal underlying continuities for further investigation. Fads are explicable in terms of commercial providers competing in markets where the purchasers have not established firm tastes, and must not be confused with historical trends reflecting structural changes in young people's positions, problems and prospects. My reading of the historical evidence detects only two major trends in postwar youth cultures: the birth of commercial youth cultures based on working-class affluence during the 1950s, and, since the 1960s, the development of comparable cultures among academic youth, mainly from middle-class homes, nearly all destined for middle-class careers.

By the late 1950s, the Teddy Boy, rock 'n' roll, coffee-bar working-class youth cultures were dividing into two distinct genres. Some young people were replacing Edwardian gear, and becoming elegant dressers in Italian-style suits, ties and shoes. Other successors of the Teds were cultivating the greaser style of heavy, rough, aggressive masculinity. By the mid 1960s, exponents of these trends were known as mods and rockers, who had respectively adopted the scooter and motor bike as cult objects (Cohen, 1972). The names have subsequently changed. Each genre has hosted a succession of fads. Skinhead and punk have been developed into comprehensive styles with complete repertoires of argot, dress, music and meeting places. But the division between working-class youth cultures that foster neat, cool, elegant appearances and tastes, and those whose dress and demeanour are calculated to offend, has persisted. Successive styles have attached themselves to particular types of music, bands, football teams and even political parties, usually surprising, sometimes pleasing, but often alarming their hosts. However, all these developments have occurred within established trends. The social foundations of the division between rough and respectable working-class youth cultures are reconsidered in Chapter 8. For present purposes it is necessary to note only that this division can be traced to the 1950s, and earlier, for prewar working-class communities distinguished rough from respectable families, streets, parents and children.

Since the 1960s, student movements have lapsed from news head-lines, but they are still blending the same mixtures of literary, politi-cal, high and pop cultures. The terminology has changed, but the flower people, beatnik and hippie genres which adopt leisure wear, denim and T-shirts as everyday attire, making dressing up to 'go out' unnecessary, are still alive. Changes in the educational and employ-ment contexts have altered the blends, but not the basic ingredients. Middle-class youth cultures have not evaporated. On-scene middle-class youth must take as much care to look casual, or to appear familiar with the latest gurus – Foucault or Firestone, depending on the movements to which they claim allegiance – as working-class youth who spend Saturday afternoons preparing themselves for the big night out.

There has long ceased to be any single dominant style in dress or music uniting either working- or middle-class youth. A variety of sartorial tastes are now catered for by specialist shops and market traders rather than chain stores. The rock genre has splintered. Numerous groups, radio stations and programmes appeal to special-ised tastes, not young people in general. Numerous tape- and record-producing companies, legitimate and pirate, supply shops specialising in different waves. The more persistent and popular fads are adopted by chain stores and major record companies, then mar-keted as fashionable leisure wear and family entertainment for the general public – by which time, now as always, the youth scene has moved on. The effervescence is bewildering until we realise that the flux occurs within grooves that have been running for more than twenty years.

Throughout the 1970s, the strongest impression from studies of young people at leisure was how little had changed since ten or even twenty years previously. There were new groups, hairstyles and sounds, but Saturday night remained the principal occasion for teen-age leisure when two-thirds of all young people 'went out' (Fogelman (ed.), 1976). Dancing and the cinema were still favourite destinations. In 1975, 16- to 19-year-olds were spending 50 per cent of their evenings at home, usually watching television (British Broadcasting Corporation, 1978), a virtually identical scene to that reported in Cardiff in 1960 (Crichton et al., 1962). Pop music retained and, indeed, strengthened its position at the heart of youth cultures. Trans-istor radios and cassettes took pop sounds on to otherwise quiet beaches and mountainsides, in addition to the ubiquitous discos.

Since the early 1960s young people have been taking up sport in growing numbers, as participants and spectators. At the beginning of the decade, Football League clubs were worried that they had lost a generation. Boys were still taken to matches by fathers, but soccer was not part of the 1950s teenage scene. Attendances were declining, and far-sighted directors saw no end in prospect if clubs could not capture the loyalty of young people. Would they return as adults, with their own children? During the 1960s, teenage peer groups began to colonise 'ends' and 'kops', first at Anfield and Old Trafford, then throughout the country. To the dismay of the football authorities, these young supporters refused to behave like 'proper' fans.

By the 1970s, 'football hooliganism' was a nation-wide problem. For some male peer groups, trips to 'away' matches had become major landmarks in their leisure calendars. Clubs discovered that even lower division crowds could prove troublesome inside grounds, and on their journeys to and from matches. The 'soccer hood' attracted attention from politicians, official working parties (Social Science Research Council/Sports Council, 1978) and researchers. Club managers and chairmen began to complain of hooligans driving out the true supporters. All-seater stadia and 'passports' were proposed as means of excluding the yobbos. Academics (Taylor, 1971; Clarke, 1977; Marsh et al., 1978a, 1978b) offered a variety of theories to explain the appearance of a new animal, the soccer hood, and sometimes failed to realise that, while new to football, hooliganism was a far from novel adolescent recreation. Until the 1950s, football crowds were drawn primarily from the skilled manual and lower white-collar strata (Dunning et al., 1982). Soccer hooliganism became a problem alongside changes in the composition of crowds. The teenage style is not new. It was rehearsed in cinemas, on streets and sea fronts before soccer grounds were colonised. Like other recent movements, football hooliganism has developed within an established type of youth culture.

Hooligans and vandals capture newspaper headlines. Does the public realise that many more young people play sport than watch live fixtures? During the 1970s there was a boom in sports participation, especially indoor sport, encouraged by the sports centres that appeared throughout the country. Sport has now become part of the youth scene. Sports gear is fashionable leisure wear for both sexes, but the active participants are still predominantly male and middle class (Sports Council, 1982). Working-class males predominate among football spectators. Soccer hooliganism is a working-class youth problem. In contrast, the young people who have been taking up sailing, badminton, squash, golf and other 'minority sports' are mainly middle class. Girls remain on the fringes of both sporting scenes. Levels of sports participation have changed, but the patterns still respect traditional class and gender divisions.

Another development since the 1960s has been the assimilation of alcohol into teenage leisure. Public houses have introduced juke boxes and live bands, and alongside licensed clubs and discos have largely replaced coffee bars as centres for teenage night-life. A national survey in the mid 1970s found that a half of all 16-year-olds had visited a public house during the previous week (Fogelman, 1976). Studies of 14- to 16-year-olds in secondary schools have discovered over a fifth spending regular evenings in pubs (Derrick *et al.*, 1973). It is impossible to make precise statistical comparisons, because public houses and alcohol were simply not mentioned in earlier surveys. Teenage drinking was not part of the 1950s' youth problem. During the 1970s, however, medical symposia began to discuss the growing problem of teenagers with early symptoms of alcoholism, and teachers' conferences were entertained by tales of pupils with hangovers, and groups returning drunk after lunch.

Alcohol is more widely available than formerly, for both adolescent and adult consumption. It is sold until the early hours in many of the clubs and discos where, in practice, neither admission nor sales are restricted to the over-18s. But drinking is not a specifically adolescent habit. It is akin to driving motor vehicles; the young people are participating in a broader trend. *Per capita* consumption of alcohol in Britain has doubled since 1950. Drinking in public houses has not increased. The main growth points have been licensed clubs, restaurants and, above all, off-licence sales (Smith, 1982). The British public has caught the wine habit, and spirit sales have also risen. Drink is now available in most homes, which is where young people are most likely to be introduced to the habit. Young drinkers are more likely to be emulating then defying their parents (O'Connor, 1978). Alcohol lubricates many parties held in young people's homes with parental consent. Young people are also emulating their elders when they take cans and bottles to country and seaside picnics, and to enliven journeys to football matches.

As noted previously, pills and joints have also become parts of the teenage scene in virtually all corners of the country (Plant, 1975). Glue-sniffing is cheaper, and in 1981 at least forty-five young people died as a result. The majority of young people know about and, if they wish, can purchase illegal drugs. However, alcohol (and tobacco) have survived this competition, and retain pride of place as the nation's main leisure drugs, among all age-groups. The popularity of these commodities transcends gender and class barriers. Among adults these social divisions are reflected in what, where and how much, rather than whether people drink (Smith, 1982). Middle- and working-class, male and female teenagers also assimilate alcohol into their characteristic leisure styles.

The following chapters will show that we can learn more about the sources and consequences of youth cultures by dwelling upon their enduring features than by struggling to keep pace with every fad and fashion. One persistent feature has been the divisions between the rough and respectable youth cultures of early school-leavers, and the middle-class youth styles nurtured by young people who continue to further and higher education. These divisions have been blurred, but they have never disappeared. Another persistent feature is that all postwar youth cultures have been male led. Girls have been invited to participate by dressing, dancing and otherwise acting to appeal to different types of male youth. Why have these features of youth cultures proved enduring? What can they tell us about the sources and consequences of young people's leisure practices? These are the principal questions raised by surveying postwar youth cultures. The theories of youth and leisure, particularly their interpretations of class and gender divisions, reviewed in the next chapter, suggest possible answers.

The likelihood of patterns and divisions that have bounded young people's leisure since the 1950s persisting into the future will become clearer once we have established their sources and consequences. Will young women begin using leisure to liberate themselves from traditional feminine roles? The 1970s was a decade of stagflation – high rates of inflation accompanied by economic stagnation and, after 1979, a period of decline. It was a decade that brought about major changes in the circumstances of young people. Must we anticipate profound repercussions on leisure habits during future decades? Will higher rates of male unemployment lead to more examples of role reversal? Or will unemployment force young women back into domestic roles and dependence on males? Will wagelessness lead to 'rough' working-class youth cultures overwhelming elegant styles? Or will the fiercer competition for jobs, and young people's dependence upon parents and grants, make them less defiant, more conformist? If and when unemployment threatens middle-class youth, when working-class school-leavers enter schemes or courses rather than employment, and as ethnic minority youth develop their own youth cultures, will the working/middle-class schism become increasingly blurred, less significant than other cleavages?

Firm answers must await further research, and the analysis to follow will specify the types of evidence for future investigators to collect. They cannot anticipate the findings, but the following chapters will permit informed speculation on the implications of current trends. As will become evident, my own guess is that established patterns and divisions among young people at leisure will prove resilient and adapt rather than be dissolved by emergent problems and opportunities.

3
Theories of Youth and Leisure

(A) On Youth

The rise of postwar youth cultures made young people a problem for many adults and an issue for academics. Biologists, sociologists, criminologists, psychologists, psychiatrists and educationalists have compiled an immense literature. Youth research is a well-established social-science industry that has been sliced into specialisms. There are experts on young people and education, the family, work and delinquency, but writers on all these topics recognise that the behaviour on which they focus – criminal, educational, vocational or sexual – is influenced by the youth cultures in which adolescents become involved. Investigators who have studied Teddy Boy, rocker, mod, punk and skinhead cultures have therefore not been carving out another specialism so much as trying to synthesise and generate a total understanding of young people's lives and values. Students quickly learn that in this, as in so many other fields, the experts are divided, and the main divisions are not all tidily organised along subject boundaries. Competing theories within subjects, especially sociology, have bred fiercely disputed interpretations of youth cultures. There has never been one proven and generally accepted theory explaining the significance of postwar developments among young people at leisure. Nor will there be, until the properties of leisure are taken fully into account.

Bio-Psychological Approaches
Biologists and psychologists have the longest track records in youth research. The initial statements of their still orthodox explanation of adolescent behaviour predate the First World War (Hall, 1916). These begin by noting the physical changes that accompany puberty, then trace the emotional and behavioural upheavals (Blos, 1962; Miller, 1969). Young people's bodies change shape. Hormones circulate, and reproductive organs come alive. It is argued that adolescents must learn to live with their new bodies and emotions, redefine their 'selves' and develop new answers to the identity question, 'Who am I?' Youth is regarded as the life-stage when individuals must relinquish childhood roles, experiment and form adult identities, convince themselves

and peers, then find congruent roles, usually as spouses, parents, citizens and workers. It is argued that this process is unavoidably traumatic – a period of storm, stress and turmoil for young people, and anyone who shares their company. Parents and teachers are advised that they must tolerate adolescent tantrums and defiance, even 'proving offences', as young people assert independence and test out developing personalities, sometimes using adult figures and authorities as negative reference groups.

According to this theory, postwar conditions did not create adolescence: the phase is seen as an expression of biological and psychological facts of life. However, it is accepted that the affluence and greater freedom of the postwar years made adolescence more visible than formerly. Young people act out their problems in public, and have their solutions broadcast by the media. As a result, youth may have become a greater nuisance, but the bio-psychological theory offers the consolation that it is merely a phase. Except in cases of 'fixation', troublesome teenagers become normal adults.

Adolescence as a Social Phenomenon
The sociology of adolescence was born as a critique of the above bio-psychological theory. Reuter's 1937 article was the first systematic attempt to conceptualise adolescence as a specifically social phenomenon. He queried whether growing into adulthood was really as stressful as biologists and psychologists were claiming, and whether the latter might have been misled by evidence mainly from disturbed and delinquent cases. Most important of all, Reuter noted that adolescence was *not* a universal life-phase. He quoted social anthropologists' evidence (such as Mead, 1935) from societies where individuals moved directly from childhood to adulthood, and noted that the chronological ages varied between cultures where adolescence was recognised. The inescapable conclusion appeared to deny that adolescence could be neither more nor less than an inevitable corollary of biological and psychological maturation. In his interwar study of *Plainville*, a small rural town in mid America, West (1945) observed that the word 'adolescent' never occurred in the local vocabulary. Subsequently sociologists have argued that the type of adolescence with which we are now familiar is a product of industrial civilisation, and have developed Reuter's tentative ideas about the features of industrial societies that create a disjuncture between childhood and adulthood.

First, children are segregated from many areas of adult life. Most occupations are practised behind closed doors, in offices and factories. Families and neighbourhoods no longer introduce the young to life in general. Schools cannot fill all the gaps. Rather than preparing children for adulthood, families and schools tend to 'shield' the young from many of adult life's realities. There is often a marked difference between the 'ideal' behaviour recommended and sometimes practised by parents and teachers, in front of children, and how adults deal with each other in politics, at work and in marriage. At home and school, children are often expected to enact values contrary to those required in later life. Childhood is an 'unreal' world of tolerated parasitism, legitimate dependence, submission and irresponsibility. As adults, by contrast, individuals are expected to be independent and accept responsibility for their decisions and actions.

Secondly, modern societies have a highly developed division of labour in which most positions are achieved, not ascribed. Marital partners are self-selected. Entry into most occupations depends on qualifications, not birth. Knowledge of a person's family background, schools attended and place of residence allows us to predict, with well-above-random odds of success, his or her future employment and the social group from which a spouse will be selected. Nevertheless, we subscribe to an ideology of free choice, and the *exact* positions any child will occupy are unknown. We feel that individuals ought to have scope to create their own futures. 'Training' children too narrowly would be resisted as restricting their opportunities, which limits the extent to which individuals can be prepared, during childhood, for their adult roles.

Thirdly, there is the problem of 'future shock' – the predicament of discovering that the societies for which we were socialised no longer exist – (Toffler, 1970). Industrial societies are forever changing. Today's children cannot be fully prepared for their adult lives, not only because the specific positions they will occupy are unknown, but also because the types of role that will be available may not yet exist.

Fourthly, social change always leaves a 'generation gap'. Young people are sensitive to new ideas, tastes and patterns of behaviour. The majority adopt their parents' political party loyalties, but if individuals are going to change, the chances are that they will 'deviate' while young (Butler and Stokes, 1969). As we move into adulthood, we become progressively 'set' in our political, domestic and leisure ways. In changing societies, each generation is reared in a different environment from its predecessor. For today's young people, the Great Depression is as much part of history as the Chartist movement. The same applies to the Second World War, the Cold War, the age of the Beatles and the student unrest of the late 1960s. Events that made a strong impression on older generations are beyond the personal experience of today's youth. The latter are exposed to new formative experiences, like entering labour markets in affluent societies that are unable to provide sufficient jobs for all school-leavers. The young cannot be adequately socialised within relationships of dependence on older generations because the latter are inevitably 'out of touch' with some situations, problems and opportunities that confront young people.

Fifthly, modern societies have no single ritualised point of transition. There is no age or ceremony following which juniors become adults – politically, economically and sexually. In 1967 the Latey Commission considered the possibility of rationalising the various ages of majority in Britain. The Report recommended enfranchising 18-year-olds, but concluded that there was no possibility of defining one age when all young people would become entitled to marry, vote, terminate education, financially independent and subject to adult rather than juvenile justice. Individuals acquire different adult rights at different ages. Physical maturity is reached at different ages by different individuals. The result is that young people occupy an ambiguous status 'betwixt and between', neither children nor full adults, which is why we need words like 'youth' and 'adolescence'. This life-phase begins when children first begin to assert independence from teachers and parents – normally, as later chapters will emphasise, through leisure activities in the company of peers – and it lasts until they assume the rights and responsibilities associated with adulthood, which usually, though not always, involves passing the age of political majority, marriage and, for males, entering employment, thereby becoming financially independent.

One point of agreement between biologists, psychologists and sociologists is that adolescence cannot be defined in terms of precise chronological ages. Psychologists and biologists explain that the onset of puberty and the socio-emotional responses vary between individuals. They also recognise that the ages when individuals enter adult roles and establish adult identities are equally variable. Sociologists agree, and add that there can be no precise beginning and end to adolescence, even for particular persons. One of the social sources of adolescence is the absence of any unambiguous conclusion to childhood, and any single point in time when all adult rights and responsibilities are conferred.

The Conflict of Generations

Some sociologists accept the 'storm and stress' version of adolescence. They concur with psychologists that, between childhood and adulthood, self-consciousness is heightened, self-esteem lowered and self-images become unstable, that young people are highly sensitive to others' opinions and often worry lest they are regarded unfavourably (Simmons and Rosenberg, 1973). Sociologists who share the disturbed and turbulent view of adolescence simply replace bio-psycho-logical with social-psychological explanations. Modern societies fail to provide youth with secure and stable roles. Hence, it is argued, if these same societies endow their young people with freedom and money, the inevitable result will be unstable and unruly youth cultures.

Teddy Boys, rock 'n' roll, juvenile delinquency, pre-marital sex, mods and rockers, blackboard jungles, student militants, punks, skin-heads, drugs and squatters – the series of youth movements men-tioned in the previous chapter, have stirred postwar public opinion, and as sure as night follows day, each wave of concern has been followed by a book or article analysing 'Generation X' (Hamblett and Deverson, 1964), and explaining that traditional institutions and values are threatened by teenage rebellion. Some politicians have lent their authority to the alarm. Spiro Agnew, the former US Vice-President, consolidated his conservative reputation by accusing the pop industries of corrupting young minds, spreading unrest, deviance and dissent. Academic writers have joined the chorus with forecasts of the generation war replacing class struggle. 'The conflict between generations is, today, more pronounced than the conflict between races, and, as a source of popular disturbances, it has eclipsed the class struggle' (Wilson, 1970). Some analysts claim that a latent conflict of generations exists in all societies, between the young seeking freedom, wealth and power, and elders who are reluctant to concede. This conflict is not a postwar phenomenon, but, according to one school of thought, it has subsequently become manifest rather than latent, the former equilibrium having been disturbed by young people with the resources to act, and by a changing society that generates new ideas, to which young people are particularly receptive, which 'de-authoritise' parents, teachers and established politicians (Feuer, 1969).

There are many versions of the inter-generational conflict theory. Instead of predicting collapse, an alternative scenario envisages fine, idealistic young people laying the foundations for a new, humane social order (Bednarik, 1955; Roszak, 1970; Paloczi-Horvath, 1971; Reich, 1972). Another variant approves of young people's idealism and defiance allowing society to conduct a continuous internal dia-logue about the validity of its norms and institutions.

Most versions of the intergenerational-conflict theory portray young people as the offensive party. In opposition, Musgrove (1964) has explained how, since the nineteenth century, lower fertility and mortality rates have reduced the proportion of children in the popula-tion, and permitted care and resources, as in education, to be provided on an unprecedented scale. He then draws attention to how these same demographic trends have left contemporary youth at the foot of long seniority ladders, and given adults a vested interest in keeping the young in their 'proper places' – in schools and colleges, in training for longer than is technically necessary, and other junior posts. Musgrove argues that modern societies have manufactured adolescence, then created the myth of youth as in an inevitably rebellious phase in order to justify the oppression of the young. Friedenberg is another writer who argues that teenage irresponsibility and instability are produced by the treatment young people are accorded by adult oppressors. 'Adolescents are among the last social groups in the world to be given the full colonial treatment' (1963, p. 4). In many schools, teenagers are presumed irresponsible. Their lives are regulated in minute detail. Uniforms are often compulsory, even for 16- to 19-year-olds. Even talking at mealtimes is sometimes defined as a privilege. How can young people be expected to act responsibly if they are denied the right to control their own lives?

Prescriptions for addressing the 'youth problem' depend upon who is blamed for any intergenerational conflict. Is the answer to persuade adults to relinquish their power and superior status? Should idealistic teenagers be encouraged to challenge conventions? Writers who fear anarchy advise adults to assert themselves, to oppose 'teenage tyranny' (Hechinger and Hechinger, 1964) and ensure that, as far as possible, the inevitable turmoil of adolescence is contained within harmless recreations.

Continuous Socialisation

Functionalist interpretations of youth cultures were first offered during the 1950s by researchers who found their evidence endorsing Reuter's doubts about strain, stress, rebellion and intergenerational conflict as *general* features of adolescence, even in industrial societies. The 'myth' of rebellious youth sub-cultures was attacked initially in 1955 by Elkin and Westley, who offered an alternative account of adolescence as a process of 'continuing socialisation'. These authors admitted that their fresh evidence was from a small and unrepresentative sample of 14- to 15-year-olds in a Montreal suburb, but all their main findings have subsequently been replicated in larger, more representative inquiries.

First, Elkin and Westley found that close relationships with parents were the norm, not the exception. This was noted in the more recent British National Child Development Study (Fogelman, 1976), based on a sample of individuals born in 1958. When interviewed at age 16, 86 per cent claimed to 'get on well' with their mothers, and 80 per cent with their fathers. In Schofield's (1965) survey among 14- to 19-year-olds, which dealt primarily with sexual behaviour, 79 per cent of the boys and 73 per cent of the girls agreed that, 'People should realise their greatest loyalty is to their family.'

Secondly, Elkin and Westley discovered that their young people respected parents' opinions on education, jobs, politics and even choice of friends. Once again, this finding has been repeated in subsequent inquiries (Remmers and Radler, 1957; Brittain, 1963). Peers are used as principal reference groups only for relatively 'trivial' decisions, like how to dress for a party. Far from 'immersing' their participants, 'youth values' appear limited to situations that young people themselves regard as transitory. In 1978 a National Opinion Survey asked Britain's 15- to 21-year-olds to name their most important influences. Only 6 per cent gave pop stars, whereas 66 per cent named one or both parents (quoted in Open University, 1980). Young people's loyalty to 'youth values' is confined to transitory adolescent situations, and even this limited loyalty appears to contain a strong ritual element. In the company of friends, young people often choose to appear 'on scene'. They do not wish to jeopardise their popularity by appearing odd, and this desire to conform and appear 'normal' obliges some to conceal their conservative 'private selves' from peers (Turner, 1964).

Thirdly, subsequent attitude surveys have confirmed Elkin and Westley's finding that most young people's values are thoroughly conventional. On education, they usually reflect whatever support and interest their parents display. Attitudes towards employment –the types of jobs young people rate as satisfying and desirable – are similar to adults' and usually, once again, reflect home influences. In politics, young people usually follow their parents' partisanship. Youthful extremists are untypical of their age-group. In the National Child Development Study, only 3 per cent of Britain's 16-year-olds rejected the idea of marriage (Fogelman, 1976). Nearly all young people support the family, expect to marry, and do so by their mid twenties. It is difficult to discover any issues, apart from tastes in dress, hairstyles and music, where it is possible to identify specifically adolescent points of view. On most issues young people express the same range of opinion as adults. Texts that treat older generations as uniformly conservative, then focus upon delinquent or otherwise ostentatious youth, portray a misleadingly wide generation gap. Over 90 per cent of teenage boys are *not* convicted of criminal offences in any year. Kandel and Lesser's (1972) study of young people and adults in Denmark and the United States found that attitude differences between these countries were much sharper than intergenerational differences within the societies.

Fourthly, independent inquiries have confirmed Elkin and Westley's doubts as to whether youth is a period of psychological turmoil. Peer relationships may be fluid, adolescents may possess slightly lower self-esteem and their self-concepts may be more changeable than those of adults, but it is misleading to imagine that young people possess no stable values and ideas about their interests, abilities and futures. Following his research among 15- to 19-year-olds from various parts of Britain, Kitwood (1980) has argued that young people's main problem is not establishing but protecting self-identities. Their lives, like many adults' in contemporary societies, are fragmented. They receive different treatment from different teachers, parents and employers. Sometimes they are assumed to be sexually experienced and politically aware; on other occasions they are treated as naïve innocents. Kitwood argues that the main function of peer groups is not to challenge adults, but to act as secure bases where young people can receive predictable treatment which enables them to handle and survive persistent assaults on their self-esteem from adult sources.

Writers who treat youth as a period of continuous socialisation argue that, however conventional their values and aspirations, it is impossible for individuals to step directly from childhood to adult-hood in modern societies. Childhood is now an inadequate prepara-tion, for the reasons listed earlier. A further process of socialisation is required, and, it is argued, this is why we now recognise youth as a separate phase (Parsons, 1954, 1962; Eisenstadt, 1956). According to this theory, youth cultures are not seed-beds of rebellion, but socialis-ing milieux which consolidate attitudes, aspirations and identities developed during childhood, and impart the additional skills and knowledge necessary for a phased entry into adult roles in the economy, polity and family.

'Continuous socialisation' has similar policy implications to older bio-psychological interpretations of adolescence. It encourages accepting and coming to terms with rather than opposing the spread of youth cultures. Redemption, it is argued, can be reserved for exceptional cases where normal adolescent socialisation breaks down, or where individuals prove unable to cope with normal youth pressures and environments as a result of inadequate socialisation during childhood. Postwar youth cultures are seen as basically healthy developments which institutionalise adolescence and facilitate the transition to adult statuses.

It has been suggested that adult society, maybe influenced by con-trary theories, is unnecessarily suspicious and hostile towards its young. A degree of 'separateness' may be essential to allow young people to establish independence. But, it is claimed, the antagonism of some adults impedes adolescent socialisation. There is no doubt that their elders have mistrusted postwar youth and their ways of life. Adolescents are not deceiving themselves if and when they feel that the world is against them. Schofield (1965) collected press reports mentioning young people during a four-month spell in 1961–2: 55 per cent were critical, 30 per cent defensive, and only 15 per cent approving or neutral. In their studies of young people's values and relationships with adults, the Eppels (1966) found the latter expressing more hostility towards the young than flowed in the opposite direction. In its *Young School-Leavers* study, the Schools Council (1968) found that the most important things to the young people were their families and obtaining satisfying jobs. The teachers who were questioned did not dissent from these priorities, but neither did they believe that their pupils were so conventional.

However, the continuous socialisation theory does not suggest that youth has been artificially manufactured primarily to defend older generations' privileges, and that adolescence would disappear if only their elders offered young people normal adult rights and responsibilities. This theory insists that, in modern societies, youth is a necessary phase which old and young must live with.

Class Theory

Until the 1950s, intergenerational conflict, variously explained in biological, psychological and sociological terms, was the leading theory in youth studies. Then, during the 1960s, continuous socialisation became the orthodox interpretation. At the time functionalism was American sociology's dominant theory, but 'continuous socialisation' struck additional chords in societies that were learning to live with, and beginning to see, virtues in their flamboyant younger generations. The 1970s was a period of consolidation rather than innovation in youth cultures, but academically turbulent. A 'New Wave' (Brake, 1980; Smith, 1981) in youth theory made social class, not adolescence, the central concept. This theory rejects functionalist arguments, not because their evidence is wrong, but on the ground that the data are selected, filtered and interpreted through a misleading theory of society which treats all institutions and processes as operating to maintain the totality, with some invisible hand preserving homeostasis.

The New Wave's momentum has been generated by sociologists who consider it more realistic to treat societies as arenas for conflict, divided into dominant and subordinate groups – classes with antagonistic interests, according to orthodox Marxists. During the 1970s Marxism was the ascendant theory in British sociology, and was applied to the study of youth cultures, especially working-class youth *sub*-cultures, to build the New Wave (Hall and Jefferson, 1976; Mungham and Pearson, 1976). Its authors insist that youth sub-cultures are not off-shoots from a general youth culture, created to solve the problems of moving from childhood to adulthood, but from the cultures of dominant and subordinate classes.

This theory's evidence and arguments are discussed fully in Chapter 8. In the meantime it is necessary only to note its main feature, which is the subordination of youth theory to class analysis. The theory accepts that young people are exposed to ambiguous, often contradictory pressures, and recognises that the details of these contradictions depend upon age, gender, race, place of residence and other circumstances, but insists that these additional variables, for the most part, simply mediate the overriding realities of class predicaments. Male working-class youth are urged towards educational and occupational achievement but offered limited opportunities. They are taught the virtues of hard work, then simultaneously advised to have a good time. The young people need to resolve these contradictions, which, it is argued, are rooted not in age divisions, but in class inequalities and conflicts. Available solutions depend upon gender and other statuses. Hence the plethora of youth sub-cultures. But, the New Wave insists, the main resource that all working-class groups, including young people, employ to solve their problems is a general working-class culture. Young people learn this culture in their homes and neighbourhoods, then subsequently at work, but, the argument runs, this heritage often proves inadequate. Social changes result in young people facing different predicaments from their parents (Cohen, 1976). In addition, some problems and opportunities available to working class youth are age-specific. For example, they are not laden with family responsibilities. Pop culture is treated as an additional resource that young people use creatively, to fashion solutions to their problems. Rather than gullible victims of commercial trivia, it is argued that punks, skinheads and Teddy Boys have been making important statements about their predicaments in a class society, and these styles are offered as proof that the oppressed can express their own radical, oppositional meanings (Willis, 1978).

According to this theory, youth sub-cultures are class divided. Correspondences are noted between working-class youth styles and more general forms of working-class consciousness, including the awareness of 'us and them', and interest in 'beating the system', sometimes achieving victory through humour. To understand the alarm that working-class youth sub-cultures inspire, New Wave theorists argue that we must recognise how the authorities are responding not to adolescent turbulence, but to incipient class uprisings which threaten established structures by penetrating and rejecting the dominant strata's definitions of reality.

By the end of the 1970s the New Wave theory had become the orthodox perspective in British sociology of youth, vigorously stated by a generation of (necessarily middle-class) sociologists, who had been involved in and had not lost touch with (often working-class) youth cultures. The New Wave has not been rolled by responsible and concerned onlookers from sheltered ivory towers. Its authors have taken sides with their subjects, usually working-class male youth, instead of treating the young people as 'a problem'.

Naturalistic Tendencies

Youth research has avoided the sterile battle between theorists and fieldworkers that has disfigured many other areas of sociological inquiry. Even the architects have been aware of the danger of their theoretical equipment submerging, distorting, devaluing, completely overlooking or otherwise failing to understand young people's own points of view. Theoreticians have respected evidence from formal surveys and naturalistic, hermeneutic inquiries, employing participant-observation and other unobtrusive methods where the researchers attempt to lay their own preconceptions aside, adopt adolescents' own language (Schwartz and Merten, 1967), and, in the first instance, allow young people to explain their behaviour.

Youth research can boast a splendid record of detailed ethnography. There have been numerous forays into the worlds of street-corner delinquents, student militants and, more recently, football hoods. The latter, according to one group of researchers, turn out to be rational and orderly rather than anarchic, with individuals struggling for a status and dignity denied by the wider society (Marsh et al., 1978). 'Hard data' social scientists and theory-builders sometimes dismiss these contributions as offering mere subjective impressions. But in youth research, its compelling authenticity has made it impossible to ignore the evidence of fieldworkers who have spent months, sometimes years, becoming well acquainted with their subjects, however unrepresentative or few in number.

Naturalistic inquiries are sometimes criticised for perpetuating their subjects' naïvety. It may be interesting to learn young people's points of view, but will these individuals be aware of how their attitudes and behaviour are influenced by their homes, schools and jobs, and of the political, economic and legal restraints on their opportunities? In youth studies, ethnographers have rarely been so naïve as to try to let their evidence speak for itself. They have endeavoured to interpret their findings by relating hard data and qualitative evidence to larger theories. The still unresolved problem is to make the parts mesh together.

Youth theorists have not treated evidence with contempt. This is not the reason for the theoretical dissensus. The situation here is that much of the evidence proves susceptible to alternative interpretations. It is easy to place ethnographic material, obtained from close observation and depth interviews, alongside theoretical arguments. The problem is that functionalists and Marxists are equally capable of using case-study evidence to add 'flesh and blood' to their theories. It is one thing to assert, but much more difficult actually to prove, connections between a handful of young people's dating behaviour and the functions of the modern family, or between teenagers' demeanour in city centres and the class struggle.

Some exponents believe that semiotics/semiology (Barthes, 1967), the study of signs and symbols, may one day resolve the problem of systematically relating naturalistic evidence to broader theories of society and personality organisation. Virtually all social interaction is symbolic; it involves the exchange of words and gestures whose effects depend upon their meanings to the receivers. We are all competent coders of our own meanings and, usually, decoders of messages received. Most of us have sufficient mastery of everyday codes to generate occasional original ideas, to construct original sentences and make them understood. Yet we remain, as best, only half-aware of the codes themselves. If semiologists could 'crack' the codes, it might become possible to trace the parents of different youth sub-cultures and reveal, for example, how particular economic or class interests structure young people's meanings and intentions, and even their most creative endeavours (Hebdige, 1979). As yet, however, even enthusiasts must admit that semiotic analyses bear more resemblance to statements of religious faith than scientific proof.

Uses and Abuses of Youth Theories
Theories of adolescent rebellion and intergenerational conflict, functionalist accounts, then class analyses appeared in this historical sequence. It is tempting to prefer the latest, especially when, as in youth research, successive theories have tried to reinterpret and assimilate rather than reject earlier evidence. The 'continuous socialisation' theory explains how superficially rebellious adolescents are really learning adult skills and identities. Class theories add that young people do not all learn the same skills and values, or face identical contradictions, but operate within different class situations and cultures. However, the earlier perspectives have never been totally displaced or absorbed.

'Which is right?' is an obvious but, in my view, a misleading question. Which works best depends upon which aspects of behaviour, and which young people, are selected for examination. This is why advocates of all the theories can offer supporting evidence. We need further research to develop the theories, but not more inquiries designed to illustrate favoured and dismiss suspected approaches. We need research to define the limits within which each theory is valid, and thereby shape their contributions so that the evidence and arguments become compatible and mutually supporting. Why has this advice never been acted upon previously? Another of this book's principal arguments is that, to unravel youth cultures' sometimes contradictory tendencies, we must supplement youth theories with analyses of leisure and the consequences of its growth.

(B) On Leisure

Compared with youth studies, leisure research is too new and under-developed to have been divided into clearly defined schools. Writers on leisure, whether economists, sociologists or geographers, mostly agree that leisure is difficult to define, but has definitely grown, that they are unsure of the consequences, and that more 'fundamental' research will be necessary before youth workers and other public-sector professionals can be advised on how to enhance their clients' leisure (Social Science Research Council/Sports Council, 1978a). The following chapters agree that more research is needed, but not 'straight' leisure research, building a body of field-specific leisure theory, to be applied among young people and other groups. They argue that the effects depend upon who receives any extra leisure time and money. Granting young people more leisure does not lead to the same consequences that would occur among older age-groups. We will see that the consequences also depend on which young people are offered more leisure, and to explain these differences it is necessary to blend, not just place side by side, the theories and evidence from youth and leisure studies.

What is Leisure
Defining terms precisely before commencing any discourse is not always sound advice. Precise definitions sometimes fudge reality. Invitations to define leisure are as likely to produce treatises as short, snappy phrases, and this is not because the writers are muddle-headed. People's lives and social systems are less tidy than dictionaries. It is mistaken to assume that, because we possess simple words like leisure and adolescence, they must correspond to phenomena which, like chemical elements, display the same properties, whose presence can be rigorously tested, in all times and places. Concise definitions claiming universal application invariably distort leisure because, first, it is not a phenomenon whose character has remained unchanged throughout history. Water possessed the same properties in the Stone Age as it does today. It boils at 100° C in Greenland and Brazil. By contrast, leisure's character has varied between societies. Secondly, leisure is not precisely bounded. It is more akin to learning than schooling. The beginning and end of a school day may be punctuated with a bell. By

contrast, learning is ubiquitous, like work and play. Any sharp definition which clearly separated leisure from the rest of life would distort its own subject-matter.

The definition offered below is my own, like the subsequent account of leisure's growth. No short presentation could represent the combined wisdom of leisure scholars. But neither the definition nor the review of leisure's growth are deliberately controversial. All writers agree that leisure is difficult to define, and therefore that its growth cannot be measured or even described precisely. Most are willing to present their own efforts as provisional, and will be prepared to accept the following on these terms, as means of leading into issues where opinion is more clearly divided.

Like most social-science concepts, the word leisure is also used by laymen, and what ordinary people mean by leisure, plus work, politics, religion and social class, is part of the reality for sociology to explore. Plants, atoms and electrical currents do not possess ideas about their conduct, but people do, and sociologists cannot ignore everyday knowledge. Rituals become religions, and assortments of wood and fabrics become 'cultural' objects, like tables and chairs, only when combined with everyday knowledge of their uses. Leisure time and activities are not physically distinguishable from other occasions and events. Weekends may be occasions for work or leisure. Soccer may be a paid occupation or a leisure pastime. Social scientists would be unable to distinguish the relevant activities and artefacts without taking account of what ordinary people mean by leisure, religion, politics and furniture.

Sociology must take account of, but cannot be limited to, everyday understandings. It must explain how and why, not just adopt whatever meanings become attached to particular times and activities. Sociology must entertain the possibility of the causes and consequences of people's actions differing from their conscious motives and intentions. Its definitions, therefore, are usually stipulative rather than lexicographic, stating how authors intend to use their terms, and in the following passages leisure will be employed as a second order concept, to refer not to any single set of things, but to describe the relationships between separable phenomena – the elements of leisure. The term 'social class' is often used in a comparable way to analyse the configurations formed by inequalities of income, wealth, power, status, educational opportunity and so on.

The definition stipulated below treats leisure as the product of a number of primary elements: types of time, activity and experience. Leisure occurs when these elements form certain configurations, and the reason we need such a word is to describe the product of their combination. This method of defining leisure enables us to explain, while transcending common sense. Laymen may not be aware that the meanings of leisure in their lives are historically specific, or that, within their own societies, leisure's properties are not identical for men and women, children and workers, and the retired. The definition to be adopted allows us to treat leisure's meanings to laymen as a problem to be explored, not passively accepted.

The Elements of Leisure

One element of leisure is a type of time – spare or free time, the residue after physically necessary acts such as eating and sleeping, plus work and other social obligations, including household chores, have been discharged. In the after-hours we please ourselves, within limits, for freedom is never absolute, a point to which we shall return. Opportunities are always constrained by geography, income, the law and other social norms, but no civilisation has ever regimented every moment of every citizen's lifetime. All societies have left their members with *relatively* free time, during which individuals' activities have not been prescribed by law, custom, religion or morality, and the specific uses made of these occasions have therefore been matters of choice.

The second element of leisure is a type of activity – play or recreation. We play games, which are separated from ordinary life by some combination of time, place and rules. Since it is 'only a game', the result never really matters, meaning that the consequences can be contained within the field of play and need not interfere with our work, political or family lives. Needless to say, some people treat their games very seriously. Enjoyment depends upon commitment. Victory at soccer is only satisfying if the opposition is playing to win. Yet, however wholehearted our commitment, defeat at Monopoly does not involve losing all our worldly assets. Play allows us to step outside our normal selves. It enables us to develop and express aspects of our characters that would otherwise remain hidden. During play we can experiment with new roles and persona. Play can be educational in the broadest meaning of the term, for children, and for adults. In many societies, certain types of play have been obligatory military and religious training. Physical education, which normally includes team games, is compulsory for schoolchildren in contemporary Britain. Play may not be absolutely essential, but all societies have used it to encourage the acquisition of valued skills, and to allow their members to release physical, social and psychological tensions generated in other spheres.

The third element of leisure is experience that contains its own reward, where the intrinsic satisfactions are considered sufficient justification. Writers who advocate unidimensional experiential definitions

(Neulinger, 1982) are seeking to avoid tying leisure to any particular times or activities. Gardening may be work to one person, leisure to another. Some people may find work-days more exhilarating than weekends. Hence the case for treating the activities and occasions that are experienced as leisure by different people as matters to be resolved by research rather than by definition.

Adopting the quality of the experience as one element of leisure enables us to accept this advice. Indeed, the definition being outlined allows us to treat all the relationships between the elements – free time, play and intrinsically satisfying experience – as matters for investigation. The elements need not co-exist. Indeed, throughout the greater part of history they have not been closely related, which is why a concept of leisure was unnecessary. We only need such a term when the elements overlap and coalesce, which has been the tendency in industrial societies. Industrialism packages the elements to blend a distinctive type of leisure, and in Britain the term began to be applied to the lives of working people only during the second half of the nineteenth century (Cunningham, 1980). Previously, when the word was used, 'leisure' conveyed a different meaning from that which the term has now acquired. The pre-industrial man of leisure was an educated individual, who developed all aspects of his character, and whose way of life permitted full expression of all his talents. Following the Industrial Revolution, leisure was given a new meaning, though some of the word's former connotations were retained. Leisure was applied to the intrinsically satisfying experiences individuals derived from recreation during their free time. They tend to coalesce, but even in industrial societies, leisure's elements do not always co-exist. Free time is not devoted wholly to games. Neither games nor free time are always intrinsically satisfying. This is why there are occasions, activities and experiences that we feel are only partly leisure, which is why it is pointless to seek a definition that would clearly separate leisure from other domains.

Industrialism and the Growth of Leisure

How and why does industrialism forge the leisure package? First, industrialism compartmentalises work within offices and factories, where individuals sell their labour for agreed units of time and become subject to the discipline of employers and machines. It is only when work is organised in this manner, with the employee relinquishing control of his muscles, skills, abilities and knowledge, that spare time becomes a complementary and valued part of life (Thompson, 1967). Secondly, industrialism rationalises work. Play is driven from workplaces. Production is geared to efficiency, not job satisfaction. Some workers find their jobs interesting, even fulfilling, but this is a for-

tuitous by-product rather than a prime purpose of industrial organisation. Thirdly, consumption is made a private matter. Employees
receive money wages to spend at their discretion. Uses of personal
income and free time are not prescribed by employers, custom,
morality or religion. The time that remains when work has been
performed therefore becomes free time, to be used as individuals prefer.
This part of life becomes the location for play and a major source of
intrinsically gratifying experiences.

Once people's lives are structured in this manner, specialised leisure
industries can be created, selling fun, amusement, entertainment and
other playful experiences to be enjoyed during free time. Sport and
recreation have a longer history, but following the Industrial Revolution most of our games were redesigned as leisure interests, to be
enjoyed at the end of the working day or week. Specialised leisure
industries were not unknown prior to nineteenth-century industrialism. The 'modern' leisure package had existed in ancient Rome and
medieval towns. But for most people, before industrialism, playfulness
was blended into, and intrinsic satisfactions were extracted from work,
family, community and religious life. Even if modern survey instruments had been available, it would have been impossible to measure
exactly how much leisure time pre-industrial man possessed, or to
ascertain his preferred leisure activities. The questions would have been
meaningless, which is why they were never posed.

It is impossible to say whether we now enjoy more leisure than our
pre-industrial ancestors. Modern leisure is qualitatively different. But
there is no dispute that the type of leisure created during the Industrial
Revolution has subsequently grown. The demands of work have been
gradually rolled back. In mid-nineteenth-century British industry, a
sixty-hour, six-day work week was normal, with no paid vacations,
and trade unions, particularly in textiles, struggled to prevent working
hours being lengthened. Working life began during childhood, and the
right to a pensioned retirement was still two generations ahead.

Today the five-day week is standard, and a normal three-day
weekend is predicted. Trade unions are negotiating further reductions
in basic hours beneath the forty-hour barrier. Three or four weeks'
holiday entitlement, in addition to public vacations, have become
normal. Schooling until the age of 16 is compulsory. Male workers
become eligible for state retirement pensions at 65, and women at 60.
Trimming the working day, week and life began in the nineteenth
century, and the trend is still in process. Between 1961 and 1975 leisure
time grew by 18 per cent (Gershuny and Thomas, 1980).

While working time has shrunk, incomes have risen. Since 1900 the
real *per capita* value of Britain's Gross National Product has tripled. The
relatively poor still lag as far as ever behind average standards of living.

The 'tail' has not been drawn up, but both rich and poor have benefited from overall economic growth. One consequence of these trends in hours of work and income levels has been an explosion of recreational spending and activity. Leisure has become big business. By 1960 virtually all households possessed televisions, and video recorders are now becoming standard domestic equipment. Tourism and gambling have become major industries. More people are playing more sports, particularly the indoor varieties. The family car has swept a wave of leisure across the countryside. *Per capita* consumption of alcohol has doubled since 1950, but not at the expense of more cerebral types of leisure. Sales of books, classical records, visits to art galleries, concerts and museums have all risen (Roberts, 1981). The well-publicised cases of decline – the cinema and football attendances – owe their problems, like Blackpool, to their exceptional popularity in the past. As the public's scope for choice has widened, so leisure spending has been distributed across a wider range of options.

Postwar youth cultures have been products of leisure's growth. Rolling back the demands of work has given employees more free time during evenings, weekends and vacations. Simultaneously, it has allowed certain groups to be wholly released from the workforce. Compulsory schooling has been gradually extended, until the age of 16 since 1973. Growing proportions of young people have been 'staying on' voluntarily, taking A-levels and, in some cases, proceeding to higher education. The wealth generated by economic growth has created affluent workers, and enabled students in higher education, since 1949, to be awarded mandatory (though means-tested) maintenance grants. Higher wages and working wives have allowed parents to indulge teenage children. Since the 1950s, schoolchildren have been recognised as an important leisure market. Their sources (pocket money and spare-time jobs), amounts and uses of income are regularly monitored by market research. During the 1950s and 1960s, 15- and 16-year-old school-leavers benefited from the full employment that prevailed in most parts of the country. Beginning workers' wages rose more rapidly than most other incomes. With their minimal domestic responsibilities, these teenage spenders became the leisure industries' prime market. The young people, assisted by commercial providers, were able to cultivate styles of elegance in dress and appearance that often left older generations gasping in amazement. Chapter 2 described the development of postwar youth cultures. Leisure has been one of their foundations, and one of this book's principal arguments is that, to explain youth cultures, we must first of all understand leisure's properties.

Unfortunately, as in youth research, when we ask leisure scholars to list their subject's properties, we find the experts offering rival theories about the implications of leisure's growth. As we shall also see, another similarity is that the alternative interpretations of leisure need not be treated as mutually exclusive. Young people must be used not as a decisive test, but to develop leisure theory by showing how the effects of its growth depend upon who receives any extra leisure.

Leisure Issues
Leisure research has grown alongside other leisure industries. The latter, public and private, have commissioned surveys to identify actual and potential markets, to predict trends in demand, to tailor their provisions and publicity accordingly. Representatives from established academic disciplines have launched parallel, usually smaller-scale inquiries, with concepts, theories and questions from their parent subjects. All agree that leisure has grown. So what? Exactly how does leisure change people's lives? With this question the consensus collapses.

Leisure researchers could present a huge list of topics where more information and research are needed. These passages select just three controversies that must be settled in making sense of youth cultures. The first concerns the extent and quality of the freedom leisure confers. Researchers, like this chapter, normally define leisure in terms of freedom. Then they investigate uses of 'free time' when individuals can select activities according to their personal preferences. Recreational activities are assumed to be freely chosen, for their intrinsic satisfactions. All leisure scholars realise that freedom is never absolute, and that no one can ever do 'anything'. They have charted the limits to individuals' scope for choice imposed by time, spending power, geography and knowledge. But many dwell upon the character and reasons for individuals' choices, within whatever limits operate, and justify this preoccupation by arguing that the growth of leisure has gradually widened people's ability to nurture and express their own interests. Indeed, according to one school of thought, the growth of leisure is enabling people to choose not only preferred recreations but entire life-styles. The trends, it is argued, are towards where to work and in which occupation, where to live, whether to marry, and whether and how to rear children, all becoming matters for personal decision (Dumazedier, 1974).

Occupations, income levels and life-cycle stages continue to impose limitations, but, according to some investigators, the predictive power of these statuses has become progressively weaker as all social groups have benefited from the growth of leisure (Kelly, 1978). Modern leisure, as conventionally defined, was originally a product of industrialism, but, according to this argument, its growth is now resulting in leisure's influence rippling beyond the residual time to which it was first confined. It is argued that the post-industrial society, whose threshold we are said to have reached, could become a 'society of leisure' where leisure-values – doing things playfully, for their own sake – penetrate family life, education and even work. The transition to post-industrialism is supposedly breaking the package forged during the Industrial Revolution and returning play, plus the quest for intrinsically satisfying experiences, back to life in general, making leisure a quality of total life-styles rather than a subsidiary sphere. Should the young people who have been accused of irresponsible attitudes and behaviour in employment, and when liberating sex from traditional domestic roles, be treated as a social vanguard?

Other writers focus on the limits to leisure choices, and judge these too persistent and narrow to justify stressing 'freedom' in social-science definitions. Rather than bestowing freedom, leisure is seen as a modern system of social control. It is argued that leisure is a set of meanings that have become attached to certain times, activities and types of spending to serve specific interests, and that these meanings have never been constructed by the public at large, but by educators, government agencies and, in particular, by the leisure industries (Coalter, 1980; Henderson, 1980).

The function of the ideology of leisure, critics argue, was and remains to convince workers that wages and free time are sufficient reward for working, and to persuade them to use their leisure 'rationally', in worthwhile activities that reproduce rather than destroy labour power, and sustain consumer demand for the products of their alienated labour. Demand can be raised and channelled by advertising which tells people their lives will be enhanced by purchasing and displaying appropriate leisure commodities. If the primary uses of products cannot be made sufficiently attractive, the goods can be surrounded by images so that consumers buy social status or sex appeal with their toiletries and tobacco. In reality, it is argued, most people's scope for choice is trivial, but the ideology of leisure persuades people that their discretion is significant. Should social science celebrate, by incorporating in its stipulative definitions, a freedom that is confined to spare time, and to playful activities that are devoid of economic and political consequences? Critics suggest that the proper job of sociology is not to accept and consolidate, but to expose the ideological character of leisure's contemporary meanings, and reveal the ideology's true rule of reconciling individuals of social orders which remain basically exploitative and oppressive. Rather than anticipating and exploring the wider freedom to be offered in an imminent society of leisure, this critique implies that participants in postwar youth cultures have been manipulated and exploited, and simultaneously blinded to the sources of their oppression.

A second controversial issue in leisure studies concerns whether, during its growth, leisure has been 'democratised' and, in the process, has helped to dissolve former social divisions. The leisure democracy thesis (Roberts, 1981) alleges that, as all sections of the public acquire greater scope for choice, formerly exclusive pastimes are transformed into mass recreations. Democratised does not mean equalised. No one claims that all citizens now enjoy equal amounts of leisure time, spending power and access to recreational opportunities. The leisure democracy argument is that the distribution of leisure no longer corresponds with other contours of inequality. Professional and managerial employees, plus the self-employed, now work longer, on average, than manual workers (Gershuny and Thomas, 1980). It is the latter who are time-privileged. Young people, the unemployed and the retired enjoy exceptional amounts of free time, but none can be described as social, economic or political élites. On average, white-collar occupations still pay better than manual jobs, though the gap narrowed during the 1970s, but leisure spending depends upon 'commitments' in addition to income, and intra-class inequalities across the life-span now rival life-time inter-class differentials.

This is why, it is argued, despite the middle classes still 'doing more', mainly because they continue to enjoy the higher incomes, there remain few 'exclusive' middle-class recreations. In general, the middle classes do more of the same things that occupy working-class leisure. Symphony concerts and pigeon racing draw their followers overwhelmingly from the middle and working classes respectively, but these pastimes involve only minorities within each class, and account for only small proportions of most participants' leisure. Popular working-class pastimes, like watching television and taking holidays away from home, feature among the more common middle-class recreations.

The leisure democracy thesis does not deny that different sections of the public, including men and women, still use their leisure in very different ways, but queries whether the differences always fall into hierarchical patterns. Democracy need not mean homogeneity. Women are less active in masculine recreations. Is this because they have less leisure and narrower opportunities? Or do the sexes have different preferences? It has been argued that women's leisure is different, but no less satisfying; that their play is often blended into, and intrinsic satisfactions derived from, family obligations and neighbourhood relationships (Gregory, 1982).

The leisure democracy can be linked to the post-industrial 'society of leisure' scenario, to suggest that rather than patterned by other social roles, the trends are towards leisure activities and interests becoming autonomous sources of identity and social relationships, possibly acting as a sub-structure for the rest of life. If leisure is a democratising force, we would expect to find young people's personal tastes and interests, rather than the constraints associated, for example, with social origins and educational attainments, shaping youth cultures.

Some scholars remain sceptical of claims that a leisure democracy is here or imminent. Social class is still the most frequently used predictor in empirical and theoretical sociology. The oppression of women has now joined the subject's sensitive issues. Whatever some researchers claim, others are reluctant to believe that uses of leisure fail to reflect persistent inequalities associated with capital, occupations and gender. There are many dimensions of inequality, whose interaction produces a kaleidoscope of life-styles that may create an illusion of democracy with everyone acting on their personal preferences. In reality, sceptics insist, leisure is patterned by a social system that is still highly stratified by class and gender.

Chapter 2 explained that boys and girls make different uses of leisure, that middle- and working-class youth are involved in different youth cultures, and that these differences have persisted since before the Second World War, but this does not seal any argument. The existence of class or gender differences among young people at leisure is not in dispute. The controversy is about the significance of these differences. Are girls and working-class youth constrained? Or are the sexes and social classes expressing tastes and exploiting opportunities that are simply different, rather than deprived and privileged? If some young people's uses of leisure are relatively constrained, is this in spite of, or because of, leisure lacking democratising qualities?

The third controversial claim is that leisure enhances the quality of life; that self-selected activities, practised for their own sake, governed by participants' own natural rhythms, within a sphere of life separated from work and other commitments where individuals can display their private selves, boost psychological well-being. Quantitative evidence has been gathered showing that participation in leisure activities enables individuals to develop and practise skills, to express their interests and 'be themselves', thereby increasing life-satisfaction (Dower *et al.*, 1980). Have youth cultures been spreading these blessings? Could it be the older generations, who have accused young people of squandering their time and money on trivia at discos, pop festivals and boutiques, who have grown 'way out' of touch? Most adults still spend their leisure in conventional ways. Between the world wars, the cinema and radio displaced the public house and music hall. During the 1950s television superseded radio and the cinema. Fortnights on the Costa Brava have replaced Wakes Weeks at Blackpool. Upon acquiring motor cars, families have driven miles

into and around the countryside, often never venturing more than
twenty yards from their vehicles. Can young people be blamed for
seeking alternatives? We have seen that, on young people's own
admission, their leisure is not all fun and excitement. 'What to do?' is a
perennial topic of conversation in many peer groups. Young people
often complain that their spare time is drab. They may not have
discovered all the answers, but, it can be argued, young people have at
least begun exploring the new opportunities to express their talents and
interests, and thereby enjoy life, created by the growth of leisure.

Sceptics query leisure's alleged benefits. Some point out that modern
leisure was an unplanned by-product of industrialism, and argue that it
remains unwelcome in so far as our industrial civilisation is still
governed by a (now secularised) Protestant work ethic (Anderson,
1967). Others argue that industrialism's division of labour splinters life
into meaningless fragments, and when individuals anchor and
endeavour to express their selves in private life, they only devalue other
experiences and diminish their personalities (Sennett, 1977). Another
school of thought insists that humans need constraint and direction by
social norms, and that the very freedom of leisure is a threat to well-
being (Davies, 1975). People may welcome respite from unsatisfying
jobs, but are these same individuals happier when 'forced' into retirement or short-time working? It is argued that, in the absence of clear
goals, spare time hangs heavily, like a wasteland, and that the stranded
masses therefore anaesthetise themselves with television programmes,
alcohol and other leisure drugs, or are driven to compulsive activity in a
quest for distraction, touring across continents, motoring aimlessly
around the countryside, or jogging their hours away (Glasser, 1970).

Is leisure therapeutic, or must free time and activities be controlled
for individuals' own good? Is well-being maximised when individuals
possess maximum discretion? Or does happiness increase as individuals
structure otherwise spare time around domestic, community and educational 'work', treat these pursuits seriously rather than playfully, and
develop them into 'obligations'? Are we really free to pursue happiness
when at the mercy only of our selfish desires? Has the growth of leisure
made adolescence more satisfying, or a more stressful, desultory and
restless life-phase than ever? Successive youth cultures, offering trivia
and superficial experiences, could indicate that young people have been
floundering in a leisure wilderness created by the logic of industrial
capitalism rather than in response to their own needs.

The Synthesis
We have already noted that young people possess considerable leisure
time compared with adults, that they have been major leisure spenders
in the recent past, and that youth cultures are constructed primarily

through leisure activities. It is hardly surprising, therefore, that youth and leisure researchers' debates should have converged. Their routes and problems have differed, but some controversies that divide analysts of youth cultures are now mirrored in leisure studies.

First, there is the quality-of-life issue. Does greater leisure increase young people's enjoyment of the 'time of their lives'? Or does leisure accentuate the boredom of the betwixt and between years? Secondly, there is the democracy controversy. Are all young people acting out the same adolescent problems in youth cultures which, like other leisure milieux, cannot be ranked into the same hierarchies as jobs, income levels and traditional gender roles? Thirdly, there is the freedom debate. Do youth and leisure confer the freedom to allow individuals and peer groups to rebel against conventions, and maybe change society? Or are the freedoms of youth and leisure so tightly bounded as to ensure that youth cultures are basically conservative phenomena, reflecting broader social patterns, linking childhood to adulthood? Youth and leisure research have developed independently to a point where each can benefit by cross-fertilising their theories and evidence. Young people may also benefit if the hybrid allows us to predict the likely consequences of current trends, provisions and policies.

It is tempting to collapse the youth and leisure debates into two easily understood sides: the 'optimists', who believe that young people and leisure are sufficiently free to permit the spread of democratic youth cultures which enhance the quality of life, against 'pessimists', who regard the freedom of leisure as an illusion, insist that young people's opportunities are determined by traditional class and gender divisions, and argue that leisure does not alleviate so much as reconcile individuals to unsatisfying existences. This simple polarisation must be resisted. Youth cultures contain contradictory tendencies, which is why their significance has never been agreed. Likewise, ever since the Industrial Revolution, the growth of leisure has been accompanied by hopes of fulfilment and fears of anarchy, and each side has been able to marshall corroborating evidence. The propositions that divide youth and leisure researchers are essentially descriptive generalisations. They cannot be likened to scientific laws, which means there is no reason why any should be universally valid. The controversies must be used to analyse and separate tendencies, not to suggest that there are only two possible answers.

The following chapters present the evidence piece by piece, but it may help to outline the overall argument that will unfold. My own view, fully stated elsewhere, is that, all other things being equal, the growth of leisure spreads a genuine though always finite freedom, that its uses enhance the quality of life and can transcend other social divisions (Roberts, 1979, 1981). There is evidence of leisure's growth spreading these properties beyond playful, spare-time activities into family life and education, but few signs of paid employment becoming leisurely, and talk of a 'society of leisure' probably exaggerates the magnitude of the trends. The argument to be developed holds leisure responsible for the radical aspects of youth cultures. These are less clearly divided than young people's family backgrounds, educational careers and types of employment. The freedom of leisure permits youth cultures' contra- and counter-cultural tendencies which violate 'good taste', offend and defy teachers, parents, employers and law enforcers.

However, in actual societies as opposed to academic treatises, all other things never remain equal. The growth of leisure does not have uniform implications among all sections of the public. The consequences depend upon who receives any extra free time, disposable income and opportunities to play. Whether free time enriches or blights the quality of life depends upon how it is mixed with other resources such as income and access to leisure skills and facilities. The following chapters argue that youth is not a period of maximum freedom. This reputation is deceitful. Young people's freedom is relative to the total dependence of childhood. Whether teenagers receive pocket money, grants, training allowances, wages or salaries, the levels usually keep them dependent upon parents. Prior to marriage, most young people continue to live at home, under parental supervision. Young people are not political heavyweights. They are not enfranchised until the age of 18. Young voters have never been mobilised on 'youth issues'. Indeed, a feature that distinguishes the youngest voters is the frequency with which they abstain. Young people have watched passively while their jobs have disappeared, with government acquiescence. Leisure may draw young people together, but they are well divided in education, then into students and workers, apprentices and others, office and manual workers. Education is gender divided, and employment even more so.

Subsequent chapters explain how most young people have no real alternative to putting their leisure to conservative uses, and that there is no way in which adolescent leisure might be harnessed to initiate radical changes – feminist or socialist, for example. Attempted rebellions are invariably unsuccessful, whether against class barriers, gender divisions or the law. Young people's resistance is transformed into accommodation. They are given just enough freedom to resist and establish independence from adults – parents, teachers, the police and employers, to allow them to acquire the very skills, including the art of treating other adults as equals, that are required for entry into established adult roles. Family backgrounds, educational attainments and job opportunities set young people apart, on masculine and feminine, then separate social class trajectories, and youth cultures do not overwhelm but respect these boundaries, and assist in transporting young people to conventional adulthoods.

Leisure's ability to enhance well-being by allowing individuals to express themselves, depends upon actors already 'knowing their own minds' – their interests and abilities. Young people, with no established adult identities, are typically uncertain of their abilities and interests. This is why they often use their free time and money not to 'do their own things', but to prove their normality by conforming with whatever norms their peer groups are enforcing. The only stable sources of interests and self-concepts to which young people can resort are the roles prescribed by the wider society. The following chapters will not argue that leisure is completely wasted upon the young. However, if there is extra work-free time to be distributed, there are probably more deserving cases, like the many women who care for children, homes and husbands once their paid shifts are finished, whose work weeks can total seventy hours and more – schedules that would be condemned as inhumane for male breadwinners. If there is extra income to distribute, are young people more deserving than the many families where the child-rearing phase still involves descent into relative poverty? Are they more deserving than ageing citizens who lack the capacity to work, or for whom retraining would be uneconomic, and who are left to survive on subsistence pensions and other social-security benefits?

All generalisations, whether about the freedom bestowed by leisure, or the dependence of youth, must be qualified. Young people cannot be significantly described as a social class. They lack the collective capacity to generate historical change, not only because they are internally divided, but also because youth is essentially a stage. Young people always become adults, and are easily persuaded to identify with before joining their elders, even when the latter are youth's oppressors. Nevertheless, youth cultures are sensitive to changes with other sources – in gender roles, political alignments and class divisions – and can accelerate their diffusion. Later chapters will explain that the main class divisions among young people at leisure no longer correspond to the 'traditional' blue/white-collar schism, but occur beneath a highly educated and qualified élite, and above sub-employed and other marginalised minorities. Young people are not creating these new divisions. They are simply responding to the contemporary contours of inequality, without older generations' sensitivity to political and industrial cleavages that were prominent in the past.

There are variations in the amounts of freedom different groups of young people enjoy, and in the extent to which they can establish secure statuses and identities. Subsequent chapters explain that, in these respects, boys are relatively privileged. This is why the youth scene's contra- and counter-cultural tendencies have been male led. Students are more liberated than their working contemporaries, and are better equipped to assault social conventions. This is not only because of the intellectual confidence that higher education fosters. One of the myths of our age is that prolonged education involves sacrifices and deferred independence. Later chapters will explain that students are recreationally privileged. Their grants and subsidised leisure facilities bestow economic power. Their congregation on campuses allows them to mobilise politically. Grants and freedom from parental supervision give students the independence to defer employment, marriage and parenthood – indefinitely, in some cases.

There are policy implications throughout the following pages that will be drawn together in the concluding chapter. Youth is a time of recreational taste and skill acquisition. It is the period when individuals build leisure capital that can extend or limit their life-long opportunities. Our first leisure interests are normally acquired at home and school. Then, during adolescence, some individuals sample a wide range of new opportunities. Many are quickly dropped. Interests tend to lapse with marriage and parenthood, but if tastes and skills have once been nurtured there is always a chance of resurrection. Part of the explanation for the very low rates of sports participation among the present-day middle aged is that, when young, they never had opportunities to develop a wide range of sporting interests (Boothby *et al.*, 1981). Sport for boys used to be limited to traditional team games requiring high levels of skill and fitness. Girls were expected to cultivate more feminine interests.

Are today's young people being better prepared for their futures? Subsequent chapters will show that we have still not developed effective means of delivering recreational interests to all young people, especially girls, and male and female early school-leavers, mainly from working-class homes. The combined efforts of the schools, the Youth Service, local-authority recreation departments and other public agencies are still failing to widen the often limited interests that these young people acquire in their homes and neighbourhoods. How can we enrich these young people's immediate opportunities, and widen their scope for choice throughout adulthood?

In youth work, non-directive styles are fashionable. Youth workers have ceased to be 'leaders' and wardens of facilities. They have made a virtue of letting young people 'do their own things'. Youth work certainly needs interpersonal skills and sympathy for the clients, but young people are the age-group probably least equipped to respond to non-directive techniques. Fortunately the commercial sector, and the sports and leisure centres, mostly constructed since the 1960s, specialise in 'facilities'. Today's youth do not need regimenting in a revived scouting movement, but they need introductions to the widest possible range of activities and facilities in order to build long-term cultural capital, and as a framework around which to form their own relationships and meanings.

If we extend the breadth and quality of the provisions considered reasonable for students in higher education to all young people, the youth and leisure services will have little difficulty in attracting clients. Chapter 12 explains that leisure facilities, whatever their scale, will never solve the problems of unemployment; but is an ulterior justification necessary? Surely leisure is important for its own sake, and the larger the role it plays in young and older people's lives, the less tolerable will social-class, ethnic and gender inequalities of opportunity become.

4
Engendered Leisure

Ask a Silly Question...
A text on youth and leisure must treat sexual behaviour, including who does what with whom, where and when, alongside other gender differences, and not only because sex is so important an object of adolescent leisure, in conversation even when the action is limited. The following chapters explain how sexuality is constructed into a powerful force which divides boys and girls at leisure, patterns their interrelationships and commits them to broader gender divisions.

Quantitative evidence on young people's sexual behaviour is reviewed below. The main gender differences in other uses of leisure were summarised in Chapter 2 on postwar youth cultures. Boys are the more involved in out-of-home recreation, especially sport. Girls' lives are relatively home-centred, and dancing is their favourite out-of-home activity. Evidence from participant observer and other intensive studies of specific peer groups relates mainly to boys. This is partly because they have posed the overt problems, particularly delinquency. It may reflect the predominance of male researchers, but even female youth workers confess that girls are more difficult to track. They 'go to ground' in their homes, and are less accessible than boys' street-corner groups. The following arguments inevitably reflect such imbalances in the available evidence. Equally, the conclusions are products of the questions asked, which are derived from the previous chapter's review of youth and leisure theories.

To what extent do youth and leisure confer the freedom to question, rebel and discard traditional gender roles and sexual norms? Are the persistent differences between boys' and girls' leisure (a) products of their *different* tastes and choices or (b) *unequal* opportunities? What quality of life and leisure do adolescent gender roles and sexual practices offer? The answers that follow are based on incomplete evidence, mostly collected to address different questions and they should, strictly speaking, be treated as subject to further debate and investigation. These chapters are not trying to deliver any last words, even when the conclusions are stated unequivocally. They argue, first, that young people at leisure are subject to such constraints that the majority have no alternative but to adopt traditional gender roles and sexual conventions. Secondly, that relationships between boys and girls at leisure are patriarchal rather than equal, like the broader division of labour by gender. Whether the gender and sexual patterns to which young people are subject enhance the quality of life can only be answered comparatively, and the speed with which individuals forsake adolescence for marriage suggests little enthusiasm for specifically teenage practices.

This chapter is primarily a ground-clearing exercise, dispensing with the misleading questions. It insists that young people are not at the forefront of any sexual revolution or movement to overhaul traditional gender decisions. Accounts of how boys' and girls' uses of leisure diverge, then intersect in sexual liaisons, must begin by clearing layers of ideas about sexual norms and gender roles having changed rapidly and radically, with young people to the fore. These ideas are not new. Fears and hopes of young people overturning traditions are as long-standing as youth cultures. Young people's sexuality has disturbed and excited older generations throughout living memory. The 'swinging 'sixties' revived these ideas. The contraceptive pill was mass marketed, legal restrictions on abortion and homosexuals were relaxed, stage and screen nudity escaped censorship, and a spate of female writers began to explain that sex could be as intrinsically satisfying for women as men. Rumours circulated of a sexual revolution creating an 'anything goes' permissive society where young people in particular were unrestrained by traditional morals which insisted that sex be reserved for marriage. Nowadays we are all supposed to be 'at it', pre- and extra-maritally. In the late 1960s women's liberation was ridiculed as the slogan of an unrepresentative bra-burning minority, but the phrase and movement have proved sufficiently resilient to persuade some commentators that equality is now all but won. Women can now control their reproductive capacities and enjoy sex. They have won legal rights to equal pay, and equal opportunities in education and employment. Within youth cultures, liberated boys and girls are supposedly relating as social and sexual equals.

The following passages explain how youth and leisure researchers who have examined these alleged trends, and, indeed, all other writers who have relied on evidence rather than anecdotes and speculation, have concluded that any changes have been far less dramatic than talk of 'liberation' and 'revolution' suggests. Most boys and girls still leave adolescence having become husbands and wives, mothers and fathers. The contemporary family may be shaking. More men and women may be seeking sexual kicks in extra-marital affairs, at spouse-swapping parties, and with home videos. Divorcees and lone parents are more numerous than ever, but among young people marriage remains tremendously popular.

For most of us, to overstate the matter only a little, it might be said that the first 20 or so years of our lives are spent in an intensifying struggle to free ourselves from one family which we usually achieve only by setting up another one which we will spend the remaining years more or less desperately trying to maintain. (Noble, 1981, p. 121)

Asking about women's liberation and a sexual revolution are the wrong questions, and not only because the phrases overstate any changes. Continuities and changes in youth, sex, gender and leisure cannot be satisfactorily examined within these issues. Adolescent leisure is usually a scene where conventional gender identities plus sexual tastes and skills are reproduced, not rejected. The questions to answer are how and why this happens.

Gender identities and sexual norms are internalised during childhood. Throughout adolescence, young people are bombarded with dominant values in their families, schools and by the media. Their incomes, whether wages, government grants or from parents, may allow young people to play and dress extravagantly, but few can afford to live independently. For the majority, full adult status is available only as a reward for conformity. We shall see that some young people possess more freedom than others. Boys have retained the power to keep youth cultures male-dominated, to act on their definitions of girls as sex-objects, and to maintain the male balance of advantage in heterosexual relationships. Girls have less cash to spend, are subjected to closer parental supervision, given a narrower choice and less freedom to select their own leisure interests. Females 'mature', court and marry at the younger ages not because they are accorded the greater independence; they have less freedom to 'run off the rails'.

Some of the evidence appears ambiguous until leisure effects and youth effects are disentangled. The economic and cultural independence spread by the growth of leisure enables young people to experiment and question some conventions. But the freedom of adolescence is sufficiently bounded to leave the majority with no real alternative to using their leisure, eventually, to perpetuate traditional gender roles and sexual practices. The freedom of leisure simply allows young people to learn then enact conventional sexual and gender roles with a flamboyance that is sometimes mistaken for rebellion.

Chapter 6 considers the possibility of putting adolescent leisure to more radical uses. Are persistent gender differences necessary and inevitable, biologically decreed, or socially desirable? Could adolescent leisure be used to teach males and females to interact on equal instead of patriarchal terms? These chapters argue that, however desirable such changes might be, they are unlikely to be instigated through young people's leisure.

A Sexual Revolution?

In the past, all forms of sexual activity outside marriage were deplored. The churches condemned lust, and were supported by a battery of medical and other pseudo-scientific arguments, plus folk-wisdom. The medical profession warned of the dangers of venereal disease and unwanted pregnancies, instead of teaching how to dissociate these risks from intercourse. Fifty years ago, doctors attributed all manner of maladies to masturbation. Football managers believed that players would take the field fatigued without pre-match abstinence. Advice columnists declared sex satisfying only within loving and stable relationships. Young people were told that their marriages would be soiled by carnal knowledge of other partners, or even by anticipating wedlock. To sustain purity of mind and body, adolescents were supervised by 'responsible' adults whenever possible, subjected to moral preaching from schools and pulpits, and given alternative outlets for their energies, including netball, early-morning swims and cold showers. There was a double standard. Extra-marital sex was considered less harmful for males. Prostitution was sometimes justified as a necessary outlet for respectable men, married and single. 'Sowing one's wild oats' could be a route to maturity for a man, whereas sexually generous girls were stigmatised as scrubbers, slags, sluts or just plain common (McRobbie and Garber, 1976). Girls were encouraged to make themselves sexually attractive, then instructed to be on their guard against boys who were 'only after the one thing'.

It would be amazing, given the spread of information, easier access and improvements in contraceptive technology, plus the wider availability of abortion, if there had been no changes in the sexual behaviour of married and unmarried individuals. The basic mechanics of contraception were known in ancient Egypt, but have only been widely employed in Britain since the 1860s (Banks, 1954). In the 1920s, 'appliances' were still middle-class gadgets (Gittins, 1982). Until the 1950s it remained common practice for married couples to use contraception 'negatively', to prevent more births once their 'planned' families were complete (Rowntree and Pierce, 1961). It is only among subsequent generations that the divorce between intercourse and conception has become a taken-for-granted, everyday matter of fact.

More people probably are 'having it' pre- and extra-maritally. It is estimated that 15 to 30 per cent of British babies are not products of the mothers' husbands (Oakley, 1981, p. 264). In Dunnell's (1979) research, among women married before 1951, 66 per cent of under 20-year-old brides and 78 per cent of the 20- to 24-year-olds reported no pre-marital sex with their husbands. By contrast, among those marrying between 1971 and 1976, only 18 and 28 per cent were inexperienced. By the 1970s, artificial birth control had won approval among three-quarters of Britain's Roman Catholics, and nearly a half argued that intercourse between engaged couples was not wrong (Hornsby-Smith and Lee, 1979). Whether couples should anticipate marriage is no longer an issue. Within working-class communities, 'home-breaking' extra-marital sex has been condemned, whereas several generations have tolerated 'home-making' pre-marital sex (Klein, 1964). The argument for sex as a normal, healthy part of stable loving relationships has been won. The only issue left for debate is whether some relationships are too casual for sex. This question may arouse the prurient, but is the suggestion revolutionary?

Some commentators interpret recent trends as a spread of promiscuity, meaning that sex is ceasing to be regulated by social norms and that people are surrendering to animal instinct. They are wrong. Chapter 6 explains that heterosexuality itself is a social norm. The promiscuous fiend is a mythical folk-devil whose appeal resides in helping the innocent to make sense of otherwise mysterious changes, while the resulting moral panics comfort traditionalists by confirming their own normality and righteousness. Casual recreational sex may be winning paper advocates and participants. A rapid circulation of sexual partners in one-night stands may be more common than formerly. Sex without emotional involvement, in fleeting and more permanent relationships, may be on the increase. More couples may be developing stable, emotionally involved and sexually active relationships without any presumption of their affairs leading to marriage, procreation or common households. If they are occurring, these trends are not towards promiscuity: the types of behaviour are socially patterned, and hardly add up to a revolution.

Talk of a sexual revolution ignores the many continuities in behaviour and attitudes. Newspapers are eager to report liberated couples who play 'spouse swapping' and acknowledge, even encourage, each other's affairs. The fact that such stories are still newsworthy only testifies that most of our lives are more conventional. Adultery in itself is no longer sufficient ground for divorce, but is still accepted as evidence that a marriage has broken down irretrievably. Rising rates of divorce and remarriage are maintaining, not destroying the traditional relationship between sexuality and the family.

Some apparent changes are the result of today's young people maturing earlier than previous generations. The mean age of puberty has fallen, and all stages of experience are now being commenced at younger ages. Apparently dramatic increases in school-girl pregnancies, which newspapers headline, must be read against this historical trend. Females in their late teens and 20s used to 'get into trouble'. Nowadays the majority of the 'high-risk' group have married, and thereby escaped risk by these ages. Until the 1970s, there was a long-term historical trend towards younger marriage. In 1901, 26·7 per cent of women aged between 20 and 24 were married. In 1971, it was 62·1 per cent, but by 1978 the percentage had fallen to 52·6. It is impossible to tell whether this will become a permanent reversal of the former trend, and eventually make teenage weddings rare exceptions. It is also impossible to tell whether young adults are simply postponing marriage, or whether a growing minority is making alternative long-term arrangements. There may be different trends in different sections of the population – one aspect (others are discussed in Chapter 10 on youth unemployment) of how Britain is becoming an increasingly divided society. In areas with high rates of early school-leaving and unemployment, there are signs of girls opting for the 'security' of parenthood while younger than ever. Among the college educated, by contrast, marriage and parenthood are being postponed for longer, or indefinitely.

It is said that sex has been liberated for free, frank and open discussion, among other uses. How many parents tell their children and how many teachers tell pupils about their own adolescent (and adult) activities? How many people have no secrets from their spouses, or even their closest friends? Today's enlightened parents inform their children about the facts of life. Sex education is now offered in virtually all secondary schools, and in many primary classrooms, but not from personal experience. When sex is thrown open for 'frank' discussion, parents and teachers become talking textbooks. They certainly do not offer practical lessons. Sexual practice is kept as a mystery which young people learn from one another. Adolescents continue to receive their most significant sex education informally. A message of the 'official' curriculum is that sex is private. We maintain a distinction between sex as a topic for public discussion, and our personal, private sex lives. Our own practices and memories usually remain locked within our private selves that we are unwilling to display to neighbours and fellow-workers. We allow ourselves to speak only in agony columns, and when doctors and researchers offer confidentiality and scientific neutrality. Researchers have no difficulty finding subjects willing to answer personal questions on sex. Many prove eager to seize the rare opportunity.

Some homosexuals have 'come out' or gone public, and demanded equal opportunities to compete for employment, to hold public office and commit consenting acts in private. Whether the proportion of the population with homosexual inclinations, and the volume of homosexual activity, has increased is less certain. Whatever the trends, there can be little doubt that heterosexuality remains *the* norm. Even liberated minds hesitate before making 'deviant' experiences public.

Among young people, homosexual behaviour is not allowed to develop into identification with the homosexual role. It is defined as a passing phase. There is no way in which parents or peers will accept homosexuality as a choice or destiny.

Schofield's (1965) national survey, which involved a total of 1,873 interviews with 15- to 19-year-olds, found that 'experienced' boys usually explained their behaviour in terms of 'sexual appetite', while the girls named 'love'. Boys may be more reluctant to reveal emotions, but teenage girls still appear to consider love a necessary condition for sex. Many believe it would indicate immoral intentions to 'take precautions' before acquiring steady partners (Ashdown-Sharpe, 1972; Lafitte, 1972). Despite the wider availability of more effective contraception, legal abortion, plus sex education in schools, the percentage of children born illegitimately has continued to increase from under 5 per cent before the 1950s, to 5·7 per cent in 1961, 8·2 per cent in 1971, and 10·6 per cent in 1979. The stigma surrounding illegitimacy and lone parenthood have lessened, though not disappeared. There must be more women than formerly, including divorcees planning future marriages, who become unmarried mothers by choice rather than pure accident. Some pre-marital teenage pregnancies are deliberate: the girls want to become mothers (Young, 1954), sometimes to accelerate their progress towards marriage by winning the support of parents and boyfriends. However, for many teenagers, ignorance and traditional morality still mean that, in practice, contraception and abortion are not available.

Many young people's physical heterosexual experience is still restricted to the partners they eventually marry. In Gorer's (1971) national survey, 26 per cent of the male and 63 per cent of the females claimed they were virgins at their time of marriage, and a further 20 per cent of the males and 25 per cent of the females reported that their only pre-marital experience was with their future spouses. Are today's young people gaining wider experience? All our evidence indicates that it is still common for young people to have only one serious relationship (Leonard, 1980). When Schofield (1973) reinterviewed his original teenage sample, after the majority were married, 56 per cent had experienced sex with only the one partner. The majority of young people are sexually initiated by steady partners, not casual pick-ups, and the most common place is at home (Schofield, 1965), Prior to marriage, during courtship, the prevailing norm is that couples' relationships are sexually exclusive (Leonard, 1980).

Any sexual revolution has not brought sexual equality. Boys may now do with respectable girls what they once had to do with slags or prostitutes, and nice girls who succumb do not lose their respectability, provided they restrict their activities to a small number of steady relationships. But girls remain disadvantaged in sexual liaisons, culturally and economically. Lower earnings and pocket money, plus the cost of maintaining feminine appearances, keep girls dependent. They still trade meals and drinks for sex. In higher education, where male and female students receive the same grants, and women have claimed the right to dress cheaply, partners enter sexual relationships on more equal terms. Expenses are shared. Later on, however, after graduation, men and women are segregated into superior and subordinate jobs, and the imbalance returns.

Even on campuses, males and females cannot meet as complete sexual equals because the sex act itself remains culturally defined in male terms, with the active male penetrating the woman's body. Sucking, absorbing and enveloping – words that emphasise women's control in copulation – are not equally acceptable in the public vocabulary of sexual intercourse. It is still assumed that men will take the lead in the sex act, perform and prove their masculinity to themselves, and women. Female sexuality is assumed, by men, to be inferior – less appetite and enjoyment, despite women satisfying themselves as rapidly and effectively as men during masturbation (Hite, 1977). It is supposedly the man's fault if the woman fails to climax. If women take the initiative, men become confused. Women are reluctant to tell partners how they are best aroused. If their enjoyment of the act becomes known, women are labelled as nymphomaniacs. These practices and assumptions are unfounded in biology but entrenched in our culture. According to Hite (1977, p. 449), the sexual revolution 'has not so far allowed more real freedom for women (and men) to explore their own sexuality; it has merely put pressure on them to have *more* of the same kind of sex'. Access to birth control and recognition of their sexual desires have deprived women of the right to say, 'No.'

The above passages are not disputing that sexual behaviour and attitudes have changed, but the changes can mostly be explained as adjustments to new opportunities, created by contraception, for example. If the meaning of sexuality had changed so that heterosexuality was no longer the norm, but just one of several acceptable preferences, it would be proper to talk of a revolution. Such talk would be equally appropriate if the relationship between sexuality and the division of labour by gender had been overhauled so that, for example, sexual activity was now divorced from family roles. More people 'having it' more often outside marriage does not change the role of sexuality, or the division of labour by gender, and the main reason why the 'sexual revolution' is beside the point is that debating the issue neither comes to terms with the ways in which adolescent and adult sexuality are controlled nor identifies the main consequences.

The Liberation of Women?
Family life is supposedly changing, with greater equality between
husbands and wives. Equal rights to possess property, plus the vote
and divorce, were won long ago. During the 1970s women achieved
legal entitlement to equal pay, and equal opportunities in education
and employment. Within the home, some researchers have noted a
trend towards symmetrical families (Young and Willmott, 1973)
where couples share interests and tasks, take joint decisions, and spend
their money from joint bank accounts. The small planned family has
become the norm, and the typical mother now has her youngest child
in school while in her thirties. The majority of wives are no longer
mere housewives but hold paid employment, and it is claimed that
housework, like breadwinning, is being shared out. Leisure is supposedly becoming available for men and women in more equal
amounts, on equal terms (Bell and Healey, 1973).

Dependent children are no longer around to share the emotional
load during the greater part of a marriage's lifetime. Kin are no longer
on hand to provide day-to-day support. Outside social and cultural
backwaters, the extended family has ceased to be a definite group with
clear rights and obligations, whose members live in close proximity.
Rising standards of living, geographical mobility and the decline in
the birth-rate have eroded these networks. Kinship is still recognised,
but has become a loose network of relationships that individuals
activate according to convenience and interpersonal attraction (Firth *et
al.*, 1970). It is argued that these trends have accentuated the importance of the conjugal relationship as the foundation for successful
marriage. Its irretrievable breakdown is now recognised in law as
sufficient ground for divorce. It is generations in Britain since 'good'
marriages were normally arranged, since women married solely for
economic security, and men to obtain housekeeping services. Even
romantic love and regular sex have become dated motives; they are
available outside wedlock. It is argued that present-day couples seek
interpersonal compatibility (Blood and Wolfe, 1960) as 'colleagues' or
'companions' rather than as 'head' and 'dependent' members of their
households.

The decline in infant mortality has been listed among the trends
encouraging sex equality. Males are the less resilient, and, in the past,
by adolescence the larger number of male births was transformed into
a surplus of women. Some were condemned to remain wallflowers at
dances, and to spinsterhood. Today there are insufficient women for
all men to marry. In market circumstances, marginal shifts in the
balance of forces can produce sharp fluctuations in the price of commodities. Hence, it is argued, their scarcity value has enabled girls to
become selective, and required boys to make themselves fashionable

sex-objects. Careful grooming is no longer peculiarly feminine. Casual dress used to be a male prerogative. In public, women were expected to be smart or pretty. Today unisex is the fashion. 'Eyeing' and 'sampling' the talent have ceased to be male privileges.

Changes in courtship and sexual behaviour among young people are said to reflect these trends towards equality. American questionnaire surveys among high-school and college students indicate that, among males, sex before marriage had been the norm at least since the First World War (Leslie, 1967). The subsequent rise in pre-marital activity has been sharper among females. Men are now less likely to be initiated by prostitutes. Today they participate with partners they are eventually likely to marry. It is claimed that dating and steady relationships accustom males and females to interacting on equal terms, and allow young people to test their sexual, psychological and social compatibility.

The problem with these alleged trends is that leisure research among young people and adults continues to uncover all the old sharp gender divisions. Women's participation rates in out-of-home recreation, especially sport, still run well beneath male levels. The twenty-four-hour housework shift, less cash for personal pleasure, and cultural restrictions still limit women's opportunities. Chapter 2 noted that gender differences have featured prominently and attracted comment ever since surveys of young people's spare-time activities have been undertaken. These differences are not disappearing. It is doubtful whether they are even narrowing, except possibly among the highly educated élite. Sportspeople still tend to be males, and the growth of sports participation during the 1970s widened the gap rather than equalised men's and women's activity rates. When they are present in the same leisure milieux, such as discos and youth clubs, males and females continue to behave in their different masculine and feminine ways. Girls still spend more time at home, and are expected to undertake household chores (Newson and Newson, 1976).

There is debate on whether women's leisure is deficient or simply different. Some writers argue that leisure, as conventionally defined, is a masculine concept, and object to women's lives and opportunities being judged against male standards. 'The starting point should be the collective achievements of women to date rather than their failure to slip from under the yoke of male "oppression".' Gregory (1982) argues that women's leisure has its own strengths; that women integrate play with family and community obligations, and even paid employment, instead of demarcating special times and places for leisure, and that this female life-style encourages resourcefulness and an ability to adjust to change that men, as well as women, may find increasingly helpful in the future. Hence the case for better provision for women's existing needs, rather than deploring their failure or inability to use male facilities.

The contrary argument, insisting that women are disadvantaged, has been vigorously stated by Rosemary Deem (1982a, 1982b), supported by evidence from 195 females, plus numerous women's organisations in Milton Keynes. Deem argues that however much it encourages resourcefulness and adaptability, the fact remains that women have less leisure, and that their uses of the leisure time and money they do possess are restricted by gender roles and responsibilities. She argues that when women derive leisure experiences from domestic roles, and by servicing husbands' and children's play, they are making the best of an objectively disadvantaged situation. Furthermore, Deem argues, the main beneficiaries of this situation are not women themselves, but men who gain housekeeping services, employers who benefit from a reserve army of cheap labour, and the state which avoids the costs of child-care facilities. Deem also points out that women's opportunities to make the best of their feminine circumstances are associated with education, adequate income and car ownership.

Where are the husbands and wives who are enjoying leisure in equal amounts, on equal terms? Even in families where both husbands and wives hold professional qualifications and employment, their roles remain asymmetrical (Edgell, 1980). Are times really a-changing? There are more wives in employment than a generation ago, but time-budget surveys show that men are doing only slightly more housework – this remains primarily 'women's work' (Thomas and Shannon, 1982). Men's domestic work-time does not increase when their wives take outside jobs. The women are left to cope by compressing domestic chores into the smaller number of available hours. Moreover, domestic gadgets for cooking, cleaning and washing do not reduce housework time. In some ways they increase the demands upon women by raising expectations and standards. Early twentieth-century feminists and socialists anticipated an industrialisation of domestic work, with crèches, laundries and restaurants provided by the state or private enterprise. This has never happened. Instead, industry has created or discovered markets for domestic appliances. Commercial manipulation of consumer demand cannot be wholly responsible. If an equally powerful latent demand had existed, capitalist entrepreneurs would have competed successfully with cheap eating and laundry services. The public's preference for domestic appliances has rested on an unquestioned assumption, by men and women, that the latter's work at home is free.

The next chapter supplies details of how teenage peer groups and leisure activities develop within, cannot be insulated from, and are indeed structured by the wider social setting described above. Patriarchal gender role models are propagated by the media, and confront young people in their childhood families. During adolescence, educational trajectories and job opportunities commit males and females to different futures. Peer groups cannot overturn; they mediate and amplify these realities. Boys' leisure is as gender typed as girls', but a wider range of activities are judged compatible with masculinity. In any case, boys are unlikely to see any serious need to question their economic and cultural dominance. Women's liberation is good for a joke. Males favour liberating women from some traditional inhibitions. Waiting time is a useful indicator of social position (Lewis and Weigert, 1981). Among girls it is an important skill. They learn to wait for boys to propose dates, to telephone, to be taken to discos, to be invited to dance and to go to bed, just as adult women wait on their husbands and children.

Is there a case for youth workers and other leisure professionals forgetting ideas about boys being naturally sporting, and that girls can only be interested in records and dancing? Would non-discriminatory leisure opportunities assist girls to escape from patriarchy, and allow males and females to explore alternative gender and sexual roles? Chapter 6 will argue that, within our present society, boys and girls have no alternative to using leisure provisions in masculine and feminine ways. Chapter 12 takes up the point that youth and leisure services are already relatively undiscriminating, but given the wider social context, girls inevitably use leisure to make themselves attractive to boys, on the latter's terms, and both sexes spend a great deal of their spare time and money nurturing relationships leading to marriage. Leisure is probably one sphere where the best way of addressing women's disadvantages is not by eradicating gender differences but by raising the status of feminine activities (Cohen, 1981). This will involve the youth and leisure services becoming more aware, sensitive and responsive, and developing a wider range of activities and milieux for girls' feminine interests.

5
The Adolescent Procession

This analysis of sex and gender, then later chapters on social class differences among young people at leisure, juxtapose a 'traditional sociology of youth' against more recent perspectives. Until the 1960s, functionalism was sociology's dominant theory. Orthodox interpretations presented adolescence as a period of continuous socialisation. Functionalist sociology endorses the social realism of defining adolescence as the 'betwixt and between years', after young people begin emancipating themselves from families of orientation, but prior to establishing families of procreation, then explains how the adolescent society which fills the gap is not a mere 'waiting room' where individuals mark time before gaining full economic independence and the legal right to marry. It describes how young people are gradually weaned from, and allowed to establish, more distant relationships with parents and kin, and simultaneously taught social and emotional skills that cannot be learnt at home or school but which are essential in building adult gender and sexual identities. Adolescence is treated as a 'process'. 'Stage' is judged too static a concept. Peer groups are constantly evolving. Leisure interests are highly volatile. Youth cultures are fluid. Young people are age-conscious; less homogeneous than they may appear from a distance.

Functionalist accounts recognise that some features of adolescent life are rigid rather than fluid, and define the boundaries within which leisure interests and social relationships change. In particular, gender divisions are strengthened as children move towards adulthood. Young people may lack sexual confidence, but they are rarely confused about gender. They know whether they are becoming men or women. Sexuality, among other skills, is learnt within prescribed and internalised gender roles. Functionalist sociology argues that peer groups are less independent and youth cultures less autonomous than older theories of intergenerational conflict suggested. Young people transport values and identities acquired during childhood into adolescence. The majority live at home until marriage, supervised and economically dependent upon parents. Young people's freedom is bounded. Teenagers are subjected to a variety of manifest and insidious controls. Youth cultures are penetrated by numerous extraneous influences, which keep them fluid and maintain the movement of young people from childhood towards conventional adult roles, while simultaneously imposing certain meanings and divisions that young people are never allowed to question.

To non-sociologists, functionalist accounts of adolescence may still sound radical in so far as they explain how young people's defiance and sexuality have conservative rather than traumatic consequences. This interpretation of the adolescent procession remains alive in sociology, but within the discipline it is now considered conservative, and has encountered growing opposition from 'radical' investigators seeking to understand what their activities mean to young people themselves as well as for the wider society, and from writers influenced by conflict theory, especially feminist versions. They have queried whether it is really 'functional' for everyone that home should be defined as feminine territory and the public arena as masculine, with all the implications for youth and leisure. Is it absolutely essential that we override demands for sexual freedom, and maintain the marriage/family institutions for the procreation, care and socialisation of children? Whose interests are served by keeping women at the lower end of the labour market, increasing men's chances of landing the top jobs, thereby making child-rearing a more attractive option for females? Would it be more crippling for us all if the state provided child- and adult-care facilities.

A theme of this book is the need for synthesis: to cross-fertilise theories of youth and leisure, and to absorb older sociological perspectives rather than abandon all that was previously known, like the stages in the adolescent procession distinguished by functionalist writers, which should prove acceptable for descriptive purposes even among those who dispute whether the causes and consequences are functional. This chapter therefore describes the developments which transform boys and girls into men and women, husbands and wives, and structure their uses of leisure. It explains how adolescent leisure reproduces conventional gender roles and forms of sexuality. Simultaneously, however, it introduces questions raised by critics of this reproduction. Do present arrangements impose unnecessary restrictions on all young people, and subordinate women in particular?

Needless to say, there is no uniform pattern of adolescent development followed by all boys and girls, from all social strata, in all parts of the country. The processes vary by region, race, parental social class and education. Personality factors account for further differences. However, the best way to introduce the variations is by explaining how and why specific groups and individuals diverge from an ideal-typical pattern. A modal pattern can be discerned, despite the numerous departures. It leads from childhood. Before they can join the adolescent procession, children must learn that they are boys and girls, and how to play.

Child's Play

Do infants really play? Or are the activities we define as play experienced as work by young children themselves? Learning to play is a work-task for the very young. Parents and teachers define certain times, activities and festivals, such as Christmas, as occasions for enjoyment. The work–leisure division is not a natural, universal rhythm. It became normal only with the advent of industrialism (Thompson, 1967). Early factory owners struggled to impose industrial discipline. Today's beginning workers are more compliant. They enter employment, when it is available, having been prepared to seek their pleasures in the after hours, and one reason is that, in important respects, schools are run like factories (Bowles and Gintis, 1976). They teach the virtues of punctuality and disciplined toil during the working day, and thereby define leisure as a separate, complementary part of life. Domestic routines reflect their members' paid employment and reinforce the impact of schooling. Children are taught to distinguish work from leisure, sometimes informally, as a result of their participation in families, and sometimes deliberately. Parents who wish their infants to grow into well-adjusted, high-achieving pupils make sure the children realise that certain times are set aside for work that has to be done, whereas on other occasions they can 'play', preferably with 'educational' toys, and 'improve' while enjoying themselves.

Children are taught to play and, in this sense, their games are organised like adults' jobs with equipment, tasks and companions · selected by supervisors – parents and teachers. If we could become full participant observers, or conduct informal depth interviews among young children, would we discover any near fit between the playtimes and activities defined by teachers and parents, and the children's perceptions? Informal observation suggests that children create their own play-space within activities and environments that adults provide for work and approved games. Children organise their own play during lessons and meals in addition to 'official' playtimes.

Middle-class parents tend to be the more deliberative and successful in controlling their children's recreation. They maintain the wider span of control over children's choices of games and friends, and are the more aware of how play can be intrinsically satisfying and simultaneously educational, with children nurturing interests and skills to transfer to their schoolwork (Newson and Newson, 1968, 1976). Infants in playgroups from different social class backgrounds make different uses of 'free play' periods. Middle-class infants are the more active: they are the more likely to be taught by parents to use materials 'constructively', and to treat adults as 'resources' to turn to for assistance (Barnett, 1981; Child, 1981). Their parents are the more assiduous readers of books and articles on, 'How to rear a bright, adjusted child'. They encourage children to play quietly, and co-operatively, often *with* adults rather than *under* the latter's supervision. Working-class children are more likely to be granted the freedom of the streets, with adults intervening, sometimes with heavy hands, only when the kids create trouble. The message internalised by children is that adults must be avoided or obeyed. As middle-class infants grow into school-age children, parents ensure that their offspring fulfil whatever potential they possess and, if possible, excel in sports, dance, music or any other activities at which the children display some talent. These are the concerned, interested and participant parents who make themselves known to their children's teachers and establish co-operative home–school relationships. The less closely supervised working-class children make the earlier transitions into adolescence.

In his research among over 5,000 American high-school students, Rosenberg (1965) found that middle-class teenagers remained the more closely attached to their parents, and one consequence appeared to be that these young people possessed the greater self-confidence and self-esteem. Working-class youth begin to 'stay out', smoke, go out with the opposite sex, enter employment and eventually marry ahead of their more carefully coached middle-class peers. Middle-class child-rearing practices delay social maturation, but those responsible are no doubt well-satisfied with the results. Working-class teenagers' lives are less structured by adults. They appear to have greater freedom to 'do their own things' – though later·chapters will argue that this appearance is deceptive – and also to worry about their personal adequacy.

Cliques and Special Friends

Working-class children are given the greater and earlier scope, but before the end of their primary-school years, most young people are being encouraged, or at least allowed, to design their own uses of 'officially' programmed leisure time, and are beginning to spend these parts of their lives in 'worlds of their own'. It is impossible to name one chronological age, or even dates when particular individuals complete childhood and begin adolescence. Children's own worlds are slowly strengthened. At any time after the age of 8, parents are likely to find their children drifting away. Teachers begin to find classes becoming difficult to control. Within peer groups, young people accord each other statuses and identities, sometimes derived from pop culture, that differ from those bestowed by parents and teachers. Young people begin to use peers rather than families as reference groups for their tastes in dress, music, hairstyles and argot. Peers replace parents and teachers as architects of the framework for play, or leisure. Parents and teachers find their efforts to advise and assert control resented as interference. Adolescence begins when young people establish this independence, which is usually won only within and by adopting the wider society's definition of leisure time.

It used to be said that boys organised themselves into mono-sexual gangs, while girls formed special friendships with individuals of the same age and sex (Douvan and Adelson, 1966). Boys were judged to be in greater need of peer-group support to assert masculine independence from female-dominated households. They have also been given the greater encouragement to 'break the apron strings', more pocket money, freedom to stay out late and to roam the streets. Parents are more protective towards daughters. However, the evidence now available suggests that juxtaposing gangs and special friends overstates the breadth of gender differences. These differences could be narrowing over time, but it is also possible that earlier investigators were misled by the greater visibility of male peer groups (Crane, 1958).

Girls' peer groups are less visible than boys'. Female 'gangs' can be observed in most city centres, but other women shoppers reduce the visibility of these hordes. Gangs of teenage boys, behaving in boisterous, masculine ways, are more likely to be noticed. In any case, girls tend to congregate with friends at school and in each other's homes rather than in city centres or even neighbourhood streets. Many girls' cliques dissolve when their members leave school and lose one of their bases for interaction (Leonard, 1980). Girls lack the resources to nurture their own networks. They have less cash to spare than boys, because of lower wages and pocket money, plus higher self-maintenance costs, and also less time, since girls are the more likely to be required to undertake household duties (Newson and Newson, 1976). They also face public not to mention parental disapproval of unescorted females in public places – on the streets and in pubs. Youth workers have directed their efforts towards boys rather than girls. There are now more boys' than girls' clubs, just as working men's clubs are not paralleled by organisations for working women. Men have been reluctant to allow women to develop and control their own leisure organisations. Even the Women's Institutes had to struggle against male opposition in their early history (Deem, 1982b). This is why, once they leave school, girls are often fragmented, separated from each other and prevented from regrouping. If boys' gangs are more common and resilient than girls', maybe this is a result of the latter being prevented rather than their lesser need of group support. At present, where they exist, girls' peer groups are the less likely to create trouble for the wider society, force themselves to the attention of police and other authorities, and thereby become problems for researchers to pursue. Female peer groups have probably been over-looked by researchers and public alike, and their scale of under-representation in the literature cannot be taken as an accurate measure of their rarity. Nevertheless, males are the more likely to maintain peer-group life in pubs, clubs and sports teams throughout adolescence, and adulthood.

'Gang' may be too strong a term for most male groups. It suggests clearly defined memberships, names, leaders, maybe initiation rituals, a capacity to 'take on' other groups and to defend the gang's own territory. Such groups exist, but often more in the imaginations of self-styled leaders and committed members, plus some police officers, journalists and film-makers, than as objective social structures (Downes, 1966; Yablonsky, 1967). Yablonsky proposes 'near group', but 'clique' is probably as adequate, and a more recognisable term, for describing most teenage males' and females' social relationships. Within their cliques, boys also have 'special friends' who 'share secrets' and are invited into each other's houses. There are differences between boys' and girls' styles of sociability, but they have more in common than the gang/special friend contrast suggests.

Another article of conventional wisdom whose validity is now questioned suggests that working-class boys, who are given the earlier freedom of the streets, organise themselves into potentially delinquent gangs, whereas middle-class males develop innocent, fun-seeking relationships. In practice, the main differences seem to be that middle-class youth enter the 'gang phase' later, and operate within the more 'protected' environments – in boarding schools, youth and sports clubs. America's middle-class parents often send their children to summer camps to learn and express their independence (Seeley et al., 1956). Working-class adolescents are indulged only in the sense of having more money in their pockets, some of it earned in casual, spare-time jobs. Middle-class boys and girls have more spent on their behalf. Working-class teenagers need personal spending money to create their own spaces in otherwise public places. No one purchases protected environments for them.

The peer group is the normal milieu for adolescents' spare-time and leisure activities, and these groups seek environments that will accommodate their own informal organisation. Homes are often inhospitable, especially towards boys' gangs. Sports and youth clubs are used, but streets and town centres are also popular resorts for teenagers, particularly boys who are seeking places to 'hang about'. One function of the peer group is to support its members and supply a reference group while they establish a limited degree of independence from adults. Another is to consolidate gender identities. Young people's first independent attachments are normally to same-sexed cliques and special friends, with whom they practise masculine and feminine behaviour. Boys spend more time than girls outside their homes. Gender norms still inhibit girls from using the freedom of the streets. Creating space through assertive behaviour in public places is unfeminine. Street-walking is considered a deviant activity. Hence the importance that teenage girls attach to possessing or lacking their own rooms at home. Those with the opportunity often retreat to the culture of the bedroom – a place to meet friends, listen to music, practise make-up and dancing, discuss clothes, compare sexual notes and generally gossip.

Winning adult independence and becoming masculine or feminine and sexually aware are interwoven in adolescent leisure. Most boys and girls first define their sexual inclinations among same-sexed peers. Within their cliques they learn to 'weigh up' the opposite sex. Boys learn to treat girls as sex-objects. The equivalent feminine behaviour is surreptitious. Economic dependence and cultural subordination deny girls the luxury of male sex-objects. Sex is more frequently a topic of conversation than direct action, but even small-talk can be important. Individuals first learn to define their sexual inclinations through conversation. It is difficult, usually impossible, for young people to establish independence without being sexualised and identifying with the gender roles prescribed for their sex.

Functionalists have assured the wider society that teenage peer groups themselves are not a problem. They have recognised the danger of young people's struggles for independence exceeding tolerable limits, but argue that modern societies must accept teenagers retreating to their own adolescent worlds, then demonstrating their autonomy. Teenagers who are 'left out', who remain tied to the apron strings and good pupils at school, have been identified as a potential problem group. During early adolescence, they may cause little trouble for adults, but they can still possess problems. Some are lonely. They lack introductions to their age-group's normal leisure activities. Some find it difficult to proceed to later stages of social development. Boys and girls who neither belong to cliques nor develop close friendships may be unable to 'go out' (Jephcott, 1955). Leisure is normally a social enterprise. There are few opportunities for the teenage loner. Advising these individuals to 'join a club' misses the point. Teenagers are normally taken to clubs by or with existing friends. Clubs have been described as 'federations of peer groups'; they reflect rather than determine adolescent group structure (Willmott, 1966).

More recently, critics of the adolescent procession have suggested that the normal pattern of social development, which eventually leads into gender and sexual traps, should be considered a problem. As the next chapter will explain, these critics do not recommend isolation, but neither do they accept as desirable or inevitable the gender divisions in which young people learn to think, feel, behave and express sexuality in masculine and feminine ways.

'Going Out': Crowds and Dates

Teenage peer groups do not obliterate family relationships, but change their character. Likewise, relationships with same-sexed peers that are cemented during early adolescence may persist throughout the life-cycle. Many males continue to meet their 'mates' in pubs, darts teams, on golf courses, at Freemasons' and Round Table meetings, where they perpetuate the out-going life-styles commenced during adolescence. Females may retain contact with the special friends, sometimes 'popping in and out' of each other's homes following marriage. Restrictions on teenage girls' out-of-home recreation prepare them for adulthoods in which they remain unable to 'go out' independently because of lack of cash for discretionary spending and long houseworking hours, reinforced by public disapproval of unescorted married women going out to play (Hobson, 1979).

They may not be eradicated, but nevertheless, peer groups *tend* to dissolve and special friendships with the same sex lose their preeminence as young people 'mature'. Monosexual cliques are normally transformed into heterosexual crowds. These are loosely structured collectivities with fluid memberships, vague boundaries, and certainly no leaders, gang names or initiation rituals. The unattached (to formal organisations) young people studied by Morse (1965) spent most of their leisure time in groups of this character. A common development is for pairs or triads of girls, whose own peer groups often disintegrate upon leaving school, to become attached to larger groups of males who congregate in customary places – cafés, discos, youth clubs, pubs or streets (Smith, 1962). When suitable accommodation is available, parties which all who are invited through grapevines can attend to talk, dance, circulate, pair off or remain in their own cliques provide environments tailored to the haphazard membership and organisation of adolescent crowds. These networks are inherently unstable. Cliques, pairs and triads attach themselves to larger crowds, taste the company, then sometimes uncouple themselves hastily. Individuals who remain for a while are constantly pairing off, then dropping out in heterosexual couples.

Young people begin chatting up then going out with individuals from the opposite sex at any age from 12 onwards, sometimes earlier. Partners are usually selected from crowds who see each other 'around and about'. Dates, then steady relationships, do not normally follow chance encounters at dances, parties or public houses. Questionnaires that ask courting and married couples where they first met can create a misleading impression when they oblige respondents to name one specific meeting place. It appears more common for individuals already known to each other in crowds drawn from their neighbourhoods, education institutions or workplaces, and who have already seen each other on numerous previous occasions, to pair off then begin going out (Leonard, 1980).

Consecutive short-lived relationships were initially made respectable by American college students after the First World War. They pioneered 'dating', and the practice soon spread into America's high schools. It was publicised on cinema screens and exported across the Western world. In a dating relationship there is no expectation of permanence, nor any assumption of emotional involvement. Physical intimacy is subject to negotiation. As the dating habit spread, American social scientists began exploring the 'dating and rating complex' (Waller, 1937), and found that many teenagers were extremely concerned, sometimes preoccupied, with their popularity among peers. The typical American high-school student was found to rate 'popularity' above excelling in class (Coleman, 1961).

All the relevant British and American inquiries have found that young people worry about personal relationships, particularly their ability to 'sell' themselves to the opposite sex (Remmers and Radler, 1957; Eppel and Eppel, 1966). They worry about their physical attractiveness, and not without cause, for many young people form first impressions, and often decide whether they desire greater familiarity on the basis of 'looks' (Hendry, 1979). On American campuses, dates are often public knowledge. Student magazines have reported regularly on who is 'dating', 'going steady' and 'serious', and this mine of information has been raided by social scientists (Larson and Leslie, 1968). They have discovered that individuals' ratings depend heavily on the quantity of their dates, and the partners' standing, and his or her 'rating' then becomes a quality that a young person carries into subsequent relationships (Waller, 1937). It becomes part of the currency in sexual negotiations. Girls sell favours and boys pay out, the terms of trade being set by the partners' relative ratings. Youth cultures mediate wider social mores, and teach females to use their sexuality to build social relationships, while males learn to use sex for personal gratification, and pay with status earned in the wider society – the man's world.

Self-respect and status among same-sexed peers become dependent upon proving oneself date-worthy. Since America's middle class-parents, who previously exercised more direct control over their children's courtship behaviour, became aware of dating and rating norms, many have been arranging parties, dances and other occasions to equip their pre-pubertal children with the necessary skills to make themselves popular and attractive to their own and the opposite sex (Seeley *et al.*, 1956).

British parents still worry, but dating relationships are now generally accepted or encouraged, daughters having been warned 'not to get into trouble' (McRobbie and Garber, 1976). Girls are expected to have a good time and acquire boyfriends. Films and pop songs encourage them to believe that Mr Right will capture their emotions and leave them defenceless. They are told that boys are 'just after one thing', and that pregnancy could mean ruin, but are not encouraged to 'take precautions' before going steady, for to do so would indicate 'loose intentions'. Boys are expected to be virile, to take the lead and show they are 'interested', if only to prove themselves normal, but are led to expect nice girls to resist early advances. The girls are told to resist, advised that true love will make resistance impossible, and this failure will diminish their boyfriend's respect. How do young people handle these contradictions? The Quines' (1966) study of 14-year-old British pupils found that 67 per cent of the girls and 23 per cent of the boys claimed to have 'steadies'. Most of these relationships must be physically innocent. In Schofield's (1965) research, only 8 and 7 per cent of the boys and girls were 'experienced' at the age of 16, and no more than 37 and 23 per cent at 19. It still seems exceptional for teenagers to go 'all the way' during short-lived dating relationships.

Most young people first define their sexuality among same-sexed peers. The opposite sex may supply the objects, whether media figures or personal acquaintances, but same-sexed friends can still act as the primary audience who approve or denigrate each other's performances. Such friends often remain a reference group with whom experiences are discussed, and 'notes' exchanged, after young people begin going out with individuals from the opposite sex. Skilled impression management is often necessary to maintain one's rating. Individuals often exaggerate their accomplishments. Total honesty can cost face. This is how the majority of young people become convinced that they are less experienced than most of their age-group, which is a statistical impossibility (Schofield, 1965).

Once individuals have acquired 'the knack' of chatting up, picking up and engaging the company of the opposite sex, they often venture afield, away from their own crowds to city-centre discos and dances. These trips 'abroad' can be exciting. The action is unpredictable. The disco at a local youth club or community centre is no real substitute (Robins and Cohen, 1978). Leisure facilities that draw young people from various quarters of cities and regions play a special role in the adolescent social calendar.

It used to be argued that dating was exploitive and competitive, embodying entirely different norms from courtship, teaching methods of handling people of use in professional and business careers, but dysfunctional in developing relationships leading to marriage. However, American social scientists have now tested this hypothesis with their customary vigour, and have been unable to identify any clear 'break' between dating and courtship relationships (Leslie, 1967). The weight of the evidence suggests that dating allows young people to develop the social skills required to attract mates in societies where partners are self-selected. It is not a universal stage. In Britain, where dating has never been as widely encouraged by parents and schools as in North America, many young people move directly into steady, albeit often temporary liaisons. But it is teenagers who never become involved in cliques, attached to same-sexed friends, or immersed in crowds, not the more active daters, who appear to experience the greatest difficulty in establishing relationships leading to marriage. These individuals tend to be 'late starters', who often seize the first opportunity to go steady and marry after short courtships (Leonard, 1980).

Cliques, crowds and dating relationships are inherently fluid. They do not offer secure, permanent statuses. Many young people find the heterosexual market-place stressful, never become full-blooded participants in the dating game and grasp the earliest opportunity to escape into steady liaisons. In later decades, some may recall the 'time of their lives' for the benefit of their successors. Youth may be at its best in retrospect. At the time, young people worry about their popularity and their ability to handle interpersonal relationships. Many dislike the charade of putting on masculine and feminine airs and graces, proving themselves and performing in front of the opposite sex. The popularity of computer dating among older age-groups who can afford this service indicates a widespread desire for relief from the burden of 'hunting' for partners. Some young people opt out of the educational, occupational and sexual rat-races, and surrender to movements such as the Unification Church (the Moonies), which then instructs them where to work, and who to marry. Is this behaviour as amazing as the press makes it sound? How much brainwashing is required? When the option is suggested, substantial numbers of 'ordinary' young people say they would consider it a relief if their marriages could be 'arranged' (Barker, 1981).

Courtship and Marriage

The nomenclature varies, but throughout Western Europe and North America young people distinguish three types of pre-marital heterosexual relationships. 'Going out' differs from 'going steady', which is different from 'courting' with its (revocable) commitment to marriage. In Britain, the vast majority of first marriages are preceded by public engagements, with the partners making their intentions known and visible, often by the bride-to-be displaying a ring (Leonard, 1980).

The stages in the heterosexual procession to which individuals have progressed are sometimes used to indicate their general social maturity. Functionalist accounts note the typical pattern of adolescent development from monosexual cliques through heterosexual crowds to couple relationships, which become increasingly stable (Smith, 1962; Dunphy, 1963), and suggest that a main function of each stage is to equip young people to progress to the next. This same idea of progression through stages has been applied to young people's sexual activities. The scales begin with 'holding hands', then progress through various forms of manual stimulation to full intercourse (Schofield, 1965). Social and sexual development, thus measured, are closely related. Intercourse becomes common, though not universal, only within steady relationships. Needless to say, individuals do not have to halt at all the stages. Social development is more variable than straightforward biological maturation. Levels can be leapt, and individuals can move backwards as well as forwards – from courting to just going out, and from 'having it regularly' to less heavy practices.

The importance attached to 'love' in Western cultures often disrupts socio-sexual development. It is considered legitimate to allow an ambiguous feeling for another person to shatter an established relationship which the partner, friends and parents assumed was leading to marriage. Young people from Asian backgrounds can find it difficult, maybe impossible, to reconcile Western cultures with their families' expectation that children will accept arranged marriages, and treat love as a bonus or duty. Indigenous youth experience comparable cross-pressures, the difference being that Western cultures encourage the young people to ignore parents' expectations. However, despite all the deviations and backsliding, there is a clear tendency for individuals to ascend the levels of social development and sexual experience with age. Instead of going about in cliques or crowds, 'mature' young people spend more of their leisure as couples.

For some girls, thinking, talking about, preparing, then actually going out with boyfriends become virtually the whole of leisure. In some communities, social convention requires girls to drop personal friends and interests on commencing serious courtship (Hobson, 1979). The 'responsibilities' of courting may force girls to relinquish other interests, but a complementary point is that many girls find they need steady partners to maintain any wider interests and relationships. Their peer groups tend to collapse when girls leave school, irrespective of whether individuals already have steady boyfriends. Spatial and social restrictions on girls' leisure make same-sexed relationships difficult to maintain, which helps to push girls into boys' hands.

In addition, Leonard (1980) has drawn attention to how girls are taught to reveal their emotions, and how their talk about boys therefore tends to be personalised. Without first-hand experience to contribute, girls can feel left out and inferior. Boys have less need of steady girlfriends. They can go out unescorted, and male peer groups are the more resilient. Courting males preserve same-sexed friendships with nights out in clubs and darts teams, and through weekend sports. Moreover, when men discuss women it is usually in impersonal, often crude terms. One can participate without offering personal details, and no one is expected to reveal emotions – that would be unmasculine. Girls have a greater need of steady heterosexual relationships to maintain any extra-domestic life: this is one reason why girls develop more quickly and eventually marry older men, though the expectation that the male will be the dominant partner and take the lead in proposing dates is also relevant.

The early 20s is now the most common age for first marriages in Britain – 25 for men and 23 for women in 1978. In Leonard's (1980) study of South Wales couples, a minority of brides and grooms were marrying their first steady partners. Another minority had experience of more than three 'old flames'. Most young people appear to meet their marital partners after only one or two 'false starts'. It remains far from unknown for young people, especially males, to experience only one serious relationship. Despite the ideology of free choice, few young people sample a wide selection of potential partners, and there is one common pattern of development from chatting up, through dating and steady relationships, then courtship to marriage in all regions, and all social classes. Individuals who 'start late' tend to catch up by the prime age of marriage by hurrying through courtships. Another function of anonymous city-centre clubs, pubs and dances is to give 'isolates' the opportunity to meet, and join the adolescent procession. There are strong pressures to conform. There is a fear of being thought immature and, subsequently, 'left on the shelf'. At the same time, it is considered undesirable to marry too hastily or too young – this suggests fecklessness or having been 'forced' to marry. Building a track record of too many 'failed' relationships can also damage a reputation.

Dating couples normally 'go out' to cinemas, dances, pubs, for walks and drives. Courting couples act likewise, but also spend evenings in each other's homes. This is a cheap leisure milieu, which helps when couples are saving to marry. Equally important, when courting seriously, young people are expected to introduce each other to their families. Taking one's companion home indicates serious intentions. When couples begin going out, it is rapidly assumed, by parents and friends, that they are *en route* for engagement, then marriage. What does love mean? Klein (1964) has argued that rather than 'falling' in love, young people who go out regularly simply take it for granted that they are in love. Once aboard this escalator, terminating a relationship can require far more effort than allowing it to develop towards its 'natural' conclusion.

Preparations for marriages and weddings are heavily ritualised. It has been argued, with justification, that young people have some choice over who to marry, though even this is normally governed by the crowds to which they are attached, whereas few genuinely choose whether and how to marry. The desirability of marriage is taken for granted. Most young people are committed to the idea before they even begin dating, let alone 'fall in love' (Broderick and Rowe, 1968). Ask engaged couples why they are marrying; they will invariably interpret the question to mean why they have chosen each other, not why they have selected a marital relationship.

The majority leave their parents' homes only following marriage. 'Living together' pre-maritally may be an option for the college educated, whose careers take them away from their parents' homes, but the remainder have no comparable opportunities to establish independent households. Immediately following their marriage, 24 per cent of the couples in Leonard's (1980) study went to live with one set of parents, but this was always regarded as a temporary expedient. The virtually universal aspiration among marrying couples is to establish independent households. For most young people, marriage and setting up a home, thereby becoming fully independent, are inseparable processes. The only route to full adulthood is by becoming heterosexual and learning conventional gender roles. Despite its reputation, adolescent sexuality is controlled with highly conservative consequences.

Social Class Differences
Homogamy rules. Individuals do not gravitate towards opposites. Like marries like. Young people date, court and marry partners with similar tastes, attitudes and social backgrounds, and exceptions to this 'rule' become increasingly rare at each 'higher' level of social development (Leslie, 1967). Marital partners are self-selected, but usually from a limited range. Status considerations apart, social equals are likely to discover common tastes and interests. Parents rarely need to actively discourage 'unsuitable' company.

Treating gender and social class separately, in different chapters, is an artificial division, though necessary in order to present and make sense of the evidence. There are class differences among boys and girls, and the implications of a given class position are not identical for males and females. Age, gender, class, race, place of residence and other factors interact to create a variety of adolescent situations. The aim as these chapters progress is to build a realistic picture of how young people's freedom to use leisure to develop and express personal interests is restricted by gender, then class and other trajectories, whose net effect is to confine most individuals' scope for choice within trivial boundaries.

Later chapters will list many additional ways in which social class differences pervade youth cultures. Choice of marital partners is just one, highly sensitive indicator. Adult class divisions are reproduced as young people pass through education, then into the labour market. In the days of the 11-plus, persons destined for different levels of employment attended different secondary schools. Private schools still enable parents who are able and willing to pay to ensure that their children make little contact with 90 per cent of the population. However, even in comprehensives, pupils are allocated to different streams and, most important of all, those destined for the higher levels of occupational achievement stay on beyond 16 and proceed to higher education. United States comprehensive schools have been described as social melting-pots, but inside these schools, in Britain and America, peer relationships divide along social class lines. In the United States, fraternities and sororities in high schools and colleges often formalise these divisions (Seeley et al., 1956).

The tendency for working-class youth to mature more quickly than middle-class contemporaries reinforces other segregating processes. Middle-class adolescents are 'retarded' by taking longer to break away from protective parents, then by remaining in education, financially dependent upon families or maintenance grants, after working-class youth have become wage-earners. When they embark upon their occupational careers, white-collar employees usually face incremental salary scales. Their earnings may not peak until middle age. Middle-class couples wishing to purchase their own houses need to save, from low starting salaries, which means postponing marriage, or at least parenthood, until they have accumulated 'deposits' and can afford mortgage repayments. Manual workers, by contrast, usually reach maximum earning power in their early 20s. Those seeking independent accommodation in the rented, council housing sector, have little incentive to delay and save. Quite the reverse: couples can strengthen their applications for council housing by marrying and/or having children. 'To get a council house what you need is to get yourself into a mess' – that is, pregnant (Ineichen, 1981).

These are among the reasons why working-class couples marry relatively young. Between 1968 and 1971, 47·3 per cent of first-marrying brides of unskilled manual workers were aged under 20, against 8·8 per cent where the groom held professional employment. Young brides are often pregnant. During 1971–6, 27·3 per cent of first births to married women aged under 20 were conceived pre-maritally, against 4·3 per cent among the over 25s. Teenage marriages are also distinguished by their high risks of divorce (Thornes and Collard, 1979). This may be partly a result of individuals marrying before they are genuinely ready to 'settle down' and embark upon homemaking. Friends who are still seeking the bright lights and sowing wild oats can be distracting. Many teenage marriages are also strained by housing and financial problems. In addition, it is possible that exceptionally young marriages, especially 'shotgun weddings', involve 'deviant' young people whose marriages would have been 'at risk' whatever the partners' ages. Brides aged 16 and 17 are exceptional, even in working-class communities. Most working-class couples postpone marriage until their early 20s, and despite the rising divorce rate, the majority of these unions prove life-long.

6
Breaking Out

What Keeps the Procession Moving?
The developmental sequence described in the previous chapter is not a product of postwar youth cultures. The gender roles and heterosexual relationships still being perpetuated predate punks, hippies and Teds. The adolescent procession is a product of the wider society's gender divisions and sexual norms, and young people's uses of leisure have remained within these parameters throughout successive styles and fads. Youth cultures have not encouraged dropping out, widened horizons or opened alternative futures, but committed young people to relationships leading to marriage. The everyday concept implies, and some leisure theories affirm, that spare-time activities are neither more nor less than personal choices. Yet it is impossible to account for adolescent leisure while we imagine that we must explain how autonomous individuals select activities matching their personal tastes and interests. In practice, adolescents' leisure patterns are powerfully shaped by gender roles which are determined by the wider society rather than by young people themselves. Threats posed by the freedom of leisure have been successfully countered.

Another everyday notion is that there are unlikely to be profound long-term consequences if males play like boys, and females like girls, with sexuality spicing their activities. This ideology of leisure helps to persuade individuals to internalise norms which, by the end of adolescence, have locked most adults into masculine and feminine futures. The adolescent procession leaves a minority of drop-outs. We will return to them later. But most travellers become husbands and wives, founders of new nuclear families, that rear new generations of young people. This was the fate of the 1950s' Teddy Boys, together with the 1960s' beatniks, hippies, mods and rockers. Adolescent sexuality only appears to threaten the family when viewed in isolation. Once located in their developmental contexts, the conservative character of teenage heterosexual relationships becomes self-evident.

The adolescent character of young people's leisure is stamped not by individuals' choices, but by the composition of their peer groups. The pairs and larger congregations, mono- and bi-sexual, in which young people are involved, shape adolescent leisure. Young people (and adults) select leisure activities not merely for their own sake but, above all else, for their compatibility with their social networks. Male monosexual cliques congregate in cafés, youth clubs and streets, wherever the group will fit, and engage in whatever activities these milieux will support. Heterosexual crowds prefer the softer lights of pubs, dances and discos. Couples seek intimate settings, sometimes in similar environments to larger groups, but also in cinemas, on excursions to the coast and countryside, and, once their 'serious' intentions are agreed, in private houses. The satisfactions obtained are not inherent in the activities, but derive from the participants' purposes, like expressing sexual interests and consolidating gender identities.

Successful commercial providers are aware of the need to tempt teenagers with environments that reflect customers' meanings. Young people would not purchase coffee, alcohol, meals or visit bowling alleys unless the environments supported the groups in which they sought to interact, and allowed them to express their masculine and feminine characters. People – in cliques, crowds and couples – frame adolescents' free time, and leisure goods and services only appeal when packaged in ways that will support the customers' social formations and meanings, which are learnt by young people and scripted by the wider society.

If youth is the great time that older generations often allege, why is it forsaken? There are many reasons, some illustrating how youth cultures are constantly disturbed by external pressures. Young people are expected to 'mature', to be their ages, and these expectations are not deflected but amplified by peer groups. Both sexes fear being left out of marriage, on the shelf. As they age, individuals find the unattached pool shrinking. By the age of 25 it can be difficult, especially for women without same-sexed peer groups that colonise public places, and who are discouraged from going out alone, to find social gatherings to meet prospective partners. The skills learnt at each stage of adolescent development can only be practised by leaving the milieux where they are acquired. For example, the cliques within which sexuality is initially defined become redundant once members have learnt their lines and can handle heterosexual relationships. The majority of young people have no real opportunity to 'break out' because the much-acclaimed autonomy of their peer groups and youth cultures is superficial, and as a result of young people's continued dependence on parents, teachers and employers. Young people are engendered by their families, plus the distribution of educational and job opportunities, and thereby encouraged to use leisure to express masculine and feminine skills and identities.

Since women's earnings remain lower than men's, girls must usually marry or settle for inferior standards of living. If males wish to become social (not just biological) parents and maintain the ways of life to which they grow accustomed during childhood and youth, marriage is equally necessary. Many men lack the domestic skills to preserve their standards of living without wives or mothers. For most young people, adult independence can only be won by accepting conventional gender and sexual roles. Youth cultures do not oppose but mediate this common sense, and simultaneously teach the skills that young people require to fulfil this destiny.

Young people at leisure engage in perpetual struggles to create space (Robins and Cohen, 1978). Girls are particularly disadvantaged. They have to suffice with space won and shaped by males. When they escape from parental supervision it is into male-dominated youth cultures. However, even boys find space difficult to secure. They have no homes of their own. Efforts to claim their own territories can lead to clashes with other peer groups and authorities. Environments cost money. Commercial providers will deliver space when customers are prepared to pay. Unhappily, their favoured environments usually cost more than teenagers are able to spend every evening and weekend. Hence the incentive for young people to use their own cultures to create private 'social' space in public places. They communicate in sub-cultural codes of dress and music. Young people do construct cultures and lives of their own, but nearly always within limits which ensure that their search for independence reproduces conventional sexual preferences, gender roles and, ultimately, nuclear families.

Gender and Sexuality during Adolescence

They are allowed no alternative, but most young people do not reconcile themselves to masculine and feminine futures reluctantly, and this is a consequence of how sexuality is controlled and constructed into a powerful force which requires males and females to identify with rather than merely enact prescribed gender roles. Distinguishing sex from gender is a well-established social-science practice (Oakley, 1972). The former biological differences between males and females are universal throughout humanity. For example, females always bear the children: alternative arrangements are biologically impossible, and will remain so until the 'test tube' becomes an option. The term 'gender' describes differences that do not arise directly from biological factors, but are produced by the social treatment accorded, and the roles assigned, to individuals depending on their sex. For instance, masculine and feminine forms of dress are cultural phenomena, prescribed by social norms, not biology. Women's physical complexions do not require make-up, but some cultures encourage its use.

Which differences are rooted in the biological facts of life and which are cultural? Are males naturally more aggressive and domineering than females? Are the latter born with a mothering instinct that men do not share? At the end of the arguments, it usually becomes apparent that nature and culture combine to produce most differences. Height and weight have biological bases, but social norms which decree it desirable for women to be trim or plump, and for men to be slim or muscular, also help to shape men and women. No one has ever argued the complete irrelevance of either biology or culture, but during the last twenty years we have become aware of the extent to which masculine and feminine qualities vary from society to society, and of the wide range of differences, previously thought to be biologically determined, which, in fact, have mainly cultural sources (Oakley, 1981). As a result, we have become alert to the main ways in which the conventional division of labour by gender could be changed, if the effects were judged socially and psychologically convenient.

Biology does not dictate that women be second-class citizens at work, that men predominate in politics, or that women perform most of the housework and rear children. The growing strength and influence of the social sciences is partly responsible for these matters becoming public issues rather than unquestioned facts of life. However, the transformation is also a consequence of women being released from former biological imperatives by technological advances, in abortion and contraception, for example, and through social engineering, as in the provision of education and nursery facilities. We now realise that the determining power of biology is not immutable, but is itself dependent upon social arrangements and knowledge.

We no longer believe that females' brains are smaller and softer than males', and that girls should not be over-taxed through exposure to educational competition with boys. No one who has examined the evidence tries to explain or justify women's underrepresentation in higher education in these terms, but many people are still reluctant to believe that their sexual preferences can have any origins apart from biology. Anyone who totally dismissed biological explanations of sexual behaviour, or overlooked the physical changes associated with puberty when explaining how young people acquire and express sexual interests, would be guaranteed to lose the argument. Sexual behaviour, feelings and activities would never arise without a supporting biological sub-structure. But we now realise that sexuality is socially patterned, like other gender differences. We learn to recognise and define our sexual appetites, and how to seek their satisfaction, as members of our societies, and exactly what we learn depends upon the societies we inhabit, and our positions in these societies, including whether we are 'typed' as men or women (Gagnon and Simon, 1974).

For present purposes, there is no need to debate whether homosexual preferences and practices are as compatible with human nature as heterosexuality. It cannot be denied that any innate tendencies towards the latter are powerfully reinforced by social pressures from families, peer groups, schools and the media, or that these pressures are as much parts of the environments within which young people become aware of, and learn to express their sexual interests, as their biological constitutions. When boys and girls 'pair off', they are not simply fulfilling their biological destinies, with society operating as a restraint. This common sense is mistaken. The young people are acting upon their society's definitions of their desires, and following a prescribed route to their presumed fulfilment. We learn to enact sexual norms in just the same way that we learn to perform our paid occupations and domestic work.

Needless to say, sexual mores, like other social norms, are often ambiguous. Different people, sometimes the same individuals, subscribe to contradictory ideas. As a result, young people, and adults, are often surrounded by cross-pressures and afflicted by uncertainty. Is it wrong to be attracted to someone of the same sex? Should sexual intercourse be treated as just another physical recreation? If we think these conflicts are simply between our natures and what society expects, we are mistaken. Individuals who feel they are just 'being themselves' when they conform with dominant expectations of the types of housework, occupational careers and sexual behaviour appropriate for men and women, can be offered as evidence of how people internalise their societies' norms, and 'deviants' are not exhibiting greater autonomy. We are all socialised beings, handling different, and sometimes conflicting or ambiguous, cultural resources, that may provoke us to generate new ideas and may give us a sense of individuality, but this is just as much a social product as the mind of the unquestioning conformist.

Gender discrimination precedes adolescence. There is evidence that male foetuses and infants are naturally the more aggressive in so far as their limbs are the more active. On average, boys are certainly physically stronger than girls of the same age. It has been argued that whenever pre-school children play together, boys 'naturally' tend to become the overt leaders, while girls learn to rely upon socio-emotional skills rather than brute force. However, any such natural tendencies are powerfully reinforced by social training. From their first days of life, boys and girls are usually dressed in different clothes, and encouraged to play with different toys, and these differences are consolidated in primary school (Sharpe, 1977). Boys are expected to be masculine; their boisterous behaviour is tolerated, even demanded. Bright boys are encouraged to take the lead and assert themselves in class. When clever girls allow less able boys to answer teachers' questions, this feminine behaviour is likely to be accepted by teachers (Evans, 1979). Boys are the more likely to receive physical punishment, while girls are taught to respond to social disapproval (Davies, 1979). It has only recently become controversial for domestic science to be officially designated as a girls' subject, while boys are tracked into woodwork and metalwork.

Long before puberty, children acquire gender identities. They learn that they are boys and girls, each with appropriate interests, rather than simply children with different individual tastes and talents. Before leaving primary school, most boys and girls are competent judges of which adult roles 'belong' to men and women. They know that men repair cars while women wash dishes, that the domestic iron belongs to mummy, that the screwdriver is daddy's (Vener and Snyder, 1966), and are anticipating appropriate futures. Little girls play at being mothers, while boys play with cars and trains. None of these differences are straightforward outcomes of biological maturation.

Gender roles are clearly distinguished, and appropriate identities are adopted by most boys and girls before puberty. Then, during adolescence, there are three interrelated developments. First, there is a process of elaboration. Gender differences become increasingly detailed. They intrude into virtually every corner of education, possibly more so in co-educational than single-sex schools. Physics and chemistry become boys' subjects, while girls drift towards English, other languages and biology. On leaving school, boys and girls enter labour markets which, despite equal-opportunity laws, remain highly segmented by gender. Few girls obtain craft apprenticeships, and few boys become typists. Previous chapters have described how uses of leisure also diverge. Adolescents are divided into same-sexed cliques. Girls' leisure remains relatively home-centred. Boys, especially from working-class backgrounds, explore the freedom of the streets. Even when apparently engaged in the same pursuits, as at parties and in cinemas, boys and girls learn to behave 'appropriately', in masculine and feminine ways.

The second development is stabilisation. 'Doctors and nurses' ceases to be just a game. When boys and girls enter different educational tracks, survive and fall at examination hurdles, and enter different occupations, these events have long-term consequences that cannot be erased at the end of playtime. By their mid 20s, most individuals have selected and married partners of the opposite sex, and 'mummies and daddies' have become real roles, not imaginary statuses. As they move towards adulthood, boys' and girls' statuses and identities become increasingly stable and specific. By the end of youth, occupational and domestic trajectories are usually set. Some individuals 'break out', start new careers or join communes, but as youth fades these opportunities narrow. Making a new start becomes increasingly difficult and exceptional. Having spent the greater parts of their lives building occupational careers and marriages, people have much to lose, economically and socially, if these structures collapse. Adolescence is a critical life-stage, when 'real' decisions are made by and for young people. Many of the roles they enter prove life-long, and virtually all these roles are gender-divided.

Thirdly, sexuality is inserted into the above socio-psychological developments. Individuals become aware of their own and their peers' sexual appetites, learn how to display their interests and intentions through language, dress and other codes, and how to 'read', respond to and influence other people's. Freud taught that pre-pubertal children, even infants, have sexual desires, and was initially misunderstood, for he was not using the word 'sexual' in its everyday sense. For present purposes, it is necessary neither to dispute nor affirm that the bodily pleasures children experience are the same kind, involving the same libidinal energies, as released during post-pubertal masturbation and sexual intercourse. The point is that adolescents develop a new type of awareness as sexual significance is attributed to their bodies and actions. Young people do not simply become aware of their 'natural' inclinations. The meanings of their biological states are defined by society. The media are prominent and persuasive, and peer groups amplify the messages.

Sexuality differs from many other qualities, such as sporting ability and studiousness, in that it is never attached to specialised roles. Individuals can become sportsmen and students, but not sexualists. Sexuality is expressed through other social roles, particularly gender roles. Indeed, the only acceptable expressions of sexuality are according to ascribed gender. Among young people, all gender-divided activities – recreational, occupational and educational – acquire sexual connotations. There is no necessary reason why boys who learn typing or enter nursing should be considered sexually queer. Neither human biology nor the recreation offer grounds for doubting sportswomen's orthodox sexual preferences. Nor is there any reason why couples who accompany each other to the cinema, dance together or live together must have mutual sexual interests. Nevertheless, in our society it is taken for granted that heterosexual couples who establish common households, and who 'go out' regularly, are sexually implicated. Women who do not seek economic security through marriage, and men who resist 'enslavement' as breadwinners, may possess normal sexual appetites.

In practice, however, within our society, as individuals leave childhood, they enter a world in which sexual meanings are attributed to such conduct. During and following adolescence, sexuality is attributed to virtually all male–female relationships and other gender roles.

Couples who 'go out', monopolise each other's company at parties and discos, or merely take lunch together, are assumed to be sexually entwined. Individuals can suggest these forms of conduct to would-be partners without fear of being misunderstood. Or can they? Partners in championship dancing and mixed tennis are not always sexually related. Workplaces are contested terrain. Should relationships between male and female colleagues, supervisors and subordinates, be free from sexual innuendoes? Conduct which is interpreted as harassment by one person is just part and parcel of all male–female encounters to another.

Defining sport as masculine, and attributing sexual meanings to all male–female relationships, have more than playful consequences. Young people are sexualised through gender roles, and are given no opportunity to question sexual meanings. They are offered no other way to make sense of 'themselves' – their physiques and emotions. If they reject heterosexuality, they are labelled as immature and, if they persist, as queer and abnormal. They are not respected if they try to protect themselves from sexual and gender traps. Pressures towards heterosexual conformity are amplified by peer groups. Individuals who display abnormal sexual tendencies are subjected to psychological, even physical savagery. Young people can only establish credible sexual identities by accepting conventional gender roles. Girls must demonstrate a desire, as well as the power to attract boys. This means being feminine in school and during leisure. It can also mean adopting feminine job aspirations. The net result is that, by the age of 20, the majority have lost whatever chances may once have been available to gain social and economic independence.

Sexual meanings require individuals to identify with, and forbid them distancing themselves from, prescribed gender roles. It is only through gender that they are allowed to express their sexuality and make sense of their own biology. This is why, if they are to be transformed, changes in gender roles and sexual norms will proceed hand in glove. There is no biological necessity for the prevailing relationships between sexuality and the division of labour by gender. The links are social, but so intricate and numerous that changes in one are guaranteed to undermine the other. There is no point in urging a sexual revolution without tackling gender divisions in leisure, employment, education and the family, or vice versa.

The Critical Re-Appraisal

Accounts of how youth cultures transform children into adults, equipped with masculine and feminine skills, tastes and identities, were first offered by functionalist sociology. Critics do not dispute the earlier description, or the explanations just offered, of how young people are disentangled from childhood families, then entwined with opposite-sexed partners, and eventually committed to marriage. Turning boys into husbands and fathers and girls into wives and mothers are complex operations.

Traditional sociology is congratulated for distinguishing the stages. However, critics object to the conservative implications of presenting the adolescent procession as inevitable and/or functional for society in general, thereby justifying the patterns and practices being perpetuated. They object to inferences that youth cultures are supporting nature, assisting males and females towards their biological destinies, rather than endorsing socio-cultural patterns and interests. They challenge suggestions that boys and girls learn complementary rather than dominant and subordinate roles, and object when resistance is explained away as mere transitional discomfort, creating an impression that no one's long-term interests are harmed by the perpetuation of gender divisions, and that all young people can succeed within the spheres to which they are suited. Critics argue that functional interpretations of youth cultures err by assuming instead of querying the value of gender divisions that teach young people to think and act in masculine and feminine ways. Traditional sociology is accused of accepting prevailing relationships between biological differences, gender roles and sexuality as functionally convenient if not inevitable outcomes of the former, instead of emphasising that established gender divisions and sexual conventions are biologically unnecessary, and that there could be alternatives.

Once upon a time it was widely believed that biology prescribed motherhood as the female's main role. Contrary social engineering was opposed as flouting nature and courting social disaster. These beliefs justified adolescent leisure which encouraged girls to be gentle and affectionate in preparation for home-centred adulthoods, and discouraged their involvement in aggressive and competitive sports. Once we realise that individuals who are born female may not be naturally suited to motherhood and domestic servitude, and that alternative arrangements are practical, we are likely to take a different view of adolescent leisure.

Sociologists have never considered biology a sufficient explanation of why males become breadwinners, while females concentrate on their domestic roles as wives and mothers, but some argue that this is a reasonable way for societies to build upon natural sex differences (Cohen, 1981). Until the late 1960s, gender divisions were not regarded as exploitive and oppressive in mainstream sociology, or by mainstream opinion in society. It was believed that women had already been emancipated from unnecessary restrictions. Government Reports debated whether the schools were making enough special provisions for girls' feminine interests (Crowther, 1959; CACE, 1963). Rather than treating prevailing gender divisions as social problems, functionalist sociology explained how they contributed to the economy's efficiency by freeing male workers from domestic responsibilities, while women who specialised on domestic tasks enabled the nuclear family to perform its essential functions of procreation, the primary socialisation of young children, and as a unit of consumption which satisfied its members' material and emotional requirements.

An alternative, critical interpretation of the adolescent procession stresses, first, that biology alone explains very little. How many boys and girls are sentenced to adulthoods which stifle their aptitudes and impose demands they cannot meet? Secondly, the critical reappraisal insists that the roles of male and female adults and boys and girls at leisure are unequal; that women are subordinated and youth cultures male-dominated. Thirdly, it argues that traditional sociology has exaggerated the harmony of adolescent life and the smoothness of the transition to adulthood by rendering invisible and, in this sense, suppressing dissent, especially when the dissidents have been female. The many young people who worry about their normality and popularity suggest that reconciling individuals to their futures involves sacrifices.

Sociology is still male-dominated. Could this be why it has accepted girls' treatment as appendages as 'normal'? The traditional sociology of youth says little about how girls feel. It has pursued male delinquents, but has rarely touched the subterranean world of the female teenybopper. Fourthly, traditional sociology is accused of failing to explore how leisure could be used to teach boys and girls alternative norms which, alongside wider social and cultural changes, might transform young people's engendered life-chances. Radical sociologists are committed to a less oppressive division of labour and a better quality of life for women and men. They accept that, at present, adolescent drop-outs are a minority, but see no reason to dismiss them as 'deviants'. Why not treat the rebels as pioneers of alternative lifestyles?

Should our gender and sexual conventions be scrapped or changed? If so, how should change be wrought? Could adolescent leisure be put to radical uses? If existing gender and sexual roles are imposed by society, subjugate women, and are neither biologically nor socially necessary, why not change them? Instead of reproducing familiar gender and sexual patterns, could we encourage more young people to use their leisure to break free? We know it can be done. Some individuals, young and old, are challenging established sexual norms and other forms of gender discrimination. Nonconformists are still made to feel 'left on the shelf' because of their own physical, psychological or social shortcomings. 'Deviants' are still told, and many still believe, that their unconventional sexual preferences for children and same-sexed adults are problems to be treated. But other homosexuals are now denying that their inclinations are a problem. Some highly edu-cated young people are now rejecting or choosing to delay marriage and parenthood, without feeling immature or social failures.

It is only when people begin to break out of the stereotypes, when otherwise feminine women become industrial managers, when obviously sexually normal men become nursery assistants, when leisure companions decline sexual advances without terminating their relationships, and when households free from conventional sexual and/or legal entanglements are established, that we realise how the relationships between sexuality, the broader division of labour by gender and biological differences are neither more nor less than social conventions. It is only then that we appreciate the need to explain the reproduction of gender and sexuality sociologically.

Prospects for Change

I have no reservations on three of the main propositions in the critical perspective outlined above: the rejection of biological determinism, the arguments about the subordination of women and the hidden injuries of adolescence, but I doubt whether simply disseminating these arguments will make change more likely. My hunch is that adolescent leisure is more likely to respond to gender and sexual changes initiated elsewhere than become a catalyst, and that any changes will take generations rather than years. Even revolutions, like industrialisation, have lasted for centuries. However, all predictions are best treated as issues for research. Forecasts cannot be as confident as interpretations of past and present youth cultures. We need further inquiries to establish how many and which young people are challeng-ing conventions. What are their problems? For instance, how liberated do women feel when their decisions to remain childless become irre-vocable? Identifying circumstances that encourage and enable some young people to break the gender and sexual moulds would clarify why others remain inhibited, and assist in specifying the conditions under which adolescent leisure could be used to mount wider challenges.

The hypothesis awaits systematic investigation, but I suspect that highly educated youth have been responsible for much of the 'break-ing out' that has already occurred. No one knows exactly how many are involved, but there has been a trend towards self-catering by women and men students who learn cooking, washing, ironing and other domestic arts, instead of relying on halls of residence and land-ladies. Highly educated young adults also appear to have been responsible for reversing the former trend towards younger marriage. Casual observation suggests that they are not opting for celibacy, but the men do not assume that love and sex entitle them to domestic services, and many of the women have no intention of surrendering to domestic servitude. Cash and freedom from adult supervision during leisure time are insufficient conditions for sexual and gender revolutions. Students' residential independence which permits experiments with novel life-styles rather than just spare-time activities, probably helps to explain their radicalism. Their slower-moving escalators which transport students past early adolescent pressures, and allow them to develop confidence in their date-worthiness before they achieve the economic independence to commit themselves to marriage and parenthood, may also be relevant. What other conditions favour challenges to conventional gender roles?

Ideas can help to change the world. Before individuals will 'break out', they must become aware of how they are being conscripted into predetermined roles and given a vision of more attractive futures. Workers who are dissatisfied with their wages and other conditions only become a radical political force when convinced that alternative economic arrangements are possible. Hence the case for radical cultural work with adolescent peer groups. Feminist and other women's organisations are adopting a plausible strategy when they seek to undermine gender divisions by teaching girls to enjoy leisure independently of boys – by making them aware of the possibility of an alternative division of labour and by giving them the confidence to demand opportunities to do *their* own things, as when housewives propose weekly days off. Are the highly educated leading the liberation movements because they possess the intellectual power to recognise alternatives? I suspect that there are additional, material obstacles to the diffusion of role-breaking initiatives.

It is not self-evident that alternative sexual practices and gender roles would yield net gains in well-being for all women, let alone men. The belief that young people in general could and would 'break out' if only the possibility was made apparent, assumes that they would find the alternatives preferable. Is this confidence justified? The fact that current gender divisions are socially constructed and perpetuated is not a ground for their destruction. Any other options would also be socially engineered. The possibilities must be made more attractive than traditional opportunities. Men, of course, will be a problem. Married women have been controlling their fertility and breaking into the workforce. Men have displayed less enthusiasm for change. Are they likely to buy the idea of reallocating the sexes' rights and duties when the case is made by disparaging women's work?

Confidence that all young people, male and female, who perceive alternatives will be keen and able to grasp these opportunities, resurrects the false assumption that youth and leisure confer the freedom to rebuild wider social structures. The highly educated women who are liberating themselves from traditional gender constraints have access to careers that make economic independence more attractive than seeking security through relationships with men. Partners can be persuaded of their mutual interest in women taking full advantage of their qualifications and career prospects. Deem (1982a and b) has argued that women with educational and economic advantages are relatively well placed to 'make the best' of the traditional female role. True, but surely these same advantages make 'liberation' attractive to the same women, and can help in persuading men to interact on equal terms, intra- and extramaritally. By contrast, for many 16-year-old school-leavers who become typists, low-paid shop and assembly workers in factories, marriage and parenthood continue to promise a security that feminist groups and strategies cannot match. Can males or females be expected to challenge conventional gender roles until changes in educational and employment opportunities have made the challenges potentially rewarding?

As indicated previously, I suspect that, on gender and sexual issues, changes in young people's leisure patterns will follow wider changes in employment, education and the family. The latter are changing, albeit slowly. Young people do not become identikits of their parents. Most of our grandmothers had their first experience of intercourse following marriage. In Gorer's (1971) survey, 50 per cent of adult women believed it impossible for females to experience anything resembling the male climax. The trends are towards equal opportunities in education. The attention they receive indicates widening interest in exceptions to conventional gender divisions, like job-sharing husbands and wives who take turns to care for children and earn, and role-reversal in families with male child-minders and better-qualified wives in employment. Unemployment might make this practice increasingly common and acceptable. So would an increase in the proportion of married women, now one in seven, who earn more than their husbands.

Alternatively, unemployment might lead young and older women to rediscover the dignity of the housebound wife. Recent adolescent cohorts have been the first twentieth-century generations mostly reared by working mothers. It is estimated that over a quarter of current marriages will end in divorce. Fifteen per cent of all children are now reared by lone parents. Many girls and boys must be learning from their own family histories that marriage may promise but cannot guarantee social and economic security. In the future, therefore, it is likely that growing numbers of young people will regard traditional gender roles and sexual norms as problems, and become receptive to other options.

Issues for Research

The above ideas embody some speculation. There is plentiful scope for further research on youth, leisure, sex and gender. There is an obvious case for filling obvious gaps, like the near absence of detailed studies of teenage girls' leisure. Researchers will have to pursue girls into their homes, if need be. Their absence from the street corners and clubs where boys congregate, and their underrepresentation in the criminal statistics, are not excuses for continuing to ignore females. It is unlikely that boys will become a neglected species. Nor should they be overlooked. Close-ups of male and female youth, enacting the latest styles and fads, and identifying the implications for sex and gender, will always be welcome. Further quantitative inquiries charting leisure participation rates and patterns will be most useful if based on national, representative samples, if they are repeated, making it possible to detect trends towards or away from sex equality and segregation, and if they relate sexual behaviour to other uses of leisure, instead of leaving the former to sexologists.

However, I suspect that the most productive future research on sex and gender among young people at leisure will focus on key groups as regards historical trends, and for theoretical issues, like the circumstances under which youth cultures reproduce and undermine conventional divisions and practices. What new forms of partnership are being pioneered by highly educated youth? What problems are encountered, and how are these overcome? Young people in high-unemployment areas will repay investigation, and not just into their vocational difficulties. What are the wider implications for dating, courtship and marriage? Does unemployment encourage girls to opt for the 'security' of marriage and parenthood? Or does male unemployment make marriage less attractive? Young women who are adopting formerly 'deviant' leisure activities, whether visiting pubs without male escorts or participating in sport, deserve investigation. Are their overall leisure styles non-traditional? What sexual codes do they adopt, and how do these women interpret gender?

At present the above issues are matters for speculation, but we can be more certain that, throughout the immediate future, understanding sex and gender among young people at leisure will require a combination of traditional functionalist accounts of how youth cultures reproduce engendered adults, and radical perspectives that detect opportunities to construct alternative life-styles from leisure interests and activities. Functionalism overstated the ease and inevitability of the reproduction of gender and sexual practices. Theory and research will progress by counter-balancing, not obliterating, these older findings and arguments.

7
The Traditional Sociology of Youth and Social Class

These chapters will not argue that young people at leisure enjoy the freedom to ignore or transcend the wider society's class divisions. The freedom of leisure allows young people to select records, sounds, clothing and hair-styles. The details are not dictated by youth's class positions. They do not passively inherit and perpetuate class-based cultures. But young people exploit the freedom of leisure only within boundaries defined by society's class structure. Youth are so divided by their homes, education and jobs that there is no way in which youth cultures might obliterate these divisions, however much leisure young people possess. The main debate concerns not *whether* young people at leisure are class divided, but the *significance* of divisions that, as Chapter 2 explained, preceded and have endured throughout post-war youth cultures. Different interpretations are grounded in rival theories of stratification that will be introduced in the following chapters, just as previous chapters drew upon theories about the social construction of gender and sexuality to clarify the relevant aspects of youth cultures.

Two main conclusions, backed by several subsidiary arguments, are developed in this and subsequent chapters. The first is that the main divisions between youth cultures no longer separate the manual and non-manual, the working and middle classes, but occur beneath a highly educated élite, and above marginalised lower-working–class groups, including ethnic minorities and the young unemployed. These schisms reflect underlying changes in the broader class structure, and subsequent chapters present a case for research to distinguish and define the boundaries between different youth cultures more precisely than existing evidence will allow.

The second major argument concerns the quality of young people's leisure – one of the live issues extracted from Chapter 3's survey of youth and leisure research. Some investigators have attempted to generate objective measures of life's quality through batteries of questions inviting respondents to rate their satisfaction with their homes, health, marriages, jobs, leisure and so on. The following chapters do not draw upon this type of evidence. It must mean something, but it is doubtful whether the scales can be equated with the quality of life (Abrams, 1977). Is someone content with poverty enjoying a superior life-style to individuals who are dissatisfied and striving to improve their conditions? It is difficult to see how value judgments can be completely eliminated, so the following arguments about the quality of young people's leisure correlating positively with their class positions do not rest solely on 'hard data'.

Some writers argue that leisure is a masculine and middle-class concept which inevitably devalues females' and working-class life-styles. The following chapters present and criticise the arguments of researchers who have deplored working-class youth's tendency to idle time 'doing nothing', their preference for passivity rather than activity, and their failure to develop 'worthwhile', 'fulfilling', 'constructive' interests. The failure of working-class children's homes, communities and schools to offer effective preparation for leisure has been judged 'a problem'. Is this apparent problem a product of investigators operating with middle-class concepts of leisure, then criticising working-class youth's lack of skills and interests that would be irrelevant, given their working-class predicaments?

These chapters agree that some earlier paternal judgements were based upon middle-class notions of which *uses* of leisure are enriching, but deny that leisure is a middle-class *concept*. Leisure, as defined in Chapter 3, is a product of industrialism, and is equally a part of working- and middle-class life-styles. These chapters will show that middle-class youth *are* relatively privileged and enjoy the greater freedom at leisure, which enables some to construct radical counter-cultures. Working-class youth often express defiance and opposition in contra-cultures, but middle-class youth are the more likely to nurture values and skills which assist individual and collective *solutions* to class problems. Condoning the constraints with which they contend becomes a real danger when 'appreciating' working-class youth's leisure. This book argues that delivering leisure opportunities to girls and working-class youth has been and remains an unsolved problem. Their opportunities are not simply different, but inferior to other young people's. Once we correctly identify the obstacles, we will be able to understand, then maybe prescribe effective remedies, when working-class youth (and middle-class girls) fail to take full advantage of facilities provided for their benefit.

The Myth of Classless Youth

Sociologists often encounter public opposition when debating social class. It is objected that people are no longer class conscious, and that social origins have become irrelevant to life-chances; that ability and achievements are now all-important, and therefore that the language of class is outdated. This opposition compounds factual error with conceptual confusion. Even if the public retained no vestige of class awareness, it would not follow that society was devoid of class divisions – only that people were unaware of them. Even if social position at birth was irrelevant to opportunities, this would not mean that class differences had disappeared, but that the class structure was extremely fluid. There can be no disputing the persistence of social inequalities, which are not arranged in compensatory patterns. The most highly educated individuals tend to enter the higher-status jobs, earn the higher incomes, live in the more desirable residences and so on, and the reason we need a term such as 'social class' is to examine the entire ways of life, the total patterns of constraint and opportunity, and the cultures which include beliefs, values and political aspirations that characterise different strata. Sociologists disagree on why all known human societies have been stratified. They differ on the shape of the contemporary class structure. Standard practice treats the division between manual and white-collar strata, the middle and working classes, as a major cleavage, but the depth and significance of even this schism have never been agreed. Nevertheless, sociologists agree on some matters, like class remaining an indispensable concept in analysing contemporary societies.

Sociologists also agree that youth cultures are class divided. Classless youth is a popular, but patently absurd fiction. Chapter 2 explained how, since middle-class youth began using their postwar freedom and affluence to sustain their own cultures, class divisions in adolescent leisure have been blurred, but never disappeared. Middle- and working-class teenagers often use the same leisure facilities. Their lives are not segregated. They must cope with common adolescent problems like establishing independence from parents, learning gender and sexual roles. Nevertheless, social class retains considerable discriminatory power. Laymen who believe youth cultures to be classless are very distant observers. Pop is popular in all strata, but as teenagers will confirm, there are different types of pop music, and college youth's tastes are not identical with their less academic peers'. Casual observation of each other's clothing and coiffure allows young people to distinguish students, office and factory workers. Trouble with the police is most common among early school-leavers from working-class backgrounds. Political activists are mainly middle class and highly educated. The majority of working-class youth profess disinterest in politics. Young people do not feel any strong affinity with all other members of their generation. Why should they? Parents and the middle aged do not exhibit such age-consciousness. Young people express varying degrees of contempt for each other's tastes and interests. Political activists rarely identify with punks and skinheads.

Class may not be a salient concept in youth's everyday consciousness. Young people may rarely think and talk in class terminology. Like adults, they often use a different language from sociologists, but young people are nevertheless aware of, and observe, class distinctions. Students fraternise mainly with other students. Even those on city-centre campuses rarely integrate with downtown youth. Students have their own clubs, sports facilities and parties, and marry one another – the litmus test. They are not necessarily snobbish. They may not consider themselves superior, but their lives are governed by college calendars and timetables rather than industrial employment, and, like adults and working-class teenagers, they prefer to spend their leisure among people who share their own tastes and interests. Young people who proceed to higher education and avoid employment until their mid 20s, do not share a common adolescent experience with 16-year-old school-leavers, some of whom withdraw from occupational careers for marriage and parenthood before the college educated start their initial jobs. Leisure industries may attempt to define, then aim goods and services at a general youth market. This creates a classless façade, but remove the commercial layers, examine young people's leisure tastes, interests and problems, and class divisions spring into focus.

Chapter 3 explained how, during the 1970s, a 'New Wave' in the sociology of youth made class its central explanatory concept. This theory, which is discussed in the next chapter, explains youth cultures as responses to, which help to reproduce while simultaneously challenging contradictory class relations. Attributing such importance to social class has been a new departure in youth studies, and to grasp the New Wave's radical impact, it is necessary first of all to sketch how class differences in young people's leisure were previously explained. This chapter describes how an older, 'traditional' sociology of youth saw class positions introducing differences among leisure styles which, first and foremost, addressed adolescent problems, and how the resulting youth cultures were seen as relieving tensions and socialising young people into their future positions, rather than challenging the prevailing system of stratification.

The Functionalist Model

Sociologists have never argued the total irrelevance of social class among young people. Neither has anyone adopted the other extreme position and postulated clear and rigid boundaries between social strata. Sociologists have always been more aware than laymen that, within present-day societies, class boundaries are imprecise, and that social mobility is common, albeit usually short-range. During the 1950s, some investigators argued that former class divisions were becoming *increasingly* blurred. Many hoped, and some believed, that the class structure was becoming increasingly fluid. The 1944 Education Act had decreed equality of opportunity. The defeat of the Labour Party in three successive general elections lent credibility to the 'embourgeoisement thesis', which claimed that working-class affluence, rehousing, wider educational opportunities, the Welfare State and the mass media were dissolving traditional cleavages, such as between manual and non-manual strata (Abrams *et al.*, 1960; Zweig, 1961). The demise of class-based ideological politics was predicted. A middle-ground consensus was identified: agreement on the mixed economy, a welfare safety net, on the need for incentives, and for these incentives to be open to all the talents (Bell, 1960).

At the time, functionalism was sociology's dominant theory. It portrayed the class structure as a multitude of layers, like a ladder that individuals could climb or descend according to their abilities and efforts. Social-mobility studies distinguished numerous 'rungs', and measured intergenerational and intragenerational movements. Functionalists argued that the social importance of well-rewarded positions was consensual knowledge, and likewise the desirability of everyone being able to climb as far as their talents would allow. The emergent class structure was described as a 'meritocracy', with no rigid barriers impeding the able, and no divisions of interest or ideological breaks encouraging the less successful to regard their betters as the 'other side'. Life-styles remained class-related; inevitably so, if only because of income differentials. The differences, however, were seen mainly in quantitative not qualitative terms. The working classes were acquiring motor cars and washing machines, taking holidays abroad and meals out – middle-class life-styles appeared to be undergoing stratified diffusion (Turner, 1963). Distinctive working-class communities and sub-cultures were considered 'traditional' and in decline.

Reflections of these broader social-class differences were detected in youth cultures. Young people's tastes and opportunities were inevitably influenced by childhood socialisation in families with different means. Further social-class differences were caused by some young people achieving wage-earning independence while others remained in education. Different classes of young people were surrounded by different patterns of constraint and opportunity, but, it was argued, they all faced similar adolescent problems, and, overarching the class differences, there appeared to be considerable overlap in musical tastes, preferred dress, films and sporting interests. The movement towards blurring class divisions was rated well advanced among the younger generation. Throughout the 1950s and 1960s, investigators agreed that youth cultures were primarily about growing up, not class struggle. Class differences in young people's leisure were considered fully consistent with continuous socialisation, which, by the 1960s, had become the ascendant theory of youth cultures. Researchers noted how socially mobile youth adopted the leisure habits of higher strata with little difficulty. Youth cultures appeared to lubricate social mobility by blurring class divisions, offering anticipatory socialisation and promoting individuals' social assimilation into the strata for which they were destined (Turner, 1964).

In retrospect, it is easy to appreciate that the evidence for this wisdom was always suspect. There were no large-scale surveys using time budgets, or otherwise collecting comprehensive data on adolescent leisure in all social strata. To this day, in Britain, there have been no national, longitudinal inquiries allowing us to measure, for example, the effects of school-sponsored recreation on young people's subsequent leisure habits. Nevertheless, by the 1960s, the successive small-scale, mostly local studies into different aspects of young people's leisure, whose findings were summarised in Chapter 2, had amassed sufficiently consistent findings to allow generalisations about the major class differences among young people at leisure, and how they arose.

Social Development and Chronological Age

Some differences were explained in terms of middle-class youth being the slower to develop. Investigators found working-class adolescents 'breaking away' from parents, displaying heterosexual interests and eventually marrying ahead of their middle-class counterparts (Schofield, 1965). Working-class children were given the freedom of the streets, while middle-class parents remained protective, and working-class youth's lead was accentuated by their earlier entry into employment and financial independence. Chapter 5 described how young people from all social strata progress through similar stages from involvement with same-sexed peers, through dating and courtship towards marriage, with working-class youth leading at each step. With chronological age controlled, therefore, investigators found working-class young people spending the greater quantities of time out of home – watching more films, attending more dances, becoming involved with the opposite sex, and generally 'hanging about' in young people's places like cafés and street corners. It could be argued, however, that working- and middle-class youth were really more similar than these 'controls' made them appear. They were doing similar things, at different chronological ages.

Harried versus Aimless

A second social-class difference that attracted comment throughout the 1960s contrasted the purposeful middle-class activist with the aimless, passive, often bored working-class teenager. The former possessed less free time and independent spending power, yet claimed and pursued the wider range of leisure interests. If building society and other investments had been investigated, a rather different distribution of wealth would have become apparent, but researchers concentrated upon disposable cash in hand. Working-class youth (especially young workers) commanded the greater amounts, and had more time to spare (especially the secondary-modern pupils), but did not appear to have sufficient interests to use their leisure productively. At home, television was often working-class teenagers' sole recreation. Elsewhere they sought entertainment at football matches, cinemas and dances, or idled time in cafés and streets. It was these young people who were considered susceptible to whatever trivia the commercial industries offered, however superficial and pointless.

Surveys found middle-class adolescents the more involved in school-sponsored recreation. The reasons are discussed below, but school was never the sole area where middle-class youth were and remain the more active. At home they watch less television, and spend more time doing a great many other things. They are the more likely to read, play sports and musical instruments, participate in virtually every hobby, attend youth clubs, theatres and concerts. The higher the educational ladder is ascended, the more pronounced these differences become. Young people in higher education have been described as the most recreationally aware and active section of the entire population (Hendry, 1979). Levels of activity ebb following marriage and parenthood, but the highly educated maintain their 'lead' over other groups throughout the life-cycle. They are the 'culture vultures', the migratory élite that descends on 'community' art and sports centres, even when sited in working-class areas, and dominates all manner of voluntary associations, religious bodies and local political parties (Musgrove, 1963). Secondary-school pupils destined for educational and occupational success often complain of pressure on their time. This 'time famine' experienced by 'academic' youth has been noted repeatedly since the Second World War.

Future members of the 'harried leisure class' (Linder, 1970) –affluent persons, often in dual-income households, whose main problem in life is 'finding the time' to pursue all their domestic and out-of-home leisure interests, yet who still engineer opportunities to relax – appear to receive excellent training during their school-days. In the 1940s, Ward (1948) observed that grammar school pupils found their education more demanding than young people in secondary moderns. The former had homework, longer journeys to and from school, and were the more involved in extracurricular activities. Despite this, away from school, they participated in the wider range of leisure pursuits, in and out of home. In the 1970s, Prosser (1981) discovered a virtually identical situation among 178 lower-sixthformers in Birmingham. They divided their out-of-school time in almost equal proportions between their families, friends and solitude, and expressed a desire for 'more time' to be on their own, and to pursue home-based interests, and to go out with friends.

Researchers noted how working-class youth, with more time and spending power, found 'What to do?' a persistent problem. During the 1950s and 1960s, survey after survey commented on working-class youth's lack of interests to fill their time.

The broad picture derived from the interviews was that the boys and girls spent a very considerable proportion of their leisure time doing nothing in particular. The range of activities in which their leisure was spent was very limited. (Jephcott, 1967, p. 82)

The combination of affluence and boredom was less surprising than it may sound today. The affluent young workers of the 1950s and 1960s enjoyed a limited prosperity. Once they had paid their board, transport costs and set sums aside for clothes, birthday and Christmas presents, teenagers could finance Saturday nights at the palais, week-night trips to the cinema and annual holidays at Butlins, but few could afford commercial leisure every evening. Even this affluence was temporary. Young people who achieved adult wage-levels in their late teens, acquired family responsibilities in their early 20s. They had little opportunity to construct affluent life-styles to keep and cherish.

Evidence that working-class youth, like adults, 'do less' with their leisure has subsequently been challenged. There are only twenty-four hours in everyone's day. Is it possible for the middle classes to 'do more'? Could this impression result from working-class interests being omitted from survey checklists? Could the conclusion that working-class youth's leisure is often dull, drab and monotonous be a product of researchers imposing alien middle-class values? Should 'hanging about' and 'doing nothing in particular' except watching television be treated as reprehensible wastes of time? If leisure is 'doing things for their own sake', why should the working class be criticised for non-purposive uses of time? Is 'idling time' deplorable or the essence of leisure? The middle classes 'stretch' and 'deepen' time by doing a lot of things occasionally. Should they be applauded for leading full and hectic lives and making the greatest possible use of their time? Does middle-class 'dabbling' always enhance the quality of life?

The theory discussed in the next chapter explains how working-class youth do 'a lot' that previously escaped researchers' attention, and that 'doing nothing' can be productive and meaningful. Until the 1970s, however, commentators were virtually unanimous in deploring the aimlessness of working-class youth at leisure. This was the 'teenage leisure problem' that teachers and youth workers were urged to address. The kids had no worthwhile leisure interests. As a result they either became bored, or succumbed to mischief.

How did middle-class teenagers avoid this fate? The conventional answer has been that they are offered the wider opportunities. Middle-class youth who 'stay on' at school and proceed to college may lack their working-class contemporaries' wages, but the formers' households usually enjoy the higher incomes. Their families are rarely without one car. Two-vehicle households are concentrated among the upper middle classes, and second cars are often used to ferry children at leisure. These households are also likely to contain substantial stocks of leisure equipment – books and sports gear, in addition to television sets. Middle-class parents are the more likely to take their children on trips to the countryside, museums, theatres, art galleries and concerts. As a result, the young people become aware of a wider range of leisure opportunities than 'culturally deprived' working-class youth.

For reasons discussed below, middle-class youth are also the more likely to take advantage of school-based recreational facilities, especially those that involve staying after going-home time to play badminton, squash, to take part in drama, orchestras or whatever. Those who proceed to college have privileged access to a splendid array of sporting and cultural facilities. Many working-class children never acquire even 'basic skills', like functional literacy, which some leisure activities require. Gardner's (1966) study of 838 15- to 20-year-olds attending day-release classes at a technical college, found the majority unable to read sufficiently rapidly to handle books for pleasure. It was hardly surprising, therefore, that only a minority visited libraries.

Fusion or Separation of School and Leisure

A third social-class difference in adolescent leisure was well documented by the 1960s. Investigators had noted how academically successful pupils often fuse school-life with leisure, while educational failures, overwhelmingly working class, compartmentalise these spheres. 'Good pupils' record the higher rates of participation in school-sponsored recreation, including sport (Hendry, 1978). Except among ethnic minority youth, whose leisure is discussed in Chapter 10, there is not a shred of evidence of academic failures compensating on playing fields. 'A-stream' pupils are the most likely to represent their schools at competitive sport (Start, 1966). In the United States, high-school students who are into athletics are more likely to aspire to college than non-athletic peers of equal academic ability (Rehberg and Schafer, 1968). In general, high-achieving pupils are not 'swots' who find no time for play. They are highly active in all types of extra-curricular recreation. Lower-stream, mainly working-class pupils are the more heavily involved in commercialised pop cultures. Sugarman's (1967) inquiry among 540 fourth-formers in London secondary schools found that respondents who admitted smoking and drinking, and who rated themselves 'on scene', tended to reject the 'good pupil' role. In his study of a boys' secondary-modern school, Hargreaves (1967) noted that A- and B-stream pupils often belonged to organised youth clubs, whereas C- and D-stream 'lads' preferred to spend their leisure infor-mally, and were more likely to be attached to 'unofficial' organisations, such as beat groups, than youth movements recognised by local education authorities.

The above evidence has led some commentators to condemn com-mercialised youth cultures as anti-academic (Coleman, 1961; Dolk and Pink, 1971), but the charge that youth cultures interfere with academic attainment, by deflecting students' efforts and aspirations in other directions, now appears a half-truth, at best. Young people who earn status and commendation tend to identify with their schools, and accept opportunities to participate in recreational activities that teachers spon-sor. When young people are taught to equate school with failure, is it surprising that many prefer to base their leisure interests and relation-ships in out-of-school youth cultures?

Conformity and Deviance
Traditional sociology defined working-class adolescents' leisure as a problem, like other deviations from consensual norms, and explana-tions of social-class differences among young people at leisure were linked to prevailing theories of crime and deviance. By the 1950s, sociology was explaining delinquency as an inevitable corollary of the core values of democratic industrial societies with open class systems. Civil liberties and economic growth depended on educational and economic success, and political positions lying open to all. Yet there was no way in which the majority could realise these goals. Hence, in Robert Merton's (1938) terminology, many citizens were thrust into anomic, normless predicaments, where society's values offered no practical guidance. Merton argued that this predicament would be most acute for young people, educated to compete for success, then brought face to face with limited prospects – especially males, who had to earn their families' status, and particularly working-class males who were disadvantaged in striving towards generally sought goals. Hence the concentration of delinquency among working-class, male youth.

This theory explained how society at large encouraged the formation of deviant sub-cultures among groups exposed to otherwise irreconcilable pressures, and distinguished various ways in which these sub-cultures could deviate from consensual norms. By the 1960s, anomie theory was being used not merely to explain and distinguish juvenile delinquency's different forms, but to characterise entire youth cultures (Mays, 1965). Young people's leisure was mapped according to whether it was conformist, mildly deviant or thoroughly criminal. Middle-class youth tended to conform – at school, at work and during leisure. They had orthodox routes to success in education and employment. In addition, they were taught to obtain satisfying leisure experiences in approved ways. Working-class youth found mainstream routes to educational and occupational success blocked. Then they acquired early financial and social independence from homes and schools which, for a variety of reasons, supplied insufficient or inappropriate leisure interests, skills and models. As a result, the young people 'hung about', doing 'nothing in particular' for much of their spare time, instead of involving themselves in 'worthwhile' and 'fulfilling' activities. They were available for commercial exploitation, and experimented with forms of dress and music that offended good taste. Some became undisciplined and disruptive at school and work, then on the streets. A minority was tempted into regular criminal exploits and sexual deviance.

The Leisure Safety-Valve
Some writers argued that these nonconformist working-class youth cultures acted as safety-valves – choices among less acceptable (to the wider society) delinquent solutions. During the 1960s, studies of the work–leisure relationship explained how individuals with satisfying jobs used spare-time activities to express identities and develop interests derived from employment, while others spent their leisure compensating for deprivations suffered at work (Friedmann, 1961; Parker, 1971). It was noted that young people whose roads to educational and occupational success were blocked could use leisure to celebrate independence and excitement. Any who felt oppressed could spend their leisure defying society, relieving their frustrations. According to these analyses, leisure is an arena where tensions generated by the wider social system can be absorbed, where young people can 'let off steam' without threatening other institutions. If leisure outlets were unavailable, would disadvantaged young people acquiesce before limited educational and job opportunities?

At one time, when the evidence was thin, before school-leaver research accumulated, the entry into employment was regarded as potentially traumatic. There were fears of beginning workers failing to adjust to industrial discipline, proving unstable and irresponsible. Young people had to move from schools' top forms into juvenile jobs. There was the longer working day, with no programmed recreation, or division into periods with different teachers and tasks. Moreover, education is progressive. Once mastered, skills are used to acquire further knowledge. In contrast, many job skills are learnt then practised *ad infinitum*. There was additional concern that young workers would be shocked by amoral workmates and chargehands. However, by the 1950s research had allayed most of these fears. The relevant inquiries portrayed young people adjusting to employment with little difficulty. Today, some bosses still believe that teenage employees will be difficult to control, liable to drift and generally irresponsible (Colledge *et al.*, 1977), but in practice young people usually settle quickly, when offered responsible jobs worth keeping. School-leavers' main fear is not work but unemployment (Youthaid, 1979).

The speed with which the majority of beginning workers adjust, even when entering low-status, careerless jobs, has been attributed to covert but effective anticipatory socialisation, partly in status-assenting working-class communities where it has been taken for granted that sons and daughters follow fathers and mothers, where friends and employment have been delivered effortlessly, by tradition. Parents, kin and neighbours may rarely offer formal vocational guidance, but their small-talk leaves children knowing what to expect, and may never encourage them to envisage optional features other than those available in local offices and factories.

Education has contributed to working-class youth's 'realism'. Schools have rarely treated careers as a priority subject, but they operate in a work-like manner. Children become accustomed to tasks offering little intrinsic satisfaction, and to supervisors – their teachers. Perhaps most important, young people's attainments in education allow them to anticipate their future positions in the occupational hierarchy. Early selection, apparently by merit, accustoms young people with modest prospects to subordinate positions, and teaches disadvantaged youth that their destinies are commensurate with their abilities and efforts. Losers in the educational competition become apathetic and difficult to control in secondary schools' lower streams. They acknowledge school's value for individuals with different talents and prospects, but realise how little it can offer them (Birksted, 1976). In their classrooms, the 'thickies' are often uncooperative, sometimes resistant to all authority. Some teachers are driven to despair. Others accept that their role is primarily custodial. The pupils retreat into anti-academic sub-cultures, then, on being 'released' from school, when jobs were available, they revelled in the freedom, preferring real work, being treated as adults and paid. Within weeks, 'teething troubles' with bosses and workmates, and the fatigue of the longer working day, were usually overcome. Paul Willis (1977) has written about these working–class school-leavers 'applauding their own damnation'.

In addition to the influence of home and school, some writers argue that the ease with which beginning workers have adjusted, even when facing lifetimes in routine jobs offering modest pay and few prospects, has been dependent on the existence of a leisure safety-valve. Residual tensions generated by the class barriers and labour-market experiences have been deflected outside work and expressed during leisure, through youth cultures. In 1966, Downes noted how the schools never really engaged children from the base of the class structure, and how this failure had aroused little concern; it was useful for other strata, and the young people could leave school at the earliest opportunity, become absorbed in a vast semi- and unskilled workforce, and earn good money, or so the school-leavers thought.

> The school system helped to make the prospects of these less pleasant jobs more pleasant by making education itself a massive irritant for children from culturally different and academically unsophisticated families. (p. 263)

The dullness of schoolwork and the generally restrictive atmosphere strengthened pupils' desire to leave and earn as soon as possible. The reward for those who left school early, in Downes's view, was being bought off with a few years' relatively high wages before marriage and parenthood eroded this affluence.

My own assessment is that the arguments of the traditional sociology of youth, outlined in this chapter, were never wrong but always incomplete, and need supplementing not abandoning. Sociologists operating from functionalist premises have defined working–class youth's leisure as a problem, and simultaneously explained its functions for society. In my view, this remains a genuine dilemma.

Since the 1960s, different theories of society and stratification have been ascendant. Their perspectives are introduced in the next chapter. The predicaments of young people have also changed. How young people react to unemployment and the likely consequences for society at large, rather than their uses of affluence, have become major issues of the 1980s, and are debated in Chapter 9. How do school-leavers respond when they cannot follow in their parents' footsteps, when there are no jobs for which schooling has prepared them, and when wagelessness reduces their opportunities to compensate during leisure? Once the relationship between young people's leisure and the class structure is properly understood, we will be better placed to trace the implications of current changes in school-leavers' career prospects, and to predict their likely responses to new opportunities in education, training and leisure.

8

The Reappraisal of Working-Class Youth Cultures

The New Wave

Functionalism lies discredited. It is reborn every autumn, for new generations of sociology students, only to be ritually slaughtered. During the 1970s, Marxism became British sociology's leading theory. Rather than different institutions and groups serving common interests and maintaining a social order on which we all depend, conflict theorists believe it more realistic to conceive societies as composed of dominant and subordinate groups – classes standing in antagonistic relationships to the means of production, according to orthodox Marxists. Any value consensus is judged artificial, the result of economically and politically dominant groups imposing their meanings on others. This ascendant conflict theory has overhauled all the specialist sociologies – of education, urbanism, industry, race and crime. 'Traditional criminology' has been jostled by 'critical criminologists' – critical of previous theories, and of the wider society's definition of the crime problem. It is now orthodox, within sociology, to treat crime and deviance as labels that dominant groups apply to behaviour that offends *their* interests. Delinquency has been reinterpreted as a primitive form of rebellion against class oppression, and legal apparatuses as bourgeois instruments.

The 'New Wave' (Brake, 1980; Smith, 1981) sociology of youth has been a spin-off from this critical criminology. It rejects the functionalist premises of earlier work on social-class differences among youth at leisure. Rather than treating young people with different class origins and destinies as having different levels and mixtures of resources to handle the same adolescent problems, New Wave theorists distinguish qualitatively different class circumstances with which different classes of young people must contend. Their major argument has been that youth cultures express class problems first, and youth problems only secondarily. Youth cultures are treated, first and foremost, as manifestations of class interests, conflict and struggle. Statements of this theory (Hall and Jefferson, 1976; Mungham and Pearson, 1976) have been intellectually tentative, but delivered in a polemic that dismisses not only the myth of classless youth, but all talk of generation gaps, conflicts and adolescent problems of learning independence. By the beginning of the 1980s, the New Wave had become the leading British theory in the analysis of youth cultures. To date, its authors have con- centrated upon working-class youth cultures, but later chapters will illustrate how the theory's main propositions can be applied more widely.

The following passages simple describe then comment upon how the New Wave has reappraised working-class youth at leisure. It has sought to 'understand' working-class youth, while simultaneously transcending the (limited) perspectives of all lay individuals and groups. New Wave writers do not treat their subjects as deviants, or any other kind of problem group who need educating into worth- while pastimes, and reject the view of working-class leisure as passive and pointless.

There is no single authoritative statement or source of the New Wave theory. Different writers have examined different groups of young people, though predominantly working-class males, and have focused upon different processes. They do not all say exactly the same things. To present, then assess, it is necessary to compress the argu- ments into a coherent package that inevitably does less than full justice to some contributions, like the preceding chapter's overview of earlier writing on youth and social class. But neither treatment constructs a straw man. New Wave writers acknowledge their membership of a common school, quote each other's works, subscribe to the same symposia, and have floated a new and influential theory of youth that makes social class the central, not a peripheral concept in a series of related arguments.

Contradictions
The theory contends that Teddy Boy, punk, skinhead and other working-class youth cultures are correctly read as collective attempts to resolve contradictions in the participants' class circumstances, experienced while at school, then in the labour market. What are these contradictions? The young people are encouraged to seek success – to 'get on' in life, to obtain and hold 'good jobs', and make money, but offered limited opportunities. At school many are told they are fail- ures. In the labour market they are restricted to low-paid jobs, often with no prospects. Apprenticeships which, in time, allow them to attain skilled status are the best they can hope for. They are urged to have a good time by parents and the media, but given limited spend- ing power. Their affluence permits Saturday-night glamour, but will not allow the young people to escape from factories and council estates into the life-styles flaunted in films, advertisements and other media. The same firms that tempt the young to become swingers by

night insist, by day, that they work and defer gratifications. These contradictions affect all age-groups, but can be especially acute during the transition to working life, before individuals have settled in occupations and marriages, and reconciled themselves to attainable standards of living.

Why talk of contradictions? Surely these are the same predicaments to which anomie theory drew attention long ago. One difference is that functionalists were always coy when asked the source of consensual values. The New Wave is less reticent. It claims that the cross-pressures young people experience do not arise arbitrarily as a result of different employers, media personnel, teachers and parents offering conflicting advice, but are systematically produced by a contradictory, and therefore inherently unstable class society, whose dominant institutions and values have not been created in benign attempts to deliver economic security, political liberties and equal opportunities, but to protect the privileged. It is argued that the institutions of inequality, like private property which is transmitted through the family, place occupational success and the good life beyond the majority's reach, but can only be legitimised through objectively false claims that the highest rewards are open to all who display sufficient talent and effort. Young people may not be aware of these origins, but they experience and must handle the contradictions, and the New Wave claims that youth cultures are attempted resolutions which symbolically discount some demands, or appear to reconcile the various pressures. One similarity with the traditional sociology of youth is that New Wave writers also regard leisure as a sphere for resolving frustrations. However, the theories differ in their diagnoses of the frustrations' sources, and on the long-term consequences of leisure solutions.

Class Divisions
The New Wave argues that there is no single national or international youth culture, but a series of class-divided sub-cultures. It contends that working- and middle-class young people inherit qualitatively different class cultures from their homes and neighbourhoods, and therefore develop different youth sub-cultures based on the focal concerns and values of their respective classes. Working-class youth are said to have access to a working-class culture, nurtured since the Industrial Revolution in trade unions, on shop floors, in neighbourhoods and political organisations, and this, not a societal culture or general youth culture, is identified as the main parent of their sub-cultures. The New Wave does not portray working-class youth stranded in anomic, normless situations. They are credited with their own culture to interpret their predicaments, and their society.

Correspondences are noted between the identities, styles of sociability and attitudes towards authority expressed in working-class youth cultures, and the wider shop-floor and neighbourhood-based working-class culture (Willis, 1978). The focal concerns of the latter are not rejected, but, it is argued, reworked then powerfully expressed by Teds, skinheads and punks. They all adopt the working-class style of masculinity. Young working-class males share their fathers' interest in football, and their ethnocentrism which is expressed as hatred for blacks who would take 'our' jobs, houses, streets and women, if 'we' would let them. It is claimed that working-class youth cultures absorb the puritan work ethic of the parent, which insists that work has to be done, and deplores 'scroungers'. Working-class realism – the concern for the material, the need to live in the 'real' world and the fatalism – the resignation when faced with the organisation of work, the structure of the labour market, the housing situation and politicians, are also faithfully reflected by working-class youth.

New Wave theorists acknowledge the absence of any precise fit between young people's class origins, educational and occupational attainments, and the youth sub-cultures in which they become involved. How could there be any precise fit when the class destinies of some young people are unclear? Forms of consumption certainly transcend class boundaries; inevitably, since youth has been commercially gelled into a commodity culture. But take away the commercial trappings, it is argued, and we are left with clear class differences. Young people in different class circumstances are said to impose their own class-specific meanings on music, hairstyles, clothes, dances, sports and other forms of 'mass' entertainment. The New Wave recognises a working-class fringe, attached to primarily middle-class hippie and beat cultures, and middle-class punks. The latter can be found along Kings Road, Chelsea. Successful fads need only time to spread beyond their origins and straddle class boundaries. It is argued, however, that the effect is not to merge all young people into one classless youth culture, but to stratify each trend into a series of levels, appealing to young people in different class positions, with quite different meanings for participants who are handling different contradictions (Brake, 1980).

Opposition

Working-class youth cultures are considered oppositional, like their parents, rather than subordinate. 'Youth culture is an essay in the mini-politics of rebellion against obscure social forces' (Brake, 1980, p. 177). To begin to understand working-class youth, it is argued, we must appreciate the extent to which they resent and resist the dominant culture – the statuses and meanings offered by teachers and employers. Whether playing football, listening to their 'own' music or engaged in street-corner life, working-class youth are portrayed, above all else, as attempting to create their own structures, to wrestle control of their lives from obscure powers, to engineer their own space, and establish then express their own identities (Robins and Cohen, 1978; Corrigan, 1979). This is what earlier investigators mistook for 'doing nothing'. The New Wave alleges that working-class youth inherit their parents' awareness of 'us and them' and the associated capacity to resist oppression.

No one pretends that skinheads and punks have developed a full-blooded revolutionary consciousness. New Wave writers realise that working-class youth have never internalised political vengeance against the bourgeoisie. They may not even be conscious of their objective subordination. Nevertheless, it is argued that the young people's styles 'approximate' or 'correspond' to a proletarian awareness. New Wave analyses take account of, then transcend, micromeanings by exploring their relationships with macro-structures. Leisure activities can express, without arising from a consciousness of class interests, but some New Wave writers are optimistic for the prospects of a 'cultural politics', assisted by radical cultural workers, through which working-class youth could be educated to an awareness of the real sources of their oppression, and the contradictions they are handling, and the types of political action required to erase the class relations in which their problems are rooted (Willis, 1978).

New Wave authors acknowledge working-class culture's accommodating tendencies, but insist upon its basically oppositional character; its willingness to contest the legitimacy of the reward structure, and to challenge the dominant strata's everyday values and meanings. Working-class youth inherit this cultural capital which, it is argued, gives their sub-cultures a basically oppositional, not merely deviant style. This style (see below) imparts meaning to specific tastes and activities. The meanings of the elements are products of the whole. Working-class youth cultures derive their basic style from the broader working-class culture, but, the argument runs, today's youth find their inherited culture less than fully adequate. The basic problems of being working class in a capitalist society may be common and unchanging. It is claimed, however, that these problems surface in different forms for persons occupying different age, gender, ethnic and other statuses, and for different generations. Postwar youth have found their parents' culture wanting because traditional working-class ways of life based on the three interlocking nexuses of kin, locality and workplace have been ripped apart by urban redevelopment and economic change (Cohen, 1976). Another change has been postwar youth's access to new resources: greater spending power and the pop cultures their affluence has bred.

Pop Culture as a Resource

The New Wave rejects the idea of youth cultures being artificially manufactured, then imposed on gullible teenagers who are duped by commercial providers. The market economy and the ideology of consumerism are imposed, but, it is argued, young people attach their own meanings to specific commodities, and build their own youth cultures. Pop culture is treated as a resource, which young people use creatively and blend with their inherited class cultures, to address problems which, ultimately, derive from contradictions in their class circumstances.

The theory claims that skateboarding, Kung Fu, pool and discos are far from trivial; that they are attempts to express meanings and identities outside those offered at school and work, and to resolve collectively experienced problems (Hall *et al.*, 1979). It is argued that pop industries facilitate, but cannot orchestrate, youth sub-cultures. In the final analysis, it is claimed, young people impose their own meanings upon facilities; meanings that are derived from the actors' age, gender and, above all, their class positions, rather than providers' intentions (Murdock, 1975, 1977). Hence the plurality of youth cultures. The theory notes that whenever 'fads' are assimilated as 'fashions' into mainstream leisure, they lose their earlier meanings, cease to perform their original functions for working-class youth, and are deserted for new fads. Hence the flux, the rapid cycle of birth and obsolescence in youth sub-cultures, and young people's obsession with remaining 'on scene'.

Imaginary Solutions

It is argued that Teds, punks and skinheads, even soccer hooligans, are not 'mindless yobbos', but are saying something significant about their predicaments, and about society in general. The theory claims that the young people are acting out and resolving, and, for those who can read the signs, drawing attention to contradictions in their situations. It is argued, for example, that the Teddy Boy sub-culture can be 'read' as the theft of an upper-class style to celebrate heavy working-class masculinity; that skinheads' rolled-up jeans, cropped hair, industrial boots and preoccupation with 'trouble' can be understood as an attempt to recover and assert the virtues of the traditional working-class community; that the mods' cool style with neat suits and pointed shoes can be interpreted as expropriating the consumption ethic and extracting individuals from their true class locations. It may not be self-evident that these styles are resolving class contradictions, but the New Wave claims that once the meanings to the actors are understood – the satisfactions of asserting one's presence in punk, rocker gear or whatever – and once the same actors' class situations have been correctly analysed, the correspondences are plain to see.

Of course, the young people are not really changing their class circumstances. On an objective level, all the contradictions persist. But, to their own collective satisfaction, the participants in youth cultures achieve imaginary solutions (Cohen, 1976) by using elements from their working-class culture such as the aggressive masculine style, sometimes in combination with items borrowed from super-ordinate strata, like Edwardian suits, to deny their subordination. In the young people's minds, while they are parading with their mates in city centres, seaside resorts or discos, the contradictions evaporate. They are 'on top', successful, big spenders; their self-identities are released from their school records and workplace roles. These magi-cal, imaginary, cultural solutions 'make sense' to the young people. The New Wave does not confine itself within, or even accept this common sense, but respects it, and insists that young people's mean-ings be taken into account in explaining youth cultures.

Moral Panics
Although working-class youth cultures are not explicitly political, the New Wave draws attention to their oppositional character, and argues that this, not a humane concern for the younger generation's welfare, is the threat that provokes alarm among 'the powers that be'. Teds, skinheads and punks do not really solve their class problems. Their 'solutions' are 'magical', enacted only as play, during leisure. Youth styles do not change underlying class realities. However they appear and feel when parading in mod gear, the actors have to return to factory jobs on Monday morning. However 'solidaristic' their pre-sence in city centres and on football terraces, after the weekend skin-heads have to succumb to industrial discipline. The young people's resistance to oppressive class relationships is 'ritualistic', but even rituals, given time, can begin to undermine class structures.

The New Wave argues that youth sub-cultures wage semiotic guer-rilla warfare (Hebdidge, 1979). In contemporary capitalist societies, the dominant strata defend their privileges and institutions, not pri-marily through coercion, or even by overt ideological persuasion. They make their institutions 'hegemonic' by having their dominant culture – their meanings, social relations and ways of behaving – taken-for-granted, so that the *status quo* appears natural, given, time-less and beyond question. It is argued that, without necessarily being aware of the source of the satisfaction, working-class youth express their contempt and defiance by giving radical meanings to such famil-iar objects as Edwardian suits, industrial clothes, even safety pins, by incorporating them within oppositional 'styles' – a key concept in New Wave analyses. In isolation, abstracted from their contexts, there is nothing alarming about young people's clothes, hairstyles or music.

These objects are given provocative meanings only through incorporation into the working-class oppositional style, while the style itself is preserved, invigorated and broadcast through youth cultures. An effect, it is claimed, is to break the consensus so that the *status quo* ceases to appear inevitable. Class relationships, among other things, are liable to be challenged, and this, it is argued, is why working-class youth cultures are threatening.

Why should it matter if young people adopt Edwardian suits as leisure attire, dye their hair, fasten shirts with safety pins, hang the latter from their ears, smoke 'pot', parade in denim fashions or grow beards? Why the outcries, the moral panics stirred by press, politicians, judges and teachers? Research funds have been lavished on attempts to prove marijuana harmful, only to show it less damaging than alcohol and tobacco. Studies of the consumers show that it is used by 'ordinary' youth, who simply find the experience pleasurable, not just by 'young people with problems' (Young, 1971; Plant, 1975). Why not decriminalise the drug? The New Wave alleges that the authorities' reactions become comprehensible only when seen as attempts to preserve a threatened hegemony. 'Everyone knows' that industrial boots and jeans are for factory work, and that fun has to be earned, until youth cultures demonstrate that things can be otherwise. These demonstrations have to be discredited as dangerous nonsense. Otherwise, where might the questioning end? The New Wave has transferred the revolutionary mantle from young people's sexual antics to their class contradictions and solutions.

Class Control
Finally, New Wave theorists have distinguished and appraised the strategies whereby threats to the prevailing hegemony are held in check. Youth cultures can be devalued by open ideological attacks. This usually involves labelling the participants as mindless, aimless or delinquent, thereby discrediting the styles in the eyes of the majority of the younger generation. Hence the perpetual war against teenage rebellion, tyranny and anarchy. According to the New Wave, the alarm is not the result of any straightforward intellectual misunderstanding. Rather, society's quarrel with itself, the contradictions inherent in its social relations and values, are being displaced on to terrain favourable to the dominant strata. An allegedly unrepresentative minority of 'sick', disturbed or moronic young people, rather than an oppressed class, is defined as the enemy.

An alternative way of defusing threatening youth styles is to transform them into 'fashionable commodities', so rendering them safe. When Ted, punk, hippie and mod gear are publicised by pop stars, televised, marketed by chain stores and turned into fashionable leisure wear, to be displayed just for fun, for entertainment, during leisure time, on Saturday nights, they cease to challenge the dominant ideology.

New Wave theorists can see that the succession of postwar youth cultures has not carried society to the brink of revolution, but some believe that oppositional youth styles are gradually eroding the consensus. As threatening styles are transformed into fashionable commodities, young people turn to new, disreputable fads (Hall *et al.*, 1979). Ideological warfare is always likely to fail, since young people can see for themselves that 'pot' offers harmless pleasures, and that punks and skinheads are sensible, ordinary individuals. Different methods of preserving hegemony tend to negate one another – a further manifestation of society's contradictions. Sensational reporting risks amplifying styles with which nation-wide youth can then identify (Cohen, 1972).

If other controls fail, the authorities must resort to coercive tactics, to 'policing the crisis', which, according to one group of New Wave theorists, was the trend during the 1970s (Hall *et al.*, 1978). They argue that the crisis of hegemony deepened through challenges by student militants, drug use, other youth movements, plus rent strikes, unrest in Ulster, deteriorating race relations and escalating industrial conflict. As a result, the argument runs, the authorities were obliged to move from consensus to coercive management, which, it is claimed, explains the outcry over 'mugging'. The word is a recent innovation, but the offence is not new. The moral panic during the 1970s could be attributed, in part, to the press acting on news values, to the judges' desire to wage war on permissiveness, and to the police's failure to establish a role as 'peace officers' among ethnic minorities. But the background, structural source of the panic, it is argued, was the need to justify using the law as a coercive instrument of class oppression.

The Politics of Youth at Leisure
One of the New Wave's achievements has been to inject a political dimension into debates on youth and leisure. Histories and surveys of current provisions used to proceed on the naïve assumption that benign providers were attempting to meet young people's changing needs, impeded only by imperfect knowledge and financial constraints. The politics of leisure may still await an author, but the New Wave has supplied at least a base, in so far as it portrays all attempts to control working-class youth's leisure and the latter's endeavours to wrestle control of their own time and lives, to impose their own meanings, as essentially political acts, respectively seeking to maintain and threatening to undermine existing social structures.

Ambiguities in young people's lives have not been recently discovered. For over fifty years, psychologists have emphasised how adolescents are besieged by inner and social conflicts. As the preceding chapter explained, functionalist sociologists have not only acknowledged, but stressed how consensual values often read ambiguously, and offer conflicting guidance when applied to young people's predicaments. Conventional analyses insist that adolescence is an inherently anomalous life-phase. Hence young people's worries about their normality. Hence also the case for youth services, offering protected environments, where young people can act out their problems and eventually come to terms with themselves and society.

The New Wave has ruthlessly exposed inadequacies in these analyses. All status transitions, whether from childhood to adulthood, marriage to separation, or employment to retirement, pose problems of adjustment. But straightforward transitions can be institutionalised: when conflicts and ambiguities are purely transitional, in principle they are resolvable. Can such transitional difficulties alone explain the flamboyant, 'way out' and rebellious character, and the alarm provoked by working-class youth cultures? New Wave writers explain that some adolescent ambiguities and conflicts are not transitional, but express contradictions so deeply rooted in the class structure as to be intractable, failing a revolution in class relations. They argue that young people develop solutions that the wider society cannot accept because youth's problems cannot be resolved, except on an imaginary, play-acting level.

Critical criminologists have politicised their subject, though not, as yet, the criminals themselves. They show that vandals and hooligans are not as mindless as the press, politicians and 'traditional' criminologists have assumed, and that delinquency cannot be wholly 'explained away' in terms of inadequate socialisation in broken homes and disorganised neighbourhoods, or departures from consensual values. Appreciative studies have earned a new respect for delinquent youth, among those prepared to read and listen. Superimposing class analysis explains that, however primitive the level, deviance has a political meaning; it shows that the oppressed are not meekly acquiescent, but are prepared to contest and reject society's rules. Accept this analysis, and the law, police and courts can no longer be treated as politically neutral. They are seen as enforcing rules and roles that serve vested rather than societal interests.

In an equivalent way, the New Wave has shown how the dominant strata's attempts to control young people's play do not arise solely from a concern for the latter's welfare, but to obscure contradictions and thereby reinforce class structures. Its authors will not allow young people's play to be dismissed as mindless, trivial or a response merely to adolescent turbulence. Their decoding explains why working-class youth styles are satisfying to the participants: because they contest class divisions. This theory will not reassure youth workers who hope to shepherd clients into approved clubs, community service and playing fields, thereby simply meeting adolescent needs. It recognises the possibility of different types of youth work that start on the streets, or wherever the young people define as their own ground, that accept young people's own meanings and styles, then assist the young towards a total penetration of dominant ideologies, leaving them fully aware of the realities of their class predicaments, thereby destroying hegemony, which would create a potentially revolutionary situation.

The New Wave's advances beyond previous work on youth cultures and social class are undeniable, and are not confined to inserting a political dimension. Its authors have exposed the inadequacy of treating class differences as amounting to neither more nor less than gradations of income and status. They emphasise that social classes are defined by configurations of constraint and opportunity, within which participants develop their own cultures, then pursue their own objectives in trade unions, political parties and leisure. Earlier research made little attempt to understand Teddy Boy and other distinctive youth styles. If acknowledged, they were quickly dispatched to a deviant periphery. The New Wave has taken these styles seriously, explained their appeal to working-class youth, and why we (rightly) sense the presence of these sub-cultures as a threat to social order. In addition, the New Wave's attempts to relate actors' meanings to macro-structures improve upon, by combining the respective strengths of interpretive ethnography and abstract structural analyses. I have only two debating points to raise, neither intended to undermine the New Wave. Indeed, their net effect is to extend the theory's applications and credibility.

The New Wave and Other Theories
First, if the New Wave is treated as complementing other contributions, emphasising hitherto neglected processes and aspects of youth cultures, its position will be impregnable. Presented as an alternative to virtually everything previously written, it will hand unnecessary ammunition to critics. The New Wave was launched as a critique of earlier theories, but this is no reason for the finished product claiming a monopoly of truth. Its arguments do not require the traditional sociology of youth to be jettisoned wholesale.

Some aspects of adolescent leisure are classless. Middle- and working-class youth have to address some common adolescent problems. There are similar developmental patterns in peer groups and heterosexual relations in all strata. Even some class contradictions confronting middle- and working-class young people are very similar. The majority are taught that it is desirable to make money but wrong to steal; that it is sensible to work hard for eventual success and also to seize immediate opportunities to enjoy life. Middle-class parents and children nurture higher educational and vocational aspirations than the working classes. The former start on the higher rungs of the ladder, have better cushioning, but also further to fall, and are just as likely as working-class early school-leavers to experience frustration and be obliged to compromise their hopes on entering the labour market. Are the contradictions experienced by aspirant craft apprentices facing CSEs entirely different in kind from those surrounding A-level candidates, their sights fixed on universities? Does modern advertising fail to raise anyone's consumption aspirations to unattainable heights? Not all aspects of working-class youth's leisure need explaining in terms of distinctly working-class contradictions and cultures.

Equally important, class differences are not always products of class antagonisms and struggle. Some are the result of middle-class youth being the slower to break from parents, leave school and take all the additional steps leading to employment and marriage. Others reflect middle-class families having more of the resources, like money, that enable their young people to 'do more' of activities that appeal to working-class adolescents. The New Wave's arguments do not override the evidence of traditional sociology, that working-class youth at leisure are objectively disadvantaged. Family cars, homes equipped with sports gear, and space for hobbies endow middle-class youth with the wider opportunities. Some social class differences are straightforward products of constraint, rather than class values and preferences. Working-class families are unable to introduce the range of leisure interests represented in middle-class homes. Instead of compensating, education tends to compound these inequalities. Working-class youth certainly deserve recognition for expressing their own meanings, despite the massive constraints, but deflecting attention from the latter in order to extol working-class youth's creativity could unintentionally help to entrench their disadvantages.

Methodology and Findings
Secondly, the New Wave's methodology must be regarded as more important and, indeed, detached from specific arguments about the sources and consequences of different youth cultures. The evidence with which the New Wave has been launched will simply not support any immediate firm conclusions (Smith, 1981). Its substantive arguments are mostly based on small-scale, exploratory, participant-observation inquiries among working-class boys. As yet the theory says little about any girls. Stitching on Marxist concepts illustrates

their possible relevance, without demonstrating their superiority over other perspectives, and suggests that the arguments are capable of wider application than the evidence strictly warrants. The supporting studies have vindicated the New Wave methodology. They illustrate the value of relating meanings to the wider social structure by treating cultures as resources, and inquiring how young people blend elements from pop and class-based cultures to resolve problems arising from their positions in society. By contrast, the substantive arguments are best treated as hypotheses for further inquiry.

The New Wave authors' faith in the explanatory power of class analysis is one of the issues that must be treated as open for investigation. There is no need to restrict the New Wave methodology to studying class contradictions, and there are as yet no clear empirical grounds for engaging in class reductionism. Some New Wave writers argue that age and gender 'mediate' class predicaments. Why not treat class as mediating the problems of developing gender and sexual identities? Whether other social divisions and processes are derived from a sub-structure of class relations must be decided by appeal to evidence which at the moment is unconvincing, rather than, *a priori*, by theoretical fiat. It is unnecessary for the New Wave to stake its credibility on the primacy of class. The problematic is as applicable to and, in my view, should be used to explore contradictions surrounding gender and ethnic divisions. It should be used to assess, not assert the relative importance of class divisions in structuring and imparting meaning to young people's leisure. Furthermore, the methodology could be used to investigate exactly where the main class divisions occur among young people at leisure. Is the middle/working-class juncture the great divide?

The New Wave authors present punk, skinhead and Teddy Boy styles as examples of *working-class* youth cultures. Is the label justified? In terms of conditions of employment, party-political alignments and forms of class awareness, the blue/white-collar boundary is still a major threshold, but in child-rearing practices and many adult uses of leisure, the sharpest 'breaks' now occur above a lower, unskilled working class, and beneath a highly educated managerial and professional élite. Students in higher education and, to a lesser extent, those undergoing anticipatory socialisation in secondary schools, appear responsible for middle-class youth's exceptional activity in sport, high culture, political and intellectual pastimes.

Recorded delinquency rises steeply, not beneath the white/blue-collar juncture, but only within the unskilled working class (Douglas *et al.*, 1966). Could a lumpen, rough, unskilled, lower working class, or whatever label is deemed appropriate, rather than the entire manual strata, be the pool within which punk, skinhead and Teddy Boy styles have taken root? Chapter 2 noted how, beneath successive postwar styles, working-class youth cultures have been persistently divided into rough and respectable genres. The New Wave methodology might be better employed identifying the structural sources of this cleavage, and the different meanings of each trend, rather than generalising about all working-class youth cultures.

From the existing New Wave literature, one might imagine that the working-class youth scene was composed entirely of mods, rockers, skinheads, Teds and punks. Do the majority of working-class youth identify with any such distinct types, rough or respectable? New Wave writers offer no convincing explanation of why some working-class young people become skinheads and punks, while others distance themselves from these movements (Smith, 1981). Which 'classes' of young people are involved in different youth cultures must be treated as an issue for further research rather than a matter that has already been settled. Are there just two main classes and two main types of youth culture?

Another issue for the New Wave methodology to research involves working-class culture's mixture of accommodative and oppositional tendencies. The New Wave authors have focused upon oppositional aspects of working-class youth cultures. Some have stressed the limitations of hegemony-preserving strategies. Are they correct to do so? Are skinheads and punks more likely to develop proletarian images of society than other working-class youth? Do militant youth cultures help to socialise future political and trade-union activists? Or are working-class youth cultures effectively subordinated? No one can be certain because the hypothesis has not been rigorously investigated, but I suspect that the majority of working-class youth lack the resources and are too exposed to dominant values and meanings to develop their own contra-cultural tendencies into full-blooded counter-cultures, offering visions of any alternative society or future.

There must be many young people who treat 'way-out' characters essentially as commodities, available for entertainment, offering opportunities for vicarious and ritualistic identification on nights out. Threatening youth styles which are transformed into fashionable commodities are replaced by new fads. But do most young people move through a succession of rebellious youth styles? Or is each cohort assimilated into conventional adult roles as its 'way-out' styles are absorbed into mainstream leisure? These are issues for research. The New Wave methodology enables us to pose the questions, but, as yet, the evidence will not permit definitive answers.

It is difficult to measure objective aspects of dress and musical tastes, let alone meanings. In their present form, the New Wave's propositions hardly lend themselves to verificational inquiries

employing structured questionnaires and tests of statistical significance. This is not a criticism, but it indicates a need for further
inquiries to develop the theory's concepts, to make them operational,
and to chart the social geography of different youth cultures. Such
inquiries will almost certainly modify, but in the process they will
strengthen the credibility of the New Wave's substantive arguments.
The methodology could also be employed to investigate the implications of recent trends, like the spread of youth unemployment. When
appropriately designed research has been conducted, our conclusions
will become more confident. In the meantime, however, we can use
New Wave concepts, alongside conclusions from the traditional sociology of youth, to interpret the existing evidence on how young
people at leisure are responding to the new labour-market conditions.

9
Youth Unemployment

Youth unemployment was mentioned in this book's opening pages. The spread of joblessness is a main recent change in the condition of young people: a recent consequence of the growth of non-working time. Is there a leisure solution? Or will the disappearance of affluent young workers erode adolescent leisure as surely as employment is being withdrawn? Are we producing a bitter, restless, alienated younger generation, unable to resolve its problems through leisure, which will superimpose and intensify class and intergenerational conflicts? Functionalist ideas about leisure as a safety-valve, and conflict theorists' arguments about the imaginary resolution of contradictions in youth cultures, suggest that the disappearance of young people's jobs should disturb the entire community. For once, sociologists have not been alone in sounding the alarm. Commentators are virtually unanimous in deploring unemployment, especially youth unemployment. Politicians and the media dispute its inevitability and debate remedies, but agree that youth unemployment is a disaster, certainly in the short term, and maybe with life-long implications.

All the circumstances that once helped to reconcile school-leavers to their often limited prospects have changed. Traditional working-class communities which reared status-assenting young people have been destroyed by urban and industrial 'progress'. The rigidities of the 11-plus have gone. Educational selection is now delayed. The school-leaving age was raised to 16 in 1973. Less than a fifth of today's school-leavers, a minority even within the working class, have no qualifications. The majority possess GCEs and CSEs. Young people remain in the educational contest for longer, and develop higher aspirations. Few now leave school content to accept any unskilled job. Young people have become more ambitious and better qualified, while their employment opportunities have narrowed. Some have been condemned to joblessness and wagelessness – excluded from adult roles in the economy, and from many leisure activities by poverty. In addition to the immediate problem of surplus time but little cash to spend, school-leavers who are denied training may suffer throughout careers spent chasing a diminishing number of unskilled jobs, excluded from relatively secure and better-paid occupations in expanding industries based on the latest technologies.

This chapter focuses on unemployment's implications for leisure, but these cannot be divorced from who suffers unemployment, why, and how the victims feel about their circumstances. Contemporary youth unemployment is still too recent a national issue for the young unemployed to have developed, let alone for researchers to have identified characteristic responses.

However, there have been exploratory studies of the young unemployed's spare-time activities, which can be interpreted using existing knowledge of how young people's leisure is shaped by their class positions, and the following analysis develops two principal arguments, which dovetail with those of previous chapters. These are, first, that youth unemployment is not provoking unprecedented responses so much as strengthening certain tendencies and deepening divisions that already existed among youth at leisure, and that the class division being accentuated is between young people in all types of 'regular' work, whether in education, white- or blue-collar jobs, and marginalised strata where young people are rich in time but lack income, whose life-styles are not dominated by the rhythm of continuous employment. Secondly, this chapter infers that youth unemployment is intensifying problems that both traditional and New Wave sociology have attributed to working-class youth, that the latter's 'solutions' are typically contra-cultural and therefore can be expected to provoke repression rather than nourishment from the wider society. Needless to say, these 'conclusions' from the available but incomplete evidence will be best treated as propositions for further investigation.

Sub-Employment and Long-Term Joblessness

The best-known items of unemployment information are the rates and grand totals: three million out of work, representing over 12 per cent of the labour force, for example. These figures, the bread and butter of political debate, can mislead in several directions. Some youth (and adult) unemployment is unregistered. The numbers of young people failing to sign on vary from area to area, but official statistics always understate the true volume of unemployment, usually to an unknown degree (Roberts *et al.*, 1981). National rates are also misleading in that few young people inhabit localities where unemployment's severity equals the national average. In 1980–1, notoriously high-unemployment districts in Brixton, Toxteth and Mosside had up to 45 per cent of their under-21-year-olds out of work. In more privileged areas, by contrast, unemployment was still something that happened to other people's children.

The easiest way to translate an unemployment rate of, say, 17 per cent into human predicaments is to imagine that approximately a sixth of all school-leavers are sentenced to long-term idleness, which is another misleading impression that official statistics create. Most youth unemployment is short-term (Daniel and Stilgoe, 1977). It consists of transitory episodes following school-leaving, then between jobs and schemes, and local unemployment rates of 15, 20 and 25 per cent mean that considerably larger proportions of school-leavers are experiencing joblessness at some time or another.

There can be no precise boundary between transitory and long-term unemployment, but there is a qualitative difference. After some period, which can vary from person to person, individuals cease thinking of themselves as 'between jobs' or 'looking for work'; they become reconciled to unemployment and abandon any serious job-searching. As jobless spells lengthen, so individuals also become locked in the 'Catch 22' situation where their histories of unemployment turn into additional handicaps when approaching employers. By 18 or 19, young people with no substantial work experience, who have grown accustomed to idleness, are less attractive to employers than 'nice fresh school-leavers'. By this age, young adults are rarely willing to work for youth wages, while no self-interested employers can be expected to hire them if seasoned adults can be attracted. This is how the long-term young unemployed become a 'hardcore'. Employment service staffs sometimes consider these individuals unemployable (Roberts et al., 1982a).

By the early 1980s, prevailing levels of youth unemployment throughout Britain meant that, in most parts of the country, school-leavers unable to obtain apprenticeships and other secure jobs with prospects faced, at best, early career histories of sub-employment (Norris, 1978), moving between schemes and insecure, unskilled, low-paid jobs, separated by spells on the dole, or worse still, descent into the hardcore. In localities where the majority of young people left school at 16 with modest qualifications, if any, these prospects awaited them. Even in the districts most severely affected by unemployment, a minority of school-leavers, usually the better-qualified and/or those with relatives who can pull strings, obtain secure jobs and avoid unemployment completely, but by the end of the 1970s, in some neighbourhoods, these young people were a small minority and unemployment had become a normal experience.

As local youth unemployment rises to 10, 20 and 30 per cent, the majority of those affected remain 'afloat', using the available jobs and schemes to stay above the hardcore (Roberts et al., 1982a). The real function of special measures is not to train young people for skilled or other permanent jobs, but to keep them 'circulating', available for (mostly unskilled) work as and when required. These early career histories of sub-employment do not necessarily scar individuals for life (Cherry, 1976). The 'children of the Great Depression' recovered regular work habits quickly when steady jobs became available (Elder, 1974). In the past, as young adults have overcome employers' prejudices against hiring teenagers, become eligible for shift work and jobs requiring driving licences, and as family responsibilities have encouraged 'responsible' work habits, those still 'in circulation' have been gradually absorbed into better-paid, more secure employment. Unemployment rates are much lower among the over-25s than for teenagers. But there can be no guarantee that time alone will solve the problems of today's sub-employed youth. Much will depend upon what happens to the general level of unemployment.

While local youth unemployment remains at 'modest' levels, below 25 per cent, long-term unemployment remains the fate of a small minority. The victims are usually the least competitive job-seekers among the poorly qualified: individuals with physical and mental handicaps, who are poor interviewees and repeatedly rejected applicants, and persons who are unable to settle in jobs even for short periods, whose unstable work histories soon make them unattractive to employers with scope for choice. However, there is a level, which cannot as yet be precisely defined, above which youth unemployment can no longer be 'absorbed' in transitory episodes, and long-term joblessness spreads among young people who, in more favourable labour markets, would obtain and retain jobs without difficulty. By the early 1980s, in areas with exceptionally high-unemployment levels, a third and more of all young people were sinking into hard-core predicaments. Government special measures were incapable of containing the hardcore. Young people graduated through schemes and courses, then became unemployed, sometimes 'permanently' (Roberts et al., 1981).

It surprises some observers that young people in high-unemployment areas do not always 'stick' to the posts they manage to obtain. Why do young people risk perpetuating sub-employed work histories, and even descent into long-term joblessness? In some cases the young people have no choice. Many of their posts are temporary schemes. In addition, the mostly unskilled 'real' jobs open to modestly qualified school-leavers tend to be short-lived. Redundancies and dismissals are common, with minimal protection for young workers who have not built 'job property rights'. Other departures are voluntary, because the threat of unemployment is not always sufficient to discipline young people to make the best of any bad job. They leave, having grown 'fed up' with the work, bosses, or wages.

Employers who recruit young people for unskilled jobs are invariably seeking cheap, often temporary labour. They realise that they are not offering the wages, conditions or prospects to attract anyone they would wish to engage permanently. Frequent job-changing by young unskilled workers reflects the quality of their employment; a depressing situation alleviated only by job-hopping spreading unemployment around. In urban areas, even with local youth unemployment at 30 per cent and more, job-seekers do not face completely blank prospects. There are always jobs being vacated to seek and apply for, though not necessarily through the statutory services. How long individuals remain unemployed depends partly on the standards they insist on maintaining – the types of work, levels of pay and travelling distances they will consider. There is no contradiction between 25 per cent unemployment being structurally inevitable because of a shortage of jobs, and some out-of-work individuals considering their own unemployment voluntary, believing they retain control of their destinies.

What does youth unemployment mean? It means all school-leavers, even college graduates, experiencing greater difficulty in finding work, often being obliged to 'trade down' and accept second or third best, sometimes after spells of unemployment. But the burden of unemployment is distributed unequally. In areas where the majority leave school at 16, and are unsuccessful or never compete for secure and progressive jobs, sub-employment and long-term joblessness have become the normal early career prospects. National rates conceal this grim reality.

Coping with Unemployment
There is a growing literature stressing young people's ability to cope with unemployment, which is best read as a reaction to the forecasts of disaster that first appeared when mass youth unemployment returned, after the mid 1970s. Some commentators drew upon the only theories at hand – developed in the 1930s, emphasising the social and psychological damage that involuntary joblessness can inflict (Jahoda, 1979; Sinfield, 1981). Subsequent investigators (Pahl, 1978; Pahl and Wallace, 1980; Wallace, 1980) have been able to explain that society has changed: that today's young unemployed are not enduring the same grinding material hardship that spread during the Great Depression, and that it is no longer uncommon, even in working-class areas, for 16- and 17-year-olds to be supported by their families while continuing education.

A desire to provoke government action, and outrage at its absence, may have encouraged exaggeration of unemployment's injuries. It has been argued that denial of wage-earning status is particularly demoralising for out-of-school youth, who are still being educated for work, not leisure. Adults suffer similar injuries, but for young people the damage has been judged particularly acute; their self-concepts and attitudes are still being formed (Eggleston, 1979). There have been forecasts of youth unemployment undermining other institutions,

even destabilising the entire social system (Markall, 1979). Mounting
discipline problems for teachers have been envisaged as schooling
becomes more purposeless than ever, when even qualifications lead
nowhere.

A decomposition of labour power has been predicted as young
people who are denied the opportunity eventually lose the ability and
will to work. We have been warned that young people who are
rejected will, in turn, reject their society. Some believe that the
absence of jobs will confront school-leavers with problems that their
homes and education have not equipped them to address, and that the
young people's wageless predicaments will render them incapable of
discovering solutions, or even consolation in leisure. Some writers
argue that the spread of unemployment has added urgency to the case
for leisure education. But if immediate affluence is not available, will
young people be impressed? If they cannot afford commercial thrills,
will they accept cheaper, officially approved pastimes? Or will they
create less tolerable forms of excitement? Will wageless youth become
available for political mobilisation and challenge a society that can
offer neither meaningful jobs nor leisure? The 1981 street riots stirred
fears of the young unemployed threatening civilised urban life and
becoming fodder for extremist political movements on the far left and
right.

The studies that stress their ability to cope are not arguing that
young people are never or even rarely damaged by unemployment,
but discriminating among earlier claims which envisaged multiple
calamities. Youth unemployment has not brought every conceivable
damaging consequence. It has not led to mass suicides. The hundreds
of thousands of young people who have experienced unemployment
since the mid 1970s have not all become neurotic isolates. Street riots
have not become daily events. Most of the young unemployed retain
the ability and will to work. There are few signs of the revolutionary
consciousness that some believed was waiting a crisis to be more
manifest. *Youth* unemployment may not be especially damaging. Joblessness is probably more threatening to middle-class, middle-aged
commentators, even to working-class adults with family responsibilities, who have blended their identities with particular occupations and
cannot expect time to improve their prospects, than for the young
people most severely affected.

There is no uniform 'youth reaction' to unemployment. Many
school-leavers dread joblessness. It has been recent generations' main
fear (Youthaid, 1979). Middle-class youth, with no family histories of
unemployment, who are educated for entry into progressive careers,
and whose friends either remain in education or succeed in the competition for jobs, can find spells out of work very difficult to accept.

Other young people are less devastated. Writers who contemplate awesome consequences seem to imagine that, as unemployment spreads, the main effect is to sentence school-leavers who would formerly have become continuously employed to zero prospects. Past and present scenarios are exaggerations. Most of the young people affected are sentenced to sub-employment, not long-term idleness, and many of these young people are from neighbourhoods where, in the full-employment era, the majority of school-leavers spent their early careers moving between unskilled jobs. In these localities, sub-employment is not a novel career pattern.

'Breaks' between jobs have been common throughout living memory (Phillips, 1973). Some young people still welcome the respites. Within these areas, the main effect of rising unemployment has not been to condemn school-leavers who would formerly have entered secure and progressive careers to hardcore predicaments, but to lengthen and increase the risks of transitory episodes upon school-leaving and following job departures. This change has not been welcomed, but neither has it shattered the young people's career expectations, and, in these areas, youth unemployment has now become so common as to dissolve much of the stigma that surrounds joblessness elsewhere.

Where unemployment remained a local problem throughout the postwar decades, and where stagflation since the 1970s has simply increased its severity, young people have been able to draw upon their neighbourhoods' traditional cultures. Parents teach their young how to claim full welfare rights. At home the young people are taught by example how to subsist on low incomes. Coping with unemployment does not so much isolate these victims as bind friends and families. Local grapevines sometimes supply introductions, plus social and vocational skills for casual work and criminal enterprise. For girls, marriage and parenthood have always offered a (temporary) route out of the labour market. In high-unemployment neighbourhoods, the fact that many of the available jobs, of which most school-leavers soon acquire some brief experience, or learn about from friends, are boring and low-paid, helps to soften the deprivations of joblessness. The main problems of unemployment, boredom and poverty persist when many young people are in employment. Some adopt the view that neither work nor unemployment are tolerable for long unbroken periods, and sub-employment becomes their preferred way of life. They work for spells in order to do nothing for a while, and describe their episodes between jobs as holidays.

Structurally inevitable unemployment can be experienced as voluntary by the individuals affected. Many young people quit jobs voluntarily, knowing full well that they risk unemployment. Some of the young unemployed are not strenuous job-hunters; a fortnightly visit to the careers office or jobcentre exhausts many a job-search repertoire. Employment service staffs sometimes express annoyance when the young unemployed decline to be submitted for suggested vacancies. Many refuse to consider jobs more than a single bus ride from their homes. These young people do not enjoy unemployment. Nor are they masochists. They would 'get on their bikes', if there were jobs worth cycling to. The young people's behaviour is entirely comprehensible, given their circumstances.

Even the young unemployed maintain certain standards, like expecting to be paid for working. They hesitate before considering jobs where the wages less travelling and other costs barely exceed social-security entitlement. University teachers and other salaried professionals are well rewarded during spiralist careers that take them around, and sometimes between countries, but how many would leave their friends and families for £40 a week? Where would the young people live, assuming that jobs could be found in other areas? In practice, the only opportunity for most 16-year-olds to leave home is to join the armed forces (Youthaid, 1979). Why do some spend mornings in bed instead of seeking work? Job-stalking can be soul-destroying. Rejections are painful – more so than joblessness itself. It makes sense to await reliable tips from relatives or friends, or until the employment services can recommend vacancies for which individuals believe they will be seriously considered. Why do so many quit jobs knowing the risks of unemployment? Maintaining pride and status in the eyes of peers does not necessarily require young people to cling to any job. Self-respect sometimes demands that individuals demonstrate a willingness to tell employers to keep their shit work and slave wages and, if necessary, cope with unemployment (Pryce, 1979).

In areas without histories of unemployment, where adults have spent recent decades deploring workshy scroungers and where young people have not been taught to regard unemployment and supplementary benefit as 'rights', out-of-work teenagers often complain of the hassle and stigma of becoming claimants. These are among the reasons why some fail to register (Roberts et al., 1981). But even in these areas, where youth unemployment has now become common, young people are teaching one another not to regard joblessness itself as a stigma. Some have far more admiration for successful hustlers than individuals who 'sell out' and settle for permanent slave labour.

The impact of government measures depends not only upon official intentions, but equally upon the intended beneficiaries' evaluations and responses. Many unemployed young people regard the available jobs and schemes not as solutions but among their problems. Some are not so demoralised by joblessness that they will seize any help – any low-paid jobs created under the Young Workers Scheme – or be grateful when offered £25 a week as youth trainees. Hence the inability of current measures to eradicate all youth unemployment.

Having acknowledged young people's coping powers, it is necessary to add three large 'buts'. First, the unemployment that researchers have congratulated young people for absorbing without descending into demoralised apathy has represented short-term, transitory episodes. No investigators have concluded that 'hardcore' unemployment is anything other than demoralising, depressing and seriously damaging for young people's long-term prospects. Secondly, the young people who 'handle' unemployment are coping with a problem: reconciling themselves to, rather than approving the inevitable. If they were writing, the young people's first request would be for decent jobs. Any other options – schemes, courses, leisure facilities, more generous social-security payments – are judged second best. Despite all the obstacles and rebuffs, jobs worth keeping remain sub-employed youth's priority targets. They dislike unemployment: the time on their hands, being denied wage-earning status and their lack of income. If offered training leading to skilled status, or even well-paid unskilled jobs, most would abandon any preference for sub-employment. Thirdly, the fact that some young people can cope with unemployment does not mean they should have do so. Slaves and prisoners of war have adjusted to captivity, but this never justified their treatment.

The young unemployed are not a new leisure class, enjoying the time of their lives. In objective terms, the spread of youth unemployment has left young people at the base of the social structure more disadvantaged than ever – deprived of career openings, wages and opportunities to develop and express leisure interests.

A Divided Society

It is naïve to expect a uniform set of unemployment effects on young people's uses of leisure. The young unemployed are a heterogeneous group. The hardcore have different problems from intermittently employed youth. Other differences arise from the young people's home backgrounds. There is considerable inequality of recreational opportunity among the young unemployed. Many are reared in poor families, by parents on low wages or unemployed themselves, and are accustomed to modest life-styles, fluctuating incomes and periodic poverty. Others come from relatively prosperous homes, sometimes the result of two parents in employment. As among young people in full-time education, unemployed youth's leisure opportunities vary according to their parents' means and generosity. Among the unemployed, as among workers, levels of recreational activity are related to social class and car ownership (Parry, 1980).

Unemployment has different implications for boys and girls, because leisure is normally gender-divided. Girls' leisure is the more home-centred, and unemployment appears to accentuate this difference. Parents do not expect 'respectable' teenage girls, whether working or unemployed, to spend free time 'hanging about' on the streets. Unemployed girls who spend enormous amounts of time at home, helping their mothers, are rarely enthusiastic about their predicaments. They feel imprisoned, cut off, and resent being unable to afford clothes, visit discos and become involved in wider youth scenes. The attractions of early parenthood and/or marriage are relative to the modest opportunity costs.

There is anecdotal evidence, nothing more, of otherwise unemployed girls gravitating into the sex industries. 'The problem is becoming increasingly acute because of soaring unemployment among school-leavers who regard vice as an easy way of earning money' (*Observer*, 15 August 1982). There is more substantial evidence (see below) of unemployed youth, especially boys, becoming involved in crime and trouble with the police. In so far as joblessness helps to propel boys towards crime, and girls into sexual deviance and early marriage, it is intensifying existing social divisions and patterns in lower working-class areas rather than instigating totally novel trends.

It would be unrealistic to expect a clear division between the young unemployed's and unskilled workers' leisure habits since these groups are largely composed of the same individuals, at different points in time. Unemployment's effects operate not so much on solitary victims as throughout neighbourhoods and peer groups where spells out of work have become normal parts of life. Moreover, it contravenes everything we know about people's responses to new situations to expect youth in high-unemployment areas to develop completely novel leisure practices. They adapt roles and activities already at hand, which differ for boys and girls, and for young people from different types of home background.

Contemporary youth unemployment is still too recent an issue to have been thoroughly investigated, but the studies which have been undertaken permit three conclusions. First, for the reasons just explained, there is no uniformity, and little if anything that is novel in unemployed youth's leisure. Secondly, unemployed youth appear to 'do less' when recreational activity is measured in conventional ways, asking individuals whether they have participated in listed pastimes during the previous week, month or year. Unemployed youth's participation rates are well below national averages, and gradually decline as joblessness is prolonged. When asked to explain their inactivity, the young people usually complain of an absence of facilities they can afford (Parry, 1980). Wageless youth have little to spend on clothing, cosmetics, records, trips to sports events and holidays. The boredom and the frustrations of the young unemployed – their lack of interests to fill all their available time and their inability to realise the leisure aspirations they possess – are not new problems. Throughout the 1950s and 1960s, studies of working-class youth at leisure were highlighting the monotony. Sub-employed young people discover that boredom and poverty can persist during periods of employment. Joblessness is concentrated within social strata where recreational activity is generally low, and its 'depressing' effects can be read as a further instance of unemployment accentuating an existing pattern.

Wide disparities in young people's spending power predate the return of mass unemployment. Some, but not all parents have been able and willing to 'spoil' teenage children, whether in employment, education or on the dole. Young workers did not all earn 'good money' before the mid 1970s. Many apprentices and young unskilled workers in areas with persistent unemployment remained on 'youth wages' throughout the 'prosperous' postwar decades. All youth cultures have always incorporated different standards of living. Fears and hopes of youth unemployment provoking a 'crisis' among wageless youth who cannot afford to dress as Teds, rockers and mods, to parade on motor bikes and scooters or visit pubs and discos, and who are therefore unable to vent their frustrations and achieve imaginary solutions, underestimate the ways in which youth styles can be, and have always been, adapted to low incomes. Unemployed young people 'scale down' rather than abandon normal leisure habits (Willis, 1979). They drink less, trips to sports events become occasional, and wardrobes are not replenished, but they are not obliged to drop all former interests, many of which were always tailored to low incomes.

The third conclusion we can draw about unemployment's implications is that jobless youth's quantitatively low participation rates are incorporated in qualitatively different life-styles. Continuously employed individuals' lives – their daily, weekly and annual routines –are structured around work schedules. Remove these schedules, and objectively similar leisure activities are experienced differently. Relaxing in front of the television is a different experience after a working shift than when following an entire day spent 'doing nothing'. Compared with working friends, the young unemployed spend more time in bed, at home and on the streets. After three months out of work, individuals tend to 'get up' later, and daily routines geared to employment disintegrate (Parry, 1980). Intermittent employment, with repeated spells on the dole, creates a different life-pattern from that prevailing when holidays are predictable, annual events for which individuals plan and save. Needless to say, irregular work habits predate the spread of youth unemployment as a national malaise. Many young people in working-class areas receive anticipatory socialisation through irregular school attendance. Unemployment has simply intensified this time scheduling, and spread it more widely.

The sub-employed life-style has certain attractions. Unemployed young people cannot afford to participate frequently in 'a lot' of expense-incurring activities. In this sense their leisure is impoverished. But in areas where sub-employment has become the norm, joblessness does not isolate young people from their friends. Within other age-groups, loss of work diminishes social intercourse. This is not so among young people. It allows them to spend more time together (Morley-Bunker, 1982). Homes, if otherwise empty during the day, and, particularly among boys, streets at other times, are popular places for informal sociability. And as the previous chapter explained, 'doing nothing in particular' is not always dead time.

The main similarities and differences between the leisure patterns of unemployed and continuously employed youth are known, but a great deal of detail is still missing. More research is needed to distinguish the styles and cultures being nurtured by boys and girls from different home backgrounds, experiencing repeated episodes and long-term unemployment. The division that now follows compulsory schooling is growing as deep, and eventually will surely become as contentious as the old 11-plus. School-leavers are separated into white- and blue-collar occupations, but is this division still as significant as between all who gain any secure employment and young people who are denied regular work?

The 'harried' affluent strata are expanding. There are more families than ever with two or more adults in well-remunerated jobs, and life-styles to match, who possess the economic, social and cultural capital to give their children every opportunity of maintaining their status. Following compulsory schooling, the majority continue in education or training which will lead to progressive careers and continuous employment. Meanwhile, entire communities are being edged to the periphery of the workforce and the margins of society, employed intermittently in unskilled jobs, with living standards fluctuating around the minimum the state deems tolerable. Within these areas, young people mostly leave school without *useful* qualifications, to face sub-employment with no guarantee of ever being able to struggle into the mainstream. These young people 'do less' of the leisure activities that appeal to the rest of us, but within life-styles that often alarm an uncomprehending wider society. The young unemployed's ghettoes are becoming alien territory even for the police.

We need more information about the young unemployed's survival skills, psychological, social and economic. Unemployment is neither the sole nor a necessary cause of crime, but in localities where delinquency is already common, for whatever reasons, joblessness can hardly avoid heightening criminogenic pressures. Young males are on the streets, at risk, during daytimes in addition to evenings and weekends. Many are chronically short of cash, and unemployment supplies a 'vocabulary of motive'. Parents, teachers and community workers endorse the young people's view that, in the absence of legal opportunities, crime is too tempting to be resisted. Some US cities have borne 50 per cent and even higher youth unemployment since the 1950s (Conant, 1965). Britain now shares this problem, and some corollaries: property at risk in multiply locked homes, and the threat of street 'muggings'. The police are under constant pressure to 'do something', and their responses are often experienced as arbitrary harassment by young people on the receiving end. Some regard the police as the front line from a hostile society intent on holding them down. The opportunity to 'break out' and 'have a go' when street riots flared in 1981 was a highlight in many young lives. The wider society has no idea how to deal with the perpetrators. Short sharp shocks and social workers seem equally ineffective, and resented.

The challenge is only partly material fear for ourselves and our property. There is an ideological, cultural dimension. Can the rest of us accept and support sub-employed young people? If there are insufficient jobs, or insufficiently attractive opportunities to engage all young people continuously, why not consolidate their preference for intermittent work? Some employers, including Britain's universities, already institutionalise such work habits. A society with leisure could afford to disseminate the option. We could accept the sub-employed way of life by ceasing to use employment services and social security to pressure out-of-work individuals to seek, accept and retain any available jobs, and by guaranteeing a minimum income (Roberts et al., 1982b). But can the remainder of us accept that able-bodied young men and women, who are not preparing themselves for future careers, have no need to work continuously? Can we accept that employment often confers little advantage in standards or quality of life against hustling leisure and other opportunities from streets and clubs? This way of life is only possible while the 'other side' enacts contrary values. Will the working majority control their inclinations to harass the young unemployed with police, teachers, youth workers, other leisure professions, training schemes and trash jobs?

There has been talk of the young unemployed pioneering life-styles that others will emulate if the 'collapse of work' continues. Are the young unemployed pace-setters? There are few signs of any such status reversal. Objectively, the young unemployed suffer multiple disadvantages. They are not recreationally privileged. They lack the money, interests and skills to pursue recreations that the rest of us enjoy. They suffer all the leisure disadvantages that traditional sociology attributed to working-class youth, only more so.

The contradictions experienced by all working-class youth, which New Wave writers have analysed, are particularly acute for the young unemployed. Whatever hopes they are encouraged to entertain by parents and teachers, young people in high-unemployment areas find it difficult to climb aboard, let alone ascend the socio-economic hierarchy. Then there is the contradiction between the 'good life' of cars, motor cycles, audio equipment and fashionable clothing, and the predicaments of young people who cannot afford bus fares to claim social security. Should we be surprised if some of these young people use the meagre resources at their disposal to construct contra-cultures within which to preserve some dignity and self-respect, to proclaim contempt for a society that considers them entitled only to trash jobs, rubbish schemes, slave wages and humiliating treatment when claiming their welfare 'rights'? Youth unemployment is divisive. The victims' solutions win little approval and support. They receive continuous hassle, endless pressure from representatives of the wider society. Future research can probe more deeply, but my feeling is that the young unemployed lack the resources to stabilise, let alone justify their ways of life to the wider community, and that their characteristic leisure styles will remain subordinate, with the young people retreating into either their homes or the contra-cultures that the wider society seeks to contain and repress rather than emulate. Some of the young people at greatest risk may be able to cope with sub-employment, but I doubt whether others will even condone their coping strategies.

10
Ethnic Minorities

Casual street observation will convince all but the colour-blind that Britain's youth cultures are ethnically divided. Pupils from multi-racial classes leave in separate ethnic groups. Personal friendships cross ethnic divisions, but most adolescent peer groups have a predominant race. Mixed leisure projects are usually quick to polarise. Some organisers keep their efforts multi-racial only by conceding, *de facto*, separate sessions. Britain's non-white minorities, to which this chapter confines its attention, are not being absorbed, which makes them 'a problem', or at least a 'special case'. How and why does race divide young people at leisure?

One of this chapter's principal arguments is that we can explain racial divisions without recourse to field-specific race relations theories. Biology is irrelevant. Some people still believe that African rhythms and even special sporting talents are programmed into particular races' genes, but so much that was once reputed to be natural has turned out to be cultural that we are entitled to instant suspicions of biological explanations. The theories that explain social-class divisions among indigenous whites can cope with ethnic differences. Of course, class variables must be replaced or supplemented by ethnic factors, but as we shall see, this does not involve any change in the form of the explanations. Traditional sociology's accounts of how leisure opportunities are class-related can be adapted to explain how and why ethnic minorities are multiply disadvantaged. The New Wave methodology, which treats culture as resources that young people employ to address their problems, is as applicable among groups facing racial barriers, with access to ethnic cultures, as in analysing class predicaments. Ethnic youth cultures are not particularly difficult to explain. They arise in similar ways, for similar reasons, to other divisions among youth at leisure.

The presence of ethnic minorities does not increase the theoretical complexity of explaining young people's leisure, but this chapter's second principal argument is that ethnic divisions are certainly complicating situations 'on the ground'. Previous chapters have discussed leisure in strata positioned above and beneath one another – the middle and working classes, then young people in regular employment and those confined to the margins of the workforce. The ethnic minorities are heavily overrepresented among the latter. Blacks and Asians comprise less than 5 per cent of the British population, but they are the majority in many high-unemployment, inner-urban areas. Unlike traditional working-class communities, many of these districts are now socially and culturally heterogeneous.

There are many ethnic groups and many minority youth cultures. Young blacks and Asians share just one set of experiences: racial disadvantage and harassment. Experience of racism creates a basis for potential unity, but otherwise Britain's ethnic minorities have far less in common than indigenous whites. The former come from all quarters of the globe. Most black and Asian youth have parents who settled in Britain during or since the 1950s, but other families have been resident for generations. Immigrants from the Indian sub-continent include Hindus, Moslems and Sikhs. Members of each faith have backgrounds in different parts of India, Pakistan and Bangladesh, in urban and rural areas, and speak different native languages. East African Asians have their own heritage. West Indians are drawn from islands hundreds of miles apart. Like whites, ethnic minorities are further divided by gender and social class.

In Britain, the higher the social scale is ascended, the greater the socio-cultural homogeneity. Élites in business, politics, the civil service, law and the armed forces tend to be drawn from a limited number of élite schools and universities. They belong to the same clubs, political party, intermarry, sit on interlocking government committees and company boards. The next chapter argues that the British middle classes are becoming increasingly heterogeneous, but there are much clearer 'lateral' divisions at the base of the class structure, like between indigenous whites and numerous ethnic minorities. Asking youth workers in multi-racial areas to serve their entire local populations is expecting the impossible.

How racial barriers should be overridden is a contentious issue in racial politics. In Britain, the orthodox model of racial justice, the goal to which liberal whites aspire, envisages ethnic background and skin colour becoming decreasingly relevant to individuals' life-chances. It envisages minorities enjoying exactly the same opportunities as whites to acquire educational qualifications and vocational skills, decent housing and leisure interests, which will then permit their ascent and assimilation into the middle classes. Some students of race relations are now explaining that this is no longer an option, if it ever was (Hiro, 1971; Rex and Tomlinson, 1979). Many blacks are no longer seeking 'submersion' or 'Anglicisation'. Their preferred model of racial equality envisages ethnic differences persisting, with all groups represented at all levels in the class structure, so that individuals and entire communities can ascend the social hierarchy while retaining their ethnic cultures and identities. Britain's Jews have achieved this type of collective upward mobility. Some writers are predicting a Jewish future for Britain's Asians. Will there come a time when Britain's élites are as culturally heterogeneous as the populations in 'twilight' areas? This is one of the issues at stake in education, employment, housing and leisure policies.

Racial Disadvantage

Discrimination is an obvious reason why youth cultures are racially divided. Despite the letter of the law, British blacks and Asians face covert racial discrimination in housing and job markets (Smith, 1977). Their access to leisure facilities is often impeded by blatant hostility. Supporters of the National Front and similar movements may be a minority of their ethnic group, but their dress, marches and music make their presence impossible to ignore. Blacks and Asians know they risk physical assault on the streets. They all suffer verbal harassment; references to 'wogs' and 'niggers'. When they withdraw into their own peer groups and communities, having been excluded from wider leisure scenes, ethnic minority youth are gaining a social and physical security that is threatened every time they venture 'abroad'. Ethnic minority youth are forced into 'ghettoes' by racial hostility, and ignored by many major purveyors of recreational opportunities. Mainstream leisure industries are often unresponsive to ethnic cultures and interests. Films and television programmes, for example, are, like education, aimed primarily at the white majority.

Discrimination must feature prominently in any account of racial divisions among youth at leisure, but this explanation is not exhaustive. Race-relations researchers have found it necessary to envelop 'direct discrimination' within the larger concept of racial disadvantage. In job markets, black applicants are less successful than similarly qualified whites because the former encounter direct discrimination at the point of hiring labour. In addition to this, blacks are further disadvantaged because their homes, schools and high-unemployment neighbourhoods deny them equal opportunities to become equally qualified job applicants. Racial disadvantages in housing, employment and leisure are built not only by flagrantly discriminatory acts, but also through the positions in British society to which the ethnic minorities were initially allocated, and where the majority have subsequently been confined. Hence the case for 'positive action' to compensate for the 'indirect discrimination' that the minorities suffer.

The story is now well documented of how the primary waves of black and Asian immigrants, during the 1950s and 1960s, were excluded from private houses on which building societies are pleased to grant mortgages, and from council tenancies, and thereby channelled to 'twilight' areas in the inner cities, though some districts so described are not adjacent to city centres. The immigrants obtained privately rented dwellings, or purchased cheap older properties in 'zones of transition', where they housed their own families and other members of their communities who were unable to obtain any alternative accommodation. The minorities' dispersal from these districts has been slow, arrested by social-class disadvantages, overt and subtle forms of discrimination, and by some residents' understandable desire to remain among their own people, given the prevailing social climate. To the wider society, Britain's multi-racial areas are declining, blighted and multiply disadvantaged. Inhabitants who cope with the poor housing and inadequate services understand these reputations, but to many young locally reared blacks, Britain's problem areas are their swinging places, their spiritual homes (Pryce, 1979).

At school, Asian youth are now equalling whites' attainments. In contrast, West Indians continue to underachieve against national educational standards (Swann Report, 1981), though they often outperform the disadvantaged whites who inhabit multi-racial areas and attend the same schools (Roberts et al., 1981). Most blacks and Asians leave school with modest ambitions, then become disillusioned and frustrated by their even more modest prospects in labour markets where racial discrimination remains rampant. Jobs obtained generally fall short of minority youth's aspirations. Among young West Indians, unemployment runs at two to three times the level for out-of-school whites.

It is becoming clear that their modal response is not acquiescence. Blacks are less likely to accept their disadvantages passively than whites. Race enhances the former's consciousness of structured subordination. The majority do not abandon their aspirations. Should they be described as 'alienated' (Gaskell and Smith, 1981)? The reason many feel their situations are hopeless is that they cling to highly conventional ambitions. Among young Asians, a common response is withdrawal into family-based entrepreneurial ventures, a strategy normally considered second-best by parents and young people alike (Fowler et al., 1977). West Indians' frustrations are more frequently channelled into a general oppositional style – expressed at work, on the streets, through their religions, dress and politics – and it is only in this context that some of their leisure practices can be understood.

Ethnic-minority youth face all the disadvantages of being working class, only more so. They are mostly reared in low-income households, by parents in unskilled occupations, if employed, and attend inner-city schools that are often recreationally deprived as well as academically undistinguished. Whether their wider urban environments are recreationally impoverished is debatable. The countryside and playing fields may be miles away, but the young people are close to city-centre facilities, and older inner areas host more voluntary organisations than suburban estates. Blatant discrimination during leisure, on the streets and in other public places, adds to the disadvantages that minority youth suffer. Blacks' and Asians' predicaments are not identical to those of working class whites, but traditional sociology's explanations of social-class differences, suitably rephrased, have no difficulty in accounting for ethnic-minority youth being propelled to the periphery of mainstream leisure.

Cultural Differences
Listing the ethnic minorities' disadvantages and their barriers to leisure opportunities is not wrong, but it is an incomplete and therefore, unless given qualification, a misleading explanation of their uses of leisure, in the same way as traditional sociology's accounts of social-class differences. We cannot assume that the minorities would wish to emulate middle-class whites' leisure habits, if granted equal opportunities. It has been argued that working-class youth appear to be acutely deprived only when their leisure styles are judged by middle-class standards. This point gathers greater force when considering ethnic minorities, whose traditional religions, family patterns and uses of free time differ from Britain customs.

If the problem was simply to measure their recreational disadvantages *vis-à-vis* whites, checklists of leisure interests based on the indigenous population's habits would be appropriate research instruments. But if we want to understand and respect the minorities' own leisure aspirations, recognising that these will probably differ from those of whites, tried and tested research methods must be set aside, modified or supplemented. Time budgets require different codes to cope, for example, with Asians whose cosmologies include no concept of leisure. Overtly identical leisure activities, including sports participation, can have widely different meanings for blacks and whites. As we shall see, this is one reason why black youth's responses to school-sponsored recreation are the less dependent upon how warmly teachers respond to the pupils' academic performances.

Besides measuring disadvantages and opportunities we must, if we are to explain ethnic divisions among youth cultures, examine traditional cultures that the minorities have imported. It is difficult to understand Asians who dismiss many British leisure activities as frivolous until we realise that their religions stress the virtue of maintaining family and community patterns, and attach little if any value to pursuits offering mere personal pleasure (Michaelson, 1979). Moslems who take their religion seriously refuse to venture into working-men's clubs and pubs. To understand Bangledeshi textile workers in Lancashire, who prefer work schedules with long weekly hours, on whatever shifts maximise earnings, however unsocial, it is essential to appreciate that many have migrated without their families and enjoy returning home for visits lasting between six and twelve months. Hence their need to maximise earnings to pay for air tickets, and compensate for their lack of wages during extended holidays (Popil, 1982).

West Indians have transplanted marriage and family patterns, Rastafarianism, Pentecostal and other fundamentalist Christianities, reggae, blues parties, shebeens and their use of ganga. This Caribbean culture has now colonised many British streets, pubs, churches and record shops. Needless to say, Asian and West Indian cultures are modified by exposure to the British way of life. Maybe we are slower to recognise the extent to which our 'indigenous' leisure has been influenced by 'ethnic' cultures. The entire rock genre derives from black American music (Hebdige, 1979). Immigrants sometimes use Western technology to help preserve traditional cultures. Asians in Britain can afford cinema and video equipment to show their own films in their homes and community organisations.

But it seems more common, especially among the second generation, for traditions to be discarded. Some Asian girls who are 'closely supervised' go out secretly with boyfriends of their own choice (Sharpe, 1977). The children of first-generation immigrants are often exposed to severe cross-pressures. At school and in the wider community, many are introduced to a different language, plus recreational opportunities that parents may find offensive. The second generation rarely shares its parents' ties with the latter's countries of origin. Many Asian workers consider it important to send regular presents, and make repeated visits to their home towns and villages. Some buy property in their native countries in the expectation of eventually returning with their families.

Children reared in Britain often fail to see the attractions of village life, arranged marriages and so forth. Young Asians educated in Britain do not share their parents' isolation by lack of English language, formal education and rural backgrounds, which never supplied the basic skills and aspirations that mainstream British leisure takes for granted. Over time, traditional cultures are modified, which can solve some while posing new problems, as for Hindu women who obtain factory jobs but are still expected to perform all domestic home duties. Many complain of lacking sufficient time to rest. This is far and away the most popular use suggested for additions to their free time (Popil, 1982).

Uses of Traditional Cultures

Traditions must feature in any comprehensive explanation of ethnic minority leisure, but, alone and unaided, tradition is never a convincing explanation of anything. We need to ask why particular traditions are retained, and why they are sometimes deliberately revived. Survival is never inevitable. Traditional recreations may lapse, like cock-fighting and bull-baiting in nineteenth-century Britain.

Folk cultures can be packaged and marketed as commodities through the cinema, theatre and records, as leisure interests for the wider society. This celebration of tradition is practised in Latin American carnivals, which temporarily and ritually overwhelm entire cities, as well as in British folk clubs. But whenever they become mass-marketed commodities, traditional cultures lose another possible function: assisting ethnic minorities' quests for identity, and providing social support for individuals and families who might otherwise feel alone in societies like Britain. Traditional symbols and artefacts can be used creatively and invested with new meanings, to address new problems encountered in alien societies, as when young West Indians readopt Creole as a form of 'resistance through language'. The word 'tradition' implies that a culture is being passively absorbed and preserved through inertia. This occurs, but among ethnic-minority youth it is less than the full story. The complementary tale becomes visible only when cultures are read as the New Wave advises – as resources to be used, when necessary, to address non-traditional problems.

Ethnic-minority youth must resolve all the problems inherent in growing up – establishing independent identities, living with their changing bodies and emotions, and so on. Like whites, they must come to terms with their class circumstances. Simultaneously, the ethnic minorities must make sense of their racial predicaments. How minority youth respond depends upon their interpretations rather than the objective strength and breadth of racial disadvantages. Young blacks and Asians face class problems at school, work and leisure, then, in addition, they confront Britain's contradictory race relations. They are British, but not accepted as natives. They do not need academic surveys or government committees to tell them that racial discrimination persists, and that the goal of racial equality is not shared by all sections of the British public. They can see for themselves that their people are concentrated in inferior houses and occupations, while the occupants of prosperous suburbs and status jobs are overwhelmingly white. Any who are colour-blind find plenty of community spokesmen prepared to draw their attention to these facts of life. Governments have pledged themselves to equality of opportunity, then refused to implement policies that would eradicate racism at the same time as enacting implicitly racist immigration and nationality laws. Throughout the immigration debate, the very presence of coloured immigrants in Britain has been considered a 'prob lem'. This socio-political climate poses identity problems for native-born blacks. Britain is their homeland. Where else are they supposed to belong?

In addressing these problems, minority youth, alongside whites, can draw upon British cultures – highbrow, middlebrow and pop – but they can also resort to their ethnic traditions to appraise their circumstances and devise responses. 'Traditions' and 'positions in British society' are not independent factors, exerting separate influences among ethnic-minority youth. The uses to which traditions are put can only be understood alongside the problems the young people encounter, including racial and social-class barriers. West Indian family patterns, where men play peripheral roles and unmarried parenthood is condoned, are being re-created by some British blacks, but not through force of tradition alone, for many of their parents are 'saintly' Christians who came to Britain to escape life-styles bred under slavery (Pryce, 1979).

However, the second generation are not reaping the socio-economic rewards that their parents hoped to find. The young people are discovering different life-chances. West Indian girls have learnt that parenthood is a necessary qualification for independent council accommodation. Neither they nor their men always see the attractions in marriage, which would commit the males to permanent slave labour to sustain poverty-line existences. In 1979, 51 per cent of all births to women of West Indian origin were illegitimate. They have babies; whites have terminations. The state guarantees unmarried mothers and their children as generous a standard of living as many could hope for by relying on their men, who, excluded from the better jobs, drift and work intermittently, not always officially. Traditional West Indian family patterns were not traditionally maintained by council housing and social-security regulations.

As another independent variable, biology explains very little. But the meanings assigned to physical characteristics can have definite consequences, like racial discrimination in employment and harassment on the streets. Young blacks and Asians can use their cultures to construct and place different meanings on their racial characteristics. Some teach each other that 'black is beautiful'. They display pride in their race and heritages. This is why so many of the young people are not seeking assimilation. They use their leisure to revalue and preserve identities that challenge their treatment by the wider society.

The following passages will illustrate how some young blacks are using their leisure to 'hit back', to assert their ethnicity and challenge the dominant culture. Ethnic minorities are able to display all the resourcefulness that New Wave writers have highlighted among working-class youth. Despite their deprivations, ethnic-minority youth are developing styles which provide status and identities that the wider society is unwilling to corroborate. These aspects of ethnic minority leisure are normally incomprehensible, or vaguely threatening to indigenous whites. So are punks and skinheads, because in each case the young people are challenging everyday common sense. The details of their leisure styles can be specific to ethnic groups, without their being anything specifically racial about the explanations. Existing theories can account for the ways in which ethnic minorities have introduced new divisions among youth at leisure, and begun to modify the overall contours of stratification in Britain.

West Indians and School Sport

Our best adequately researched example of ethnic-minority youth combining a traditional culture with British leisure facilities, to assert their ethnicity against class and racial barriers, is West Indian representation in school sport. A series of investigators has responded to the surprise of many teachers and coaches at young blacks' prominence in school athletics. In general, multi-racial schools find West Indians accounting for twice their expected sports team places (Sargeant, 1972; Beswick, 1976; Carrington, 1982). Black British athletes are beginning to star in international track and field, and in the Football League. In 1982 the Football Association's chief coach predicted an England XI with seven black players. United States blacks have been described as 'twentieth-century gladiators for white America' (Edwards, 1973b). A similar situation seems probable in twenty-first-century Britain. More than academic curiosity has been aroused, and researchers have been able to accept this challenge because sports participation is easy to investigate compared, for example, with informal street life. The basic rules of play are common in white and ethnic-minority sub-cultures. Quantifying participation rates and levels of achievement poses few methodological problems. Meanings are less tangible, but not impossible to penetrate.

Some teachers and coaches subscribe to biological explanations of blacks' sporting excellence. These accounts cannot be completely ruled out, but they are not convincing explanations for the full scale of blacks' achievements across so wide a range of sports, including cricket, football, boxing and sprinting (Edwards, 1973a).

Another theory suggests that sport acts as an alternative means of social and economic ascent for young people otherwise destined for menial wage labour (Cashmore, 1981; Gallop and Dolan, 1981). Economically depressed regions, including Clydeside and north-east England, have been prominent soccer nurseries. It is not difficult to motivate talented lads to cultivate ball skills when this is one of the few means of escaping lifetimes in the pits. Rough, deprived urban areas supply the majority of professional boxers in Britain and North America. The wealth and status accompanying success can be spectacular, and lowly origins, even a criminal history, pose no handicaps for individuals with the necessary ability. The sports scholarship has often been the sole means to a college education for black American youth from poor families and low-achieving schools. Comparable motives are unlikely to be completely absent among Britain's young black sportspeople. But researchers seldom find them entertaining real hopes of professional success. The young people recognise their limitations, and realise how few can achieve socio-economic success by way of sport. Few name the praise they receive from teachers or wider social acceptance as reasons for participating in school teams (Carrington, 1982). The majority of black sports participants are not expecting to be rewarded with acceptance or success in the wider society.

A third theory argues that it is not black pupils who are forging an alternative route so much as teachers who sidetrack the young people. Many teachers believe it desirable for all pupils to find arenas where they can excel. This aim of progressive education has won general recognition. West Indian children are often (wrongly) stereotyped as lacking the ability or character for academic success (Swann Report, 1981), and it has been alleged that teachers sometimes channel these pupils' efforts into sports where they can earn credit for their schools, and for themselves. The teachers may be anxious to enhance the pupils' self-concepts and confidence, but, it is argued, this sidetracking accentuates black pupils' underachievement in academic subjects, and thereby depresses their job prospects still further. This charge is so serious that the sidetracking hypothesis clearly deserves further investigation. It would be surprising if it never occurred. But is it happening on a significant scale? In schools where they dominate sports teams, black pupils have been found expressing higher educational and job aspirations than white class-mates (Carrington, 1982). Teachers may sometimes try to deflect young blacks' aspirations and efforts towards goals that the former consider realistic, but surveys reveal black pupils seeking, first and foremost, qualifications from schooling, and expressing suspicions of 'multi-cultural curricula' that appear second-best consolation prizes (Stone, 1981).

It seems impossible to account for the extent to which black pupils nurture sports skills and dominate some schools' teams without recourse to a fourth theory, which suggests that the youth are colonising and using sport to express their ethnicity. Young people of all races list fun, keeping fit, enjoying competition and (if male) expressing masculinity among sport's attractions. In addition, some blacks see sport as an arena for ethnic achievement, where they can outplay whites at the latter's games, rules and grounds. These feelings have added a 'political' dimension to many England–West Indies test cricket series (Patterson, 1969). Young blacks who use sport to assert and take pride in their ethnic identities are not necessarily anti-white, any more than England's soccer fans hate all foreigners. They are simply using sport to claim a status for their people that cannot be derived from their housing, jobs or educational attainments. Sport cannot offer equivalent attractions to indigenous whites. They do not face comparable racial predicaments. As explained in Chapter 7, lower-stream whites are underrepresented in school teams, but among blacks, particularly males, sports enthusiasm and excellence are less inhibited by academic failure. They see the teams as representing their ethnic groups as well as, and sometimes rather than, the schools. There is anecdotal and some research evidence of whites in multi-racial schools declining to play for school teams, despite possessing the necessary talent, because sport has, in their schools, acquired an ethnic image with which they cannot identify (Carrington, 1982).

Educational researchers have noted young blacks' often 'contradictory' attitudes towards school, judged by white norms. Low-achieving whites tend to reject school wholesale, whereas blacks who are anti-school often remain pro-qualifications (Fuller, 1980), and keen to become sports representatives. The contradictions are resolved when sport is viewed as a resource, with roots in mainland British and ethnic-minority cultures, to which pupils can attach their own meanings and use to resolve their problems. Black pupils appear to regard qualifications in a similar way – as means of proving their worth and 'getting on' despite, in many cases, disliking school itself and believing that teachers could be more helpful.

Young whites who grow up in 'rough' areas sometimes exploit their neighbourhoods' reputations as one of the few resources available to establish respected if not respectable identities. Living up to their territories' notoriety can offer an otherwise elusive security (Elias and Scotson, 1965; Gill, 1977). When they create disturbances and trouble in the streets, male peer groups from delinquent areas are not always passively reflecting the wider society's expectations. They are often using these expectations to 'hit back', to express their contempt, to assert their dignity and independence.

Pop cultures can assist these rebellions by supplying meanings and models to emulate, and a language the wider society understands. Black youth can also use their ethnicity and traditional cultures. The resources are different, but they are used for essentially similar purposes. The rude-boy culture, with its standard gear of dark spectacles and wide-rimmed hats; the cool style of the downtown hustler who lives on his wits and earns a living outside regular wage labour from dope, pimping, gambling or entertainment; and the Rastafarians who have given woolly bob-hats in red, green and gold, the Ethiopian colours, a wholly new meaning (Cashmore, 1979; Garrison, 1979), all have Jamaican origins. But British-born blacks who adopt these styles are not slaves of traditions that must inevitably slide down the generations. The first-generation immigrants, the parents of present-day black youth, did not import these sub-cultures. Many are shocked and distressed when these traditions are revived by their own children, just as white working-class parents are alarmed when their offspring appear as bovver girls and boys.

Whose Gladiators?

Not all ethnic minority youth are 'fighting back', waging semiotic warfare. The heroism of the New Wave perspective must be tempered by recognising the disadvantages and constraints under which minority youth live, at work and leisure. Some are simply 'held down'. We know less about them because their problems remain invisible, and their solutions are never elevated into public issues for researchers to address. West Indians who originally came to Britain hoping to assimilate, are probably more likely to challenge the wider society than Asians, who migrated to preserve not desert their traditional cultures. Many Asian youth, and some West Indians, simply withdraw into their own communities from an indifferent, often hostile society. Males in all ethnic groups are probably more likely than females to fight back, though there are many instances of Asian girls walking out on parents who threaten arranged marriages, and West Indian girls are taught to fend for themselves rather than seek economic security through menfolk. Young West Indian females are earning renown for their persistence in education – in the job market, and in battling to house themselves and their children. Nevertheless, sport and street leisure remain male-dominated among young West Indians, Asians and whites.

Ethnic-minority youth who 'hit back' are not necessarily winning. The wider society is skilled at smothering semiotic attacks. Ask America's blacks. Challenges can be processed into mass-entertainment, or the challengers can be labelled as deviants, like the American 'gladiators' who used the Mexico Olympics to salute black power. Ethnic-minority youth cultures could simply be adding further examples of contra-cultures for young people to vent their frustrations, which are then used by the wider society for its own purposes. But I suspect that, in the long term, Britain's ethnic minorities will prove more effective 'cultural politicians' than white working-class youth. It is not inconceivable that the leisure styles being developed by young blacks and Asians could join the resources with which, in time, Britain's ethnic minorities reshape the wider system of stratification.

Investigators have noted that young blacks are well represented among the most radical elements in the younger generation, and, indeed, among the entire working class (Rex and Tomlinson, 1979). This is not solely because of their multiple disadvantages. Ethnic-minority youth have a visible explanation of their disadvantages –racial injustice.

No matter how strongly and repeatedly sociologists argue the case, social-class barriers remain invisible. It is easier to see skin pigmentation, which increases the probability of black youth regarding themselves as victims of an unjust society rather than held back by bad luck or by their own inadequacies. They do not find it difficult to discount the propaganda that Britain is a land of equal opportunity. There are additional circumstances that favour ethnic-minority youth developing their oppositional styles into counter-cultures. Their ethnic symbols and styles are more easily protected, and less easily managed – because they are less rapidly understood by the wider society – than white working-class youth's practices. Furthermore, many middle-class blacks and Asians are not being socially assimilated into white society. They remain resident, and some work within inner-urban areas, available to offer advice and leadership to young people and other adults, and to form alliances with sympathetic whites' organisations.

Some ethnic-minority youth, aspirant 'mainliners' (Pryce, 1979), use leisure to nurture mainstream interests and manners, and to assimilate with whites, thereby facilitating their individual ascent, but this strategy only works for individuals with qualifications and career opportunities. The modal response among ethnic-minority youth seems more likely to take the form of consolidating separate identities and cultures, which will be available as foundations if and when the minorities strengthen their own community organisations, then build upwards towards the political and business élites. As among white jobless youth, leisure workers among Britain's ethnic minorities will find it difficult to remain apolitical.

11
Middle-Class Youth Cultures

Why has so little been written on middle-class youth at leisure? Since the 1960s, their youth cultures have been as flamboyant as those of working-class teenagers. 'Traditional' sociological investigations have noted that they do 'a lot' and complain of pressure on their time (Prosser, 1981), but there have been few ethnographic studies of middle-class youth's meanings, satisfactions and styles (Murdock, 1975, 1977; Willis, 1978; Hall *et al.*, 1979; Brake, 1980). These have never been considered the main 'problem'. Delinquents attract public interest and research funds. An expectation of change being generated from below, which this chapter disputes, may also have deflected sociological attention from the middle classes. But another reason for their neglect has been the difficulty of decoding middle-class youth cultures. They defy all attempts to impose the one readily available middle/working-class model. Presenting hippies or beatniks as representatives of all middle-class youth would offend even the most vivid sociological imagination.

This chapter treats the complexity of middle-class leisure, not as a problem to be resolved by simplification, but as a principal argument. There is much greater diversity among middle- compared with working-class youth cultures. Middle-class youth weave pop with numerous political, religious, intellectual and artistic strands. Business, political and other élites may be renowned for their homogeneity, but most middle-class youth do not attend top public schools or Oxbridge. The contemporary middle classes are a heterogeneous bunch. The non-manual strata range from office and technical workers to company directors. By comparison, intra-working-class inequalities of income and leisure opportunities pale to insignificance.

This chapter suggests that a major division among middle-class youth at leisure – indeed, one of the main breaks in the entire class structure – separates students who continue full-time education until their early or mid-20s from the rest. However, the following passages distinguish additional sources and dimensions of variation among middle-class youth. A theme of these chapters on social-class divisions has been that no single process can account for all the differences in adolescent leisure that are related, in some degree, to young people's social origins, educational attainments and occupational destinies. Some differences arise because middle-class youth are the slower to 'develop'. Others involve young people from middle-class homes and in secondary schools' academic streams 'doing more', especially of activities approved and sponsored by parents and teachers. These generalisations are not mistaken, but need supplementing, because they leave 'flower people' and other 'way-out' styles, cultivated mainly by the college educated during and since the 1960s, as mysterious as ever. Once released from the simple middle/working-class dichotomy, the New Wave problematic can suggest the missing answers. Middle-class youth have the resources – not just leisure equipment, but also access to a wide variety of cultures – that enable them to do a lot of many different things. Moreover, they can blend these resources in numerous ways, creating various solutions to their different problems.

Middle-class youth may not be a problem group to the wider society, but they experience problems. They are privileged, like earlier generations, but today's middle-class adolescents are rarely complacent. They are subjected to contrary pressures, like working-class teenagers, the details differing because the young people's educational and career predicaments are so dissimilar, and as previously stressed, the present-day middle classes are a diverse body. There are many different middle-class circumstances, all presenting their own contradictions. The following pages explain how problems that distinguish all middle-class youth from working-class early school-leavers, many resulting from the former's prolonged education, surface in rather different forms for individuals from upper-middle-class homes against upwardly mobile youth, for those pursuing vocational as opposed to liberal higher education, and for young people who enter white-collar employment at or before the age of 18 instead of proceeding to college.

Another source of their diverse youth styles is the middle classes' access to a variety of cultures. Middle-class youth's political interests and leisure activities often express class-specific 'bourgeois' values, but these stretch from the intelligentsia's radicalism to the conservatism of bureaucratised strivers. Students encounter political, artistic, religious and intellectual genres, which other young people are never invited to take seriously. Their education insulates working-class youth from these resources. The gay movement, women's liberation, CND and ecology arouse interest, even enthusiasm on campuses, and create a cultural chasm between student and other youth cultures. Of course, many students are into the commercialised pop scene. Middle- and working-class youth share many leisure activities and are often served by the same leisure industries, but as New Wave writers argue, even when their activities are objectively similar, young people in different class circumstances can invest them with different meanings.

Middle-class youth blend diverse cultural strands into a kaleidoscope of contrasting tendencies. Radical students are renowned for their opposition to nuclear arms and war between nations, and also for their support of internal strife, even terrorism. Their alternative foods are purchased from health stores and informal street drug markets. They favour alternative technology alongside widespread use of hi-fi. They support liberation for women and gays, and civil liberties for ethnic minorities, yet extend limited tolerance to elected politicians. The reality behind such enigmas is usually that different sections of middle-class youth are responsible. Collectively they weave the cultures at their disposal into so many complex patterns that disentangling the matrix could occupy a generation of researchers. The task would certainly defeat any single project. However, the dense foliage need not obscure the shape of the forest. The following passages will illustrate how middle-class youth use their cultural capital to respond to the structural changes and continuities in education and employment that define their class predicaments.

Another of these chapters' principal arguments is that the middle classes, especially students, enjoy far greater freedom than working-class youth. The deferential, dependent student has long ceased to be the norm. Much working-class leisure, among older and younger generations, is subordinate to dominant values. Rebellious tendencies are processed into a harmless consumerism. Contra-cultural styles appear common only among lower-working-class youth, in strata fast being marginalised, and pose a nuisance rather than a genuine challenge to established structures. Ethnic-minority youth cultures are potentially more radical, but middle-class youth, students particularly, are far better placed to break conventional gender and sexual roles, to mobilise politically, and to resist the vocational futures that society offers. Middle-class youth's predicaments vary immensely in their likelihood of prompting individuals to question the wider social order. Many simply accept and enact dominant values, but other middle-class youth cultures are genuine counter-cultures supporting values, behaviour and roles which govern the actors' total life-styles, and thereby ripple outwards to influence the wider social structure.

Sources of Variation among Middle-Class Youth

Viewed from the working class, all middle-class youth are prolonging childhood by declining to leave school and claim adult status at 16. Why should working-class secondary-school pupils, who prize the freedom of the streets, envy the 'success' of swots who face up to another decade on the examination treadmill? This is not working-class youth's idea of a good time. From within the middle classes, however, the social landscape has a different appearance. Do working-class youth cultures illustrate the deferred gratifications to which the college-bound aspire? Are middle-class youth deferring rewards that *they* would find immediately gratifying?

Young people who complete full-time education before 18 may achieve adult wage-earning status ahead of the college-bound, but do they gain earlier independence and gratifications? Teenage white-collar workers in banks, insurance offices, laboratories and local government commence at the foot of long incremental salary scales. They may receive higher cash incomes than students, but must bear the costs of working forty-eight weeks a year. The vast majority live with their parents, unable to establish their own households until they have climbed several rungs up their career ladders. In many respects, students enjoy the greater independence. They live away from home and are offered leisure facilities, often subsidised, which match their means. College calendars permit working holidays abroad.

Are students' gratifications deferred? In sport and cultural forms of recreation, students are the most active section of the entire population (Hendry, 1979). They enjoy greater social and intellectual independence than young workers. Students are encouraged to think for themselves, to have confidence in their intellectual abilities, and are able to create their own social networks and cultures in which some feel responsible for world peace in addition to their own minds and bodies. Of course, students are not really responsible for the fate of mankind. No one is dependent on them, except their teachers. It is not students' dependence that is prolonged so much as their irresponsibility, which can be intensely gratifying. In Britain, the majority of white-collar employees are non-graduates. Is it surprising that many resent students' parasitism, especially when the highly educated step on to rapidly moving career escalators while others are arrested by graduate barriers?

Delayed entry into adult salaried status has different meanings and consequences for individuals from different social backgrounds. Young people from middle-class families are reared in homes and neighbourhoods where it is normal to remain in education, kept by parents, beyond the statutory leaving age. Middle-class parents often support their children into the latter's child-rearing phase (Bell, 1968). Deposits on houses, central-heating systems and furnished nurseries are not exceptional wedding and 'birthday' presents. Middle-aged, middle-class parents can often afford to subsidise their student-children's immediate pleasures with cars and holidays abroad. Why should middle-class youth resent this dependence? It is customary in their milieux.

The manual strata are now almost wholly self-recruiting (Gold-thorpe *et al.*, 1980). 'Skidders' often use further education to climb back into the middle classes (Hopper and Osborn, 1975). In contrast, over a quarter of university students are from manual homes. Many educationally successful youth, destined for middle-class careers, are upwardly mobile, but the majority of their neighbourhood friends still terminate full-time education at 16. Working-class parents do not expect to support grown-up children through marriage and the onset of parenthood. The majority, in any case, lack the means to do so. Yet, in one sense, these students have greater independence than individuals from more prosperous middle-class backgrounds. Students from poor families receive the full maintenance grant and pre-sume that they must achieve self-sufficiency with their limited means.

Working-class students must disentangle themselves from their social backgrounds. They are not expected to 'break off' relationships with parents, but these relationships must be redefined. Student cultures enable mobile youth to relocate their 'selves' relative to their origins and destinies (Turner, 1964; Abbott, 1971). Young people from middle-class homes have different problems. Even college entrants face the possibility of downward mobility – a fate that working-class students cannot share. Higher education has expanded alongside a routinisation, some say proletarianisation of not just cleri-cal, but even professional and management jobs. Middle-class youth's rewards for 'success' may not be deferred but non-existent, even in the long term. For the upwardly mobile, student cultures can assist their social assimilation into the middle classes. Students from middle-class backgrounds, by contrast, sometimes need to relinquish conventional bourgeois aspirations. For others, as we shall see, student cultures can be read as attempts to reassert and retain traditional middle-class values which are threatened by continuing occupational trends.

Students reading medicine, engineering and other vocational sub-jects offer a classic illustration of the need to work hard in education to enhance long-term careers, while consumption values, whose realisa-tion is a main prize for success, are kept tantalisingly out of immediate reach. These students know where they are heading and can anticipate futures as doctors, engineers or whatever with reasonable confidence. They enrol in college to qualify for these careers, often with strongly instrumental orientations towards academic work, which are reinfor-ced in student cultures. Their vocational goals are just three years and ten examination papers away. Consolidating instrumental orienta-tions towards lectures, classes and tests can be an effective form of professional socialisation: novice engineers learn from peers and teachers that making money is the number-one respected aim in their future profession (Becker and Carper, 1956a, 1956b, 1957). Within

campus cultures, students preparing for common vocations can practise professional styles and equip themselves with professional self-
concepts. By graduation they *are* doctors and engineers (Merton *et al.*,
1957). These students' cultures usually celebrate leisure activities in
which expressive consumption values are preserved and immediate
gratifications sampled. Science and engineering students are mostly
male, and in many colleges form the backbone of the hale and hearty,
beer and rugby cultures, which offer their own versions of
Saturday-night fever.

By comparison, the student cultures surrounding non-vocational
courses in arts and social science are effeminate. These students are
more easily attracted to politics and high culture (Musgrove, 1974).
This is partly because the subjects' reputations attract like-minded
students (Edelstein, 1962), and partly because of the uncertainty of
non-vocational students' futures. The types of independence and
gratifications they are working towards remain unclear. Occupational
destinies cannot impart meaning to their student lives and leisure. The
only identities offered by these students' college workloads are with
their subjects. Those who succumb are sometimes recruited as perpetual students, but many consider their own talents too modest to
claim company with Plato, Marx and Keynes (Becker and Carper,
1956a, 1956b). These students need to employ wider cultural resources to define 'success' and 'gratifications'. Answers are not delivered
by their educational and vocational trajectories.

Unfortunately, our present knowledge will not support even a
tentative, comprehensive social geography of middle-class youth cultures. The above sources of variation, and the characteristics and
consequences and the styles discussed below, are suggestions requiring further research rather than firm conclusions. The illustrations that
can be offered of middle-class youth using their cultural capital to
address different middle-class problems are necessarily unrepresentative; they are mainly from student cultures. The leisure practices of
young people who commence middle-class careers aged 17 or 18, on
leaving secondary school, have never attracted investigators. By comparison, we have a wealth of information, albeit partly dated, about
students. Following the 1960s' campus turmoil, students ousted
working-class delinquents from newspaper headlines and became,
temporarily, the most heavily researched section of the entire population.

Bracketing student cultures alongside rock 'n' roll and punk styles
under the label of adolescent leisure is not an attempt to dismiss
student politics as inconsequential pastimes. The New Wave's
polemic has sought to rescue working-class youth cultures from such
casual dismissal. The intrinsic satisfactions cannot be ignored in

explaining the appeal of demonstrations and sit-ins, but the main reason for placing student cultures alongside other youth movements is that campus issues and political crusades are embedded in broader styles, created through comparable processes and resting on similar foundations. As previously noted, in Britain full-time higher education is still confined to a minority, even among young people with middle-class origins and destinies. Students are not statistically typical, but they are exposed to particularly acute versions of some problems and opportunities that distinguish all middle-class youth, like the deferment of adult responsibilities. This is why students have been a vanguard in developing leisure styles, aspects of which have then undergone stratified diffusion, maybe not throughout the entire younger generation, but certainly within other middle-class segments – sixth-formers, young white-collar workers and young people in part-time continuing education.

However, in this chapter students are featured as illustrations, not representatives. They can offer excellent examples of how middle-class youth cultures are constructed and divided from one another, no matter how vastly students' predicaments differ from those of other teenagers. Students are misleading only when investigators use them as representatives, or imagine that there has ever been a single student culture.

Student Unrest

Just as there are more studies of actual and potential delinquents than of conformist working-class youth, among students the 'militants' have proved a magnet. There are other parallels. So-called militants have never been any more representative of students than the 'mindless vandals' of working-class youth. Furthermore, both minorities have been repeatedly misunderstood by writers who have refused to take their subjects' ideas and behaviour seriously.

The passage of time and mounting evidence have toppled several earlier, instant diagnoses of student unrest. Student militants have never been mindless. Their protests have never been wholly explicable in terms of mixed-up adolescents acting out sexual frustrations. Like other people, students are often intellectually confused, but, given the opportunity, their spokespersons will voice genuine grievances and fears. All young people, and adults, have emotional hang-ups which can effect their expression without automatically stripping arguments of educational and political credibility. Of course, students have to cope with adolescent stresses. Keniston (1972) advocates a psycho-historical perspective. How young people respond to the issues of their time owes something to the psycho-dynamics of adolescence. Equally, the manner in which individuals respond to adolescent prob-

lems depends upon their historical circumstances. Neither working-
nor middle-class youth cultures are wholly reducible to the turmoil of
teenage status transitions.

At the time, the media were laden with some of the blame for the
1960s student unrest, even as television was accused, following the
1981 street riots, of offering agitators the incentive of an international
audience, and supplying potential trouble-makers with an instant flow
of information on where to locate the action. The media were accused
of provoking 'copycat riots' by publicising and glamorising an exciting spare-time activity. In 1981 the broadcasting authorities quickly
commissioned research which acquitted the media of some charges
(Tumber, 1982). It showed that few young people watched the relevant television news programmes, that the majority learnt about
disturbances in which they were involved through informal
grapevines, and that film cameras were not sought but avoided and
sometimes attacked by persons with no wish to assist the police in
tracing their identities. The 1960s' student militants were less reluctant
to appear on screen. And in both cases, even if they did not engineer
specific disturbances, the media must have played a role, if only by
broadcasting the possibility of sitting-in, then of rioting successfully.

Modelling or imitation must be part of the reason why riots spread
from city to city within days, and how, in the 1960s, unrest spread
from campus to campus throughout the Western and Third Worlds.
The media publicised a new student tactic, the sit-in, which, for a
time, the authorities were unable to counter successfully. But it was
never possible to accuse the media of actually provoking unrest.
Copycats usually possess some predisposition. In 1981 the rioters'
main grievances, which they criticised the media for suppressing,
were towards the police. Why were the 1960s' students predisposed to
sit-in?

Some student discontents concerned higher education itself. They
complained about uninspiring teachers and courses, and expressed
resentment when processed as if they were neither more nor less than
digits on computer tapes. Commentators noted that small colleges
remained on the periphery of the unrest, and suggested that other
institutions might have grown too large and impersonal. Sit-ins,
demos and communes can be millennia for the otherwise lonely,
uprooted and socially isolated (Musgrove, 1974). The students'
demands included university reform; of teaching, courses and management bodies. Some protests were sparked by college authorities,
like the occupation of the London School of Economics in 1967
following the controversial appointment of a new principal (Blackstone et al., 1970). But the students made it plain that their discontents
were not wholly domestic, and researchers confirmed that organ-

isational variables could not account for the entire wave of protest
(Salter, 1973). Students who occupied administrative blocks and disrupted lectures were sometimes using domestic grievances to proclaim a commitment to wider social and political objectives.

The Counter-Culture

By the early 1970s, most writers agreed that student radicals were
inspired by counter-cultural values whose appeal, some believed,
signalled the imminent birth of a post-industrial society. In the United
States, Charles Reich (1972) described how industrialism had been
built on individualistic values. Then came the era of large corporations
and other-directed organisation men who adapted to bureaucratic
systems. According to Reich, a new type of consciousness, valuing
community and self-expression, was being nurtured in the student
movements, and was destined, eventually, to reshape Western civilisation. The 1960s was a decade of disillusion. Poverty was rediscovered in the heart of the affluent societies. It became evident that
state welfare provisions were making little impact upon the depth of
inequalities. Educational opportunities were as unequal as ever. The
black minorities of the United States remained subordinate. The state
machine began to draft youth for war instead of delivering peace and
prosperity. Was it surprising that students began challenging instead
of nestling into 'the system'?

The 'new radicals' were not demanding a greater share or more of
the rewards their societies offered. Many were repelled, not attracted,
by middle-class careers in dull bureaucracies, rewarded by salaries
enabling them to live in little boxes in respectable suburbs. Their
radicalism was a retreat, not a struggle into the rat race. They were no
longer prepared to trade their freedom, to conform at work and in
education, in exchange for 'commodities'. In 1974 Musgrove observed that,

> Ten years ago the young were fighting to get in: today they are
> often fighting to get out. The privileged rather than the deprived
> are at the centre of the new youth problem.

Musgrove also noted that youthful dissent had ceased to be a purely
teenage phenomenon and was spreading, by way of ex-students and
'permanent' students, into the young adult age-groups.

Roszak (1970) popularised the idea of student radicals leading a
counter-cultural movement, broadcasting values that would undermine the major institutions of industrial capitalism. He analysed the
students' opposition to 'technocracy'. They mistrusted technology
itself, in so far as it enslaved uncomprehending workers, students and

other citizens. They were opposed to all bureaucracies – military, industrial and educational. They wanted to 'participate', and release not only their own lives but their societies from traditions, élites, experts, officials and manipulative institutions. The struggles for civil rights and sexual freedom, against the American war machine and poverty, for meaningful work and relevant curricula, and for the right to enjoy consciousness-raising drugs and psychedelic music, all fed on one another. It was argued that these causes expressed together the new consciousness which was committed to improving the quality of life, personal experiences and interpersonal relationships – enhancing life-styles rather than the standards of living that had preoccupied industrial man.

The student movements in the United States rose with the civil-rights campaigns of the early 1960s, spread to embrace additional issues and found receptive audiences throughout the Western world. By the end of the decade, student unrest was a worldwide issue. In May 1968 the survival of the French government was threatened by student-led demonstrations in Paris. Disrupted lectures and occupied college buildings became daily news stories – apparently standard features of university life. Students began to solve their accommodation problems in high-rent, overcrowded cities by pioneering squats and communes. Mills's (1973) study of London commune dwellers confirmed their membership of the international counter-culture; they favoured spontaneity, doing things for their own sake and living for play rather than work.

What has happened to this counter-culture since the 1960s? It has become apparent that the analyses of early supporters and detractors committed major errors. First, its enthusiastic rapporteurs exaggerated the counter-culture's influence. By the mid 1970s it was apparent, contrary to Reich's prophecy of a 'greening of America', that counter-cultural values were not overwhelming Western civilisation, or even the younger generation. Appearances can deceive. Amid the unrest, student and rebel became virtually synonymous in media discourse, but not a single major sit-in or demonstration, in any country, involved the majority of the local student population, and this includes the Paris of 1968. At the London School of Economics in 1967, only 36 per cent of registered students sat-in, and no more than 18 per cent stayed in the school over one or more nights (Blackstone et al., 1970). Musgrove's (1974) British research found that two out of three male students and five out of six female students were not even sympathetic to the counter-culture. Students reading science, technology and other vocational courses – the 'silent majority' – remained overwhelmingly conservative, and inactive.

Secondly, it was hypothesised, when dissent flared, that students from working-class and/or overseas backgrounds might have imported alien philosophies, drugs and ungentlemanly conduct. One instant diagnosis of campus turmoil in Britain blamed rapid university expansion, during which, it was claimed, colleges had ceased to discriminate and had recruited all-comers, irrespective of their loyalty to traditional academic values (Wilson, 1970). This was one version of the 'more means worse' argument. However, when researchers began to identify the radicals, it became evident that students from working-class and overseas backgrounds were not overrepresented. All student cultures – highbrow, sporting and radical – introduce upwardly mobile youth to middle-class intellectual and political genres, interpersonal and organisational skills, and thereby facilitate their ascent. Radical student politics may allow some to desert their origins without feeling that they are 'selling out'. But students from middle-class homes proved just as attracted by the 1960s counter-culture, and comprised the majority of its supporters.

Thirdly, it was assumed that these young middle-class radicals were rebelling against conservative upbringings and discarding their parents' values, whereas when researchers probed their histories, it was discovered that radical students were as likely to be reflecting as kicking against their parents' politics (Lipset and Altbach, 1967). Parents and teachers often sympathised with the students' criticisms of bourgeois decadence. Some college teachers became leaders of the student movement. Richard Flacks (1971) has reminded us that student dissent can be traced to the 1930s, and earlier. Politicised youth cultures have a long history among the middle classes. These strata have always included an intelligentsia, based in idea- and people-processing rather than bureaucratic and entrepreneurial occupations, whose members have opposed the values of the market-place and embraced a variety of liberal causes.

Radical intellectuals emphasise different issues from those of the working-class Left. The former are agitated by international relations, human rights, racial equality and the predicament of the Third World. This brand of radicalism has a distinguished history, in ideas if not action. Arts and social-science courses, whose staff mostly subscribe to liberal/democratic values, have been attracting like-minded students, then intensifying their liberalism, since the interwar years (Edelstein, 1962). The democratic and expressive ideals of the 1960s' students were not as discontinuous with previous generations' as was initially supposed. Like working-class Teddy Boys, many campus radicals have not been rejecting but rekindling and asserting inherited values with renewed vigour. The middle classes have never been homogeneous, or uniformly conservative in outlook. Of course, the radical intelligentsia has always been a middle-class minority, but so were the radical students throughout the 1960s.

Identifying actors' values and their sources has never been an entirely satisfactory explanation of campus turmoil or anything else. Values alone explain neither the tactics nor the timing. Why proclaim liberal values by occupying college buildings, and why choose the 1960s? Flacks (1971) argues that the 1960s' heirs to the long tradition of intellectual radicalism faced new class circumstances and opportunities. The postwar expansion of higher education had helped to spread radical ideas from a small minority to a sufficiently broad section of the young middle classes to form a 'critical mass', a potentially significant political force. It may or may not have been coincidental that, during the 1960s, some of the intelligentsia's favourite causes became national political issues, especially in the United States. The war in South-East Asia and the campaign for civil rights at home preoccupied the Johnson and Nixon administrations, and set the scene for radical students to share their idealism with the wider society.

Whether students' causes become public issues depends partly upon whether the wider society is interested. Since the 1960s, inflation and unemployment have become the leading political issues. Who still cares if bureaucratic careers are dull? They offer regular work and income. Even student unions have become preoccupied with the real value of grants. It also depends on the mood of the entire student body. If they were a minority, how did the radicals appear to represent students in general? Why did the majority remain silent? We shall see that other students were, and are still, nursing their own discontents. One consequence has been that minorities with the necessary confidence and vigour have sometimes been able to secure the acquiescence even of colleagues who oppose the activists' objectives.

The costs of student activism must also be weighed. During the 1970s, in Britain and the United States, the expansion of higher education halted. Job markets tightened. In some countries, graduate unemployment mounted. British students' scope for occupational choice narrowed. The real value of their grants declined. In these respects, students have been subjected to tighter discipline. Maybe this has helped to persuade them to express their discontents and ideals within bounds that the wider society recognises as leisure. When the 1960s' students dropped out, it was from graduate labour markets where it was rarely difficult to opt back in. The counter-culture has subsequently disappeared from news headlines, but not from campuses. Between eruptions this culture does not evaporate, but returns to a subterranean level.

Conservatives' Discontents
It is not only young people from radical backgrounds, reading radical subjects, seeking to change society, who have found cause for dissatis-

faction with their life-chances. Students and other young salaried workers with conventional middle-class ambitions have faced different but not necessarily lesser problems. Professional career opportunities have grown, but less rapidly than higher education. The career prospects of graduates have therefore deteriorated. Credentials have been devalued by the qualification spiral. Graduates are no longer a tiny élite, with excellent opportunities for grasping the glittering prizes of economic and political power. The majority face career ladders stretching to the middle ranks of state and private-enterprise bureaucracies, then no further – prospects that fall short of the majority's aspirations. Does it make sense for these students to defer all gratifications and dedicate themselves to a qualification scramble for rewards that many will find stifling rather than self-actualising?

Some commentators have queried the counter-cultural status of allegedly radical students' values and life-styles. They have drawn attention to those who reflect their parents' and teachers' liberalism, and noted the ease with which many 'way-out' students opt into conventional careers. Partridge (1977) has attempted to explode the myth of the student counter-culture, just as, in the 1950s, the myth of the rebellious teenager was attacked. He found that his subjects –white and middle class, pot-smoking student hippies in a southern US city – remained absolutely loyal to core American values. They believed in self-expression, and called it 'doing their own things', but how radical are these intentions? Seeking meaningful work and intrinsic job satisfactions, and taking paperwork home, fusing work and leisure, are not novel practices for professional and managerial employees. It can be argued that 'doing your own thing' simply endorses and rephrases long-standing bourgeois support for individualism.

Partridge's evidence does not require us to dismiss the counter-culture. The mistake lies in attempting to compress all students into a single type, radical or conformist. Middle-class drop-outs have been a minority, not mythical characters. However, Partridge is entitled to draw our attention to the large number of students whose aspirations remained conventional throughout the years of campus turmoil. Many have been fighting their way into the rat race. Some are struggling to hold on to life-chances they believe they have earned, but which are threatened by the devaluation of credentials and the simultaneous routinisation of salaried jobs. Cultural divisions among students are obscured by certain phrases, like leisure activities, possessing different meanings for different groups. Who is against self-expression? Students have different ideas about the futures that would amount to their 'own things'. Some seek alternative careers. Others try to resolve their discontents by rescuing, reasserting and proclaiming their continued allegiance to the quest for wealth, status and power – goals that technocratic societies have been placing beyond the reach of many highly educated young people.

Some students have been shielded from the congested entry into élite careers. Family property and connections can still guarantee young people's futures. Silver spoons are as nourishing as ever. In addition, students taking vocational courses, on trajectories with certain outcomes, may have required student cultures to offer nothing beyond opportunities to 'let off steam', to break away from the grind and sample the good life. In contrast, other minorities, in total probably amounting to the majority, have been raiding political, artistic and intellectual cultures to understand and resolve their contradictory situations.

These paragraphs are not postulating one-to-one relationships between types of contradiction and student cultures. The research that might confirm these links has yet to be undertaken, and in any case, it is doubtful whether such close correspondences await discovery. Students, not to mention the remainder of middle-class youth, are exposed to numerous combinations of contradictions. A variety of cultures lies at their disposal. The result is a bewildering mosaic of sub-cultures that defeat all attempts to generalise. Just as sport can have different meanings for black and white youth, so the same forms of 'protest' can mean different things to different groups of students. Disrupting teaching and haranguing politicians enable some students to declare their commitment to an alternative society. They allow others to express anger at being denied access to the rewards existing institutions offer. For other students, physical and intellectual skirmishes are simply opportunities to 'let off steam'. Mass movements, whether on campuses, football terraces or shop-floors, are often the work of several minorities with different, sometimes incompatible objectives.

The preceding pages have said little about leisure activities as conventionally defined, because at the moment there is not a great deal of consequence to say about students' recreations, apart from their doing a lot of most things that are normally itemised on survey checklists. However, it is doubtful whether these research instruments tap the reality of student leisure, because this sphere in their lives is less clearly demarcated than among workers in industry. In any case, this book's central argument has been that activities derive their meanings, and become explicable, only through the broader cultures which young people construct from their experiences as males and females, on different class trajectories, using whatever additional resources are at their disposal, whether supplied by families, libraries or pop industries. Students' intellectual efforts, their pursuit of health and fitness, uses of alcohol and other drugs, and summer vacations can possess different meanings, like demonstrations, depending on the actors' cultural affiliations. There is little point in carefully quantifying activities until they can be situated on equally accurate socio-cultural maps.

The evidence reviewed in this chapter has been deliberately marshalled to plot an exploratory map which distinguishes two major streams or trends, analogous to the rough/respectable division among working-class youth cultures, each the host of successive styles, that have separated middle-class youth since their cultures blossomed during the 1960s. On the one hand, conformist or subordinate cultures have staked their claims to the best of the work and leisure opportunities that society offers. On the other, counter-cultural styles have mocked and endeavoured to replace the wider society's definitions of occupational success, political talent and worthwhile recreation. Individuals' affiliations are influenced by their family origins, college courses, and by the cultural resources they sample, which depend upon the peer groups to which they become attached. Students have been the most creative exponents, but each trend has been emulated by other middle-class youth. If the evidence for these conclusions is less than convincing, the map offers at least a basis for further exploration. It indicates the types of research that are required not merely to rectify the shortage of any information, but to dissect the middle classes, analyse and explain their leisure.

Leisure, Class and Social Change
Only time and further research will seal the argument, but there are already strong indications that leisure can make a difference to entire ways of life, given the opportunities of the highly educated. Much of the evidence in these chapters could be organised to stress the extent to which adolescent leisure is shaped and pervaded by social class, ethnic and gender divisions. It could be marshalled to suggest that leisure's freedom is tightly bounded, and that adolescent dissent is ephemeral; that youth cultures remorselessly transport their participants towards and encourage them to internalise values consistent with the gender roles and class positions for which they are destined, not by their own choices, but by their biological sex, family origins, educational attainments and job markets. The problem with this interpretation is that it fails to consider *all* the evidence, fails to discriminate between different youth cultures and between the role of adolescent leisure under existing conditions and what could happen if some of these conditions were changed.

Our terms of discourse sometimes seem to limit our capacity to understand. The natural sciences have supplied a vocabulary of causation and determination. Is this language always appropriate for explaining social behaviour? In particular, can it capture all aspects of the relationship between leisure and other social roles? This book has not merely recognised, but stressed that freedom is never boundless. Uses of leisure are always limited by time and money. No one is ever free to do 'anything'. Young and older women have less time and cash for personal spending than men. Working-class families have lower incomes than middle-class households. These inequalities guarantee that women and working-class families' leisure opportunities will be relatively narrow, and the imprint of gender and social-class divisions cuts deeper than this. It goes beyond ruling out certain activities through lack of time and money.

The uses that working- and middle-class men and women make of whatever free time and money they possess, reflect gender and social-class values. Nevertheless, it distorts reality to employ a language which suggests that we are programmed by our gender roles and social-class backgrounds to use our leisure in given ways. There is evidence of programming, but young people also offer examples of a different kind of relationship between leisure and other roles. Gender and social-class positions define problems, and simultaneously open access to cultures which different groups of young people and adults can use to construct solutions. These solutions are inevitably constrained, and are always liable to be smothered, transformed and rendered innocuous by work and family pressures, plus direct ideological assaults and hidden persuasion from politicians, judges, teachers and the leisure industries.

Previous chapters have emphasised that, although many working-class teenagers use their leisure to question and challenge, and refuse to conform passively with the wider society's demands, the balance of advantage in the cultural war is heavily against them. Ethnic-minority youth have a better chance of insulating themselves from the wider society's control apparatuses. Indigenous whites have carried their pop idols, including Cliff Richard and Elvis Presley, into and beyond the child-rearing phase. Young people do not become replicas of their parents. Social structures are not immutable. Occupational roles and patterns of family life are reproduced, and also changed from generation to generation. Youth cultures are not totally ephemeral. They accelerate and sometimes influence the direction of broader changes. But working-class youth cultures have broken neither traditional gender divisions nor class relationships.

These chapters are challenging the conventional wisdom that middle-class youth sacrifice immediate freedom and gratifications for long-term rewards. They have argued that middle-class youth, students particularly, enjoy the greater freedom, and that their leisure is more diverse and innovative than that of working-class teenagers. The latter select preferred games and Saturday-night outfits. Some student cultures nurture novel value systems which are worked into total life-styles. Since the 1960s, campuses have been relatively tranquil. Student militants have disappeared from television screens and newspaper headlines. The counter-culture never led to the instant social revolution that once seemed possible.

The doubts of writers who queried whether the radicals' values were capable of hosting permanent ways of life may appear to be vindicated (Mills, 1973). But future decades may still judge the radical students of the 1960s to have been more sensitive to long-term historical changes than writers who have seized early opportunities to dismiss their 'play' as inconsequential. The political views and behaviour of radical and moderate youth become increasingly conservative as they move through adulthood towards old age, but follow-up studies of the 1930s' activists have proved that student politics can leave a lasting impression. Student cultures define the starting-points from which the rightward drift commences, and this influence can last a lifetime (Lipset and Ladd, 1971). Fendrick's (1977) study of pre-1965 student activists has shown that radical orientations are tempered, but not obliterated as former students move through adulthood.

In the short term, students' solutions to their problems are as 'magical' as working-class youth cultures. Campus counter-cultures do not change society. Resolutions carried in student unions rarely sway national governments. The career prospects of students who convince one another of their talent to debate with, and gain admission to, economic and political élites, remain as uncertain as ever. But some activists enhance their prospects. By affirming their goals and values, whether traditional or counter-cultural, students can steel themselves to compete and, sometimes, eventually succeed in their chosen spheres. Student politics can be an excellent training ground for 'strivers'. Radical students sometimes discover alternative careers as academics, writers in the underground press, in community work and politics.

Student politics today may be playing a role analogous to Methodism among the nineteenth-century working class, providing training in skills that enable some individuals to escape the circumstances that inspired their protests. Maybe the majority's solutions must remain imaginary. There is only limited room at the top. But these young people are not necessarily condemned to lifetimes of frustration. Within student cultures they can learn to invest their time, and anchor their selves in primary social relationships and leisure activities, thereby establishing life-styles which make routine careers as employees and citizens tolerable. Some 1960s' students are still wearing denim. Other aspects of the counter-culture have rippled outwards, among other middle-class youth, and upwards into adult age-groups: the ideology of sexual liberation, the rejection (by women) of conventional gender roles and the use of (mainly soft) drugs.

Student movements have not been the sole vehicles for the new middle classes' discontents. White-collar unions have increased their memberships and overcome former inhibitions about militant tactics. Middle-class electors have become volatile. Britain's Conservative Party can no longer rely on 80 per cent of all white-collar votes. The opposition parties have not been automatic beneficiaries. A host of pressure groups campaigning, among other things, for the environment and abortion, against child poverty and nuclear energy, have drawn most activists from the middle classes – presumably individuals with little confidence in any established parties representing their interests and aspirations. The 1960s' students must surely have played some part in the growth of white-collar trade unions, and in breaking Britain's political mould. Is it likely that their desire to participate and ability to be part of these developments has owed nothing to their participation in student cultures?

Once upon a time it was believed that the growth of leisure would allow workers to educate themselves, organise politically, become trade-union activists and democratise the social system. None of this has happened. Leisure time and money have been spent on *Coronation Street* and family cars. The consequences of the growth of leisure depend upon who benefits. Radical consequences are most probable when the recipients also enjoy lifetime access to the economic resources, cultural capital and capacity for political mobilisation that are necessary to reshape social structures. More free time can be a recipe for boredom when the recipients lack income, cultural and political power, like ageing citizens and large sections of the unskilled working class. Among working-class youth, leisure time and spending are recipes for a flamboyant consumerism and contra-cultures. An implication is that enabling future generations of young people and adults to derive equal benefits from a continuing growth of leisure will require a redistribution of economic, political and cultural power. Alternatively, if the present distribution of opportunities and constraints must persist, leisure provisions for young people in different strata will need different styles and objectives. If not offered by the providers, these will be imposed by the customers, as at present.

12
Leisure Services for Young People

Many present-day youth clubs cater for children. Youth leaders find the over-14s less easily led. Those seeking their former flocks have detached themselves from clubs. Some can be found in pubs, discos, cafés and amusement arcades, often still searching for a role. By the end of the 1950s the Youth Service's postwar confidence had evaporated. Criticism mounted alongside recorded delinquency and commercialised youth cultures. Many youth workers felt beleaguered in a critical society that denied them the resources to perform the tasks demanded. Some have accepted the wider community's evaluation, embarked on periodic soul-searching and drawn inspiration from their alleged weaknesses. Has there ever been a time when spokespersons were not persuading the public that young people were/are in need as never before? There used to be enduring poverty. Then the young needed protection from pornographers and other commercial persuaders. Today unemployment is the scourge. It has joined the facility-bare housing estate, where formerly affluent young workers were portrayed as 'often frustrated and bored, being media-bombarded with sex and violence, within an urban system which in many areas is bent on destroying its youth' (Munn, 1978).

Youth workers used to be convinced of a need for their services, manifest or latent. Why else were they in the business? Until the 1960s, the standard pleas were for more cash and leaders, and better premises to surround clients with sufficient glamour to attract educated, sophisticated, affluent youth (Albemarle Report, 1960). Youth leaders who have subsequently been housed in modern sports and leisure complexes are now questioning this formula. Do young people feel at ease in expensive surroundings? Do these facilities meet their desire to participate, control their environments and learn independence (Field, 1978)? Small-scale, low-cost local facilities, such as kickabout areas in parks and primary-school playgrounds, and sports halls that can be adapted for many uses, have become fashionable, particularly for reaching disadvantaged car-less groups, like children and young people (Hillman and Whalley, 1977). But many of today's youth workers are uncertain. They are seeking not premises, but formulas, or wondering whether there is any recipe for success.

This chapter explains that these youth workers are part of the recipe, and that Britain's Youth Service is not the failure that its outside critics and internal sceptics imagine. Youth work is part of a wider network of public and voluntary services catering for young people's leisure, and the entire network does not need refurnishing with new formulas or structures so much as strengthening with additional resources, injected at strategic points, where the need is greatest. A variety of public organisations are in contact with young people, all potential if not actual channels for delivering leisure opportunities. These include education, the training industry now supervised by the Manpower Services Commission, and the less tidy assortment of youth, community and leisure services. It is necessary to assess the system in its entirety. The parts cannot be fairly judged as if operating in splendid isolation. The following passages emphasise the strengths of maintaining a diverse network, and argue for preserving all existing structures, sometimes combining their facilities, skills and professional styles to create new leisure experiences and careers, particularly for those young people who often slip through existing thinly spread nets.

Greater public provision for youth at leisure is unlikely to be opposed on grounds of principle, if not cost. Young people are being eased off the labour market. The majority of 16- to 19-year-olds are now supported by social security, grants, training allowances, youth wages and parents, many of limited means, and even adolescents from prosperous families must establish some independence. Young people without homes of their own need 'environments' – places where they can relate to each other without obtrusive supervision, high admission charges, pressure to purchase expensive drinks or other commodities. They need opportunities to acquire and practise leisure interests and skills, not just to occupy existing free time, but to enhance their life-styles for the remainder of the life-span. How much the country can afford will be decided elsewhere. This chapter considers how to deliver and distribute, and explains the returns that can be expected from whatever resources are available.

The Limitations of Public Leisure Services
Many 'failings' of the youth and other public leisure services owe their appearances to unrealistic objectives, particularly measured against the services' resources. The opening chapter explained why education and the Youth Service have not featured prominently in this book's organisation: they are not major determinants of young people's leisure, which is not a point of criticism. Adolescent leisure is patterned

primarily by gender and sexual roles, and class divisions that are entrenched in the wider society. Young people spend some, but not the greater part of their leisure time and money in places and on activities promoted by 'recognised' youth workers, teachers and other leisure service staffs. Clients' uses of their provisions usually occur within broader, pre-existing patterns. This must be expected, and accepted. In a democratic society with a market economy, which permits freedom of association, no system of public leisure provision will ever be the main determinant of young people's practices. Public intervention must be judged, and its goals set within what is socially possible. Whatever the agencies, the role of public leisure services will be to nudge the patterns at strategic points, and thereby extend opportunities and enhance young people's quality of life amid wider, more powerful influences.

The histories of youth work and education are graveyards of impractical objectives. Leisure services have proved barren territory for 'missionaries' hoping to rescue and redirect young people's lives. Those seeking to conserve traditional class and gender divisions have no cause to fear youth cultures. Any who seek to change society discover how quickly youth cultures can smother their efforts. Social isolates, persistent delinquents and other young people with special problems may be 'saved', but not their entire generation. There is equally limited scope for the 'leadership qualities' that youth workers once had to profess if not possess. The staple role of leisure provision is offering environments where young people can 'do their own things'. The commercial sector has never found leadership a profitable formula.

Young people must solve their own major leisure problems because older generations simply do not store all the answers. Who claims to know the most satisfying uses of leisure, even within current opportunities? Are the nineteen hours a week tele-viewing that adults average used to the best possible effect? The majority of adult countryside trippers never venture more than a hundred yards from their motor cars. Is this the best use of the great outdoors? Which sexual norms and patterns of family life will maximise well-being during the next fifty years? Adults can provide environments and support, but young people themselves must experiment, enact new roles and sometimes shape novel life-styles. Furthermore, leisure work with young people is primarily about groups, and 'personal relationships' secondarily. Some young people seek caring and attentive adults, but the relationships of greatest concern to the majority are with each other. Commercial providers remain in business only while they respond to young people's interest in environments where they can associate in peer groups, free from obvious intrusion. Adolescent social relationships are fluid.

Clients give few opportunities for youth workers to build personal bonds that last for years.

Finally, and most important, there can be no single form of leisure provision which will voluntarily attract all young people. There is no 'right' club or centre which, once discovered and marketed, will capture and retain all 14- to 21-year-olds, or any other age-span. This is not only because young people differ in their leisure interests. Class, gender and ethnic divisions result in similar interests being incorporated within contrasting styles that are not easily mixed. The more responsive any youth clubs and workers become towards specific groups of clients, the more specialised their markets. All leisure services must be content with a limited market share, and a high turnover rate, especially among young people. The latter are age-conscious: 18-and 19-year-olds distance themselves from school-age 'children'. As in other people-processing professions, youth workers must regard it as success, not failure, when clients drift away. The secret of success is constant recruitment rather than promoting brand loyalty.

The Growth of Leisure and the Public Services

Youth workers must also recognise that the growth of leisure favours forever greater diversity of public and commercial provisions, which means a more limited role for all specialised agencies. The growth of leisure might have been expected to set the Youth Service on the crest of a wave, and to consolidate the schools' role in education for leisure. In practice, leisure's growth has undermined, or required adjustments from, 'traditional' school recreation and youth movements. Postwar youth have been offered a wide range of options and cash to indulge their tastes, and many have used this freedom to decline opportunities extended by teachers and official youth leaders. Commercial providers have no captive market, and youth clubs and teachers of sport, the arts and literature are in precisely the same position. Different youth movements, and school subjects, compete against each other in addition to commercial interests. By the 1960s Outward Bound and other adventure training schemes had learnt that young people were no longer queueing for four weeks in the countryside, but debating whether to accept offers of sponsorship (Roberts et al., 1974). Many had no desire to leave boyfriends and girlfriends, and other leisure interests.

We know how to boost enrolments in official youth movements – abolish the competition. In the USSR, the Pioneers, the Communist Party Youth Organisation catering for 9- to 16-year-olds, achieves an entirely voluntary and almost universal membership. It is virtually the only organisation offering opportunities for young people to participate in sport, hobbies and watch films. Its provisions enrich the basic school curriculum, and there is a political message, but no one pretends that political motivation wins the bulk of the membership. The Pioneers cater for young people's leisure during weekends, and at the end of the school day when many parents are still working. It is not difficult to fill Pioneers' palaces, just as the prewar British youth organisations had few recruitment problems, when rival options were virtually non-existent. Youth leaders and teachers who support political and economic pluralism should welcome not deplore the growth of competition.

The fact that young people's leisure is not tidily organised by any set of dominant institutions poses problems for researchers and writers, in addition to youth leaders. A youth and leisure text that concentrated on the role of schools and the Youth Service would miss the heart of the matter. Some young people are addicted participants in their favourite sports; other teenagers structure their leisure diaries around Football League fixtures; others become devotees of the arts; and another minority makes politics a time-consuming activity. But the majority of young people devote only a small proportion, if any, of their leisure to playing, watching sport or whatever. A typical individual's leisure is serviced by dozens of organisations. In aggregate, young people pursue a huge variety of leisure interests. There is no monolithic youth culture. Young people are divided by age, gender, ethnic group, family background, education and employment. There are some common denominators. Adults spend most leisure time at home, usually watching television. Young people have no places of their own. Hence their perpetual search for environments to create defensible space. Their varied solutions defy concise description, and the more leisure time and money young people possess, the greater the variety. It is not a sign of failure when promoters of specific interests and organisations find the majority of young people remaining unattached.

The Success of the British Youth Service

Given the wider social context, and its own limited resources, Britain's Youth Service is a success story. The youth workers' problem is often their inability to perceive the breadth of their achievements. The majority of young people in Britain use the Youth Service at some time. A government survey (Bone, 1972) has shown that while only 26 per cent of 14- to 20-year-olds belonged to recognised clubs at the time of the inquiry, 65 per cent belonged to organised groups of some description, the majority outside the officially recognised Youth Service, and 93 per cent had been 'organised' at some time or another. 'Membership' of clubs is a narrow and unrealistic measure of success. Youth workers undermine their own morale when they define their objectives in terms of recruiting and retaining members, and counting the proportion of the age-group currently using their buildings and contents (Leigh, 1971).

Voluntary youth organisations are flourishing. They have not been driven out by local-authority or commercial competition. In 1969 three-quarters of all 'memberships' were still with voluntary bodies (Youth Service Development Council, 1969). Since the pre-Albemarle doldrums, youth organisations have adjusted to the postwar world by changing their styles and target groups. Between 1965 and 1979, membership of the Church Lads Brigade fell by 10 per cent, the National Association of Boys' Clubs increased its strength by just 13 per cent, whereas from 1961 to 1979 the National Association of Youth Clubs (mainly mixed) membership rose by a massive 256 per cent. During this same period, the Scouts and Cubs grew by 5 per cent, and the Guides and Brownies by 42 per cent. These 'traditional' organisations have rediscovered a role by moving down the age range and identifying groups for whom alternative provisions have been limited, such as 7- to 13-year-old girls. Between 1960 and 1978 the Youth Hostels Association membership rose by 53 per cent (English Tourist Board, 1981). Members can now use motorised transport, and are offered less spartan accommodation than was considered virtuous by prewar hikers.

In Britain, provisions for young people's recreation have, like other leisure services, grown incrementally (Evans, 1965; Eggleston, 1976). The end-product is an untidy patchwork that offends analysts who recommend clear lines of responsibility, preferably leading to single government departments and management by objectives. But their diversity is a main strength in Britain's provisions for young people. In aggregate, the youth services draw upon the ideas and initiative of full-and part-time, paid and voluntary workers while catering for an enormous variety of tastes and types of young people within many different structures, the 'club' being just one example.

The concept of one Youth Service is probably misleading. It suggests a monolith that has never existed. The Youth Service Development Council's (1969) recommendation to abolish all age limits, while promoting different types of provision for under- and over-16s, has never been implemented by administrative fiat, but it has occurred by stealth. Britain's 'Youth Service' now includes traditional single-sexed movements with uniforms and leaders. Then there are social clubs, usually catering for boys and girls. Voluntary sports associations, particularly local football leagues, cater for enormous numbers of young people, though mainly males. Arts organisations enrol, and often make special provisions for, smaller numbers. Local-authority leisure services – swimming pools, indoor sports facilities, playing fields, libraries and meeting places – add to the panorama. There are opportunities for young people who wish to devote some of their leisure time, a few hours each week or more extended periods, to community service (Housden, 1971).

Present-day youth workers do not all operate from clubs. Many are 'detached' and work from advice and information centres, arts laboratories, sports facilities, careers offices and coffee bars, wherever their clients 'hang about' (Morse, 1965; Goetschius and Tash, 1967; Lewis *et al.*, 1974; Marchant and Smith, 1977). Clubs vary immensely in their formality. Some do not require members to 'join'. Many allow young people to create their own scenes and run the show. There are examples of skinhead groups being assisted while adapting premises for their own use (Daniel and McGuire, 1972), and disused pubs being taken over by squatters and local youth with the support of detached workers (Robins and Cohen, 1978).

There is a public-relations element in the repeated protests that the Youth Service is failing. Voluntary organisations, and public-sector workers as well, must exaggerate the depth of unmet but deserving need, and their own currently limited capacity, in the battle for 'sponsorship', as begging is now described (Roberts *et al.*, 1974, Brandon *et al.*, 1980). But the air of despondency is also a product of youth workers' fascination with unrealistic objectives. Since the 1950s there has been persistent talk of using leisure services to re-create local communities, to give young people and older residents a sense of belonging and controlling their lives (Munn, 1978; Haworth, 1979). Academics whose social networks straddle continents, and whose own favourite leisure activity is fleeing from local communities to international conferences, are sometimes reluctant to concede that working-class youth may also wish to escape from their localities. Are local communities still viable? Youth workers and other leisure professionals who adopt the rebirth of neighbourliness as a prime objective are unnecessarily increasing their risks of failure.

No single youth organisation, even one with branches in every area, can hope to attract the majority of young people. It is unrealistic for any service to hope to involve the majority of its participants for the greater part of their leisure time. From within any youth club, there will always appear a vast reservoir of local unmet need, because no one type of provision can satisfy all the interests of the entire younger generation. Different organisations play complementary roles, cater for different interests, and attract young people of different ages, from different educational, social-class and ethnic backgrounds. Commercial and voluntary provisions are complementary. Youth-club discos perform a different function than city-centre haunts. The latter's attractions include the young people venturing outside their normal territories (Robins and Cohen, 1978). This is not to say that all young people are benefiting from the best of all possible leisure provisions. The entire network of leisure provisions for young people has always been underresourced, never more so than in the 1980s, with public spending restrained, local authorities under pressure to make their adult education and recreational facilities approach break-even performances, and more young people than ever in education, unemployed and receiving training allowances. Today, as always, some groups of young people are better serviced than others. But the untidiness of the system of youth services is not responsible. The system itself is not a shambles. The combined efforts of the youth, community and leisure services, public and voluntary, some of the latter not recognised as branches of the Youth Service, reach the majority of young people, males and females, from all ethnic groups and social classes. These structures are basically sound. Youth workers and their organisations are not failing. Most defects could be remedied by injecting resources into existing structures.

Schools and Leisure
Education has been winning 'the trend' – the percentage of post-compulsory age-groups choosing to enrol – but not the battle for young people's hearts and minds, if the schools' influence on leisure is a reliable guide. Many schools have broadened their recreational curricula – tennis, squash and various sports-hall games are now jostling traditional team sports. Countryside appreciation, mountain walking and orienteering are increasingly offered, sometimes from outdoor pursuit centres. Library facilities have improved – more so than stocks of basic textbooks. Some schools boast art and drama studios. A few have youth leaders on their staffs. Educational establishments have been opening their facilities for community use, some being designed as 'community schools'. But all the relevant studies continue to report the majority of young people declining to pursue school-sponsored interests during evenings and weekends. Upon completing full-time education, the majority cease daily worship, drop team games and ignore the arts as well as the 'worthwhile' books that teachers were forever recommending.

   The birth of mass education was accompanied by visions of a church-attending, cultured nation, able to enjoy Shakespeare and the remainder of the 'heritage'. These hopes have been confounded. Reviews of research into the impact of education upon leisure confess the limited influence (Hendry, 1978), or even the difficulty, of discerning any long-term effects (Grazia, 1962). One follow-up study in north-west England found that good sports facilities and encouragement in school raised levels of extra-curricular and post-school-leaving activity among girls, but had no apparent effects among boys

(Emmett, 1971). Musgrove's (1971) argument that British schools are underpowered, unable to countervail against families, peer groups and the media, appears highly relevant in leisure. Are would-be educators for leisure waging a hopeless battle? Despite their ever more impressive facilities, many schools have now abdicated responsibility for young people's leisure interests. Teachers have abandoned the battle to influence pupils' dress, hairstyles and musical tastes. Schools have thrown their doors open to the youth culture. Discos are replacing school concerts. Trendy teachers follow students' tastes in fashion.

Schooling's impotence is not analogous to the Youth Service's alleged failure. It is fact, not malicious rumour, that formal schooling makes little short-term let alone any life-long impact on most young people's leisure. Like all other organisations and families, schools could use more money, but formal education does not share the Cinderella status of external youth services. Schooling is compulsory from the ages of 5 to 16. Teachers are in charge of children's lives for at least 15,000 hours. Furthermore, it is estimated that, in the past, 50 per cent of all public spending on sport has been channelled through education (White, 1972). While in education, young people have access to more generous public recreation provisions that when 'released' into the wider community. As explained below, this is part of the problem. Another contrast with the Youth Service is that, as we shall see, the overall structure of formal education impairs the delivery of leisure skills and interests to a large proportion of the age-group. Leisure teachers and teaching find British education a hostile environment.

We know that school recreation can be influential, not merely on out-of-school leisure, but in additional spheres. Leisure skills can be transported into other activities, and vice versa. Encouraging free, unrestricted play among young children improves their problem-solving skills in other areas, including classrooms (Barnett, 1981). Israeli children who attend Kibbutz schools, which value co-operation and egalitarianism, display these qualities during spontaneous play (Eiferman, 1970). In Britain, some pupils' leisure is greatly influenced by formal education. Chapter 7 explained how successful pupils who identify with their schools, mostly from middle-class homes that support high levels of recreational activity, tend to exploit whatever opportunities their schools offer to extend leisure interests. This is one reason why students in higher education display higher levels of recreational activity than any other section of the entire population (Hendry, 1979), then retain their lead over other adults throughout the life-cycle. The obverse side of this situation, where a minority of high-fliers reap the benefits, is that most pupils passing through Britain's selective education necessarily become failures, discharged at

16 with nowhere further to travel up the academic ladder, by which time many have learnt to protect their own leisure time and interests from the disparaging influence of school.

British education is still firmly geared to qualifications to compete for jobs, and this ethos inevitably devalues education for leisure. Sport, art and music are not allowed to distract any but the exceptionally talented (in these fields), and the academically incapable from the pursuit of credentials. Within British state education, sport has never been accorded the importance that boarding establishments and entire American communities often attach to the performances of 'their' school and college teams. However, the latter are not necessarily models to emulate: competitive sport can be a wasteful method of education for leisure. A thirst for success encourages concentration on a limited number of games, as in East Germany, and suggests that sport is only worthwhile for the talented.

Britain's present-day educational institutions were not designed to educate for leisure. They were cast in an age when scarce resources had to be concentrated on enabling a privileged or capable few to gain the qualifications to become the 'officers' who built an industrial society at home and an empire abroad. Less charitably, it might be said that still dominant educational practices date from a time when Britain's élites displayed little concern for the majority's occupational or leisure futures. Following the Industrial Revolution, Britain's educational system was reformed amid indifference or outright opposition from the educational establishment, and largely in violation of values enshrined in the most prestigious forms of education. Schooling for leisure is less alien to Western civilisation's educational ideals than twentieth-century practices. Education for leisure – indeed, education as leisure – is a time-honoured value. It has been some philosophers' leisure activity *par excellence*. Education for its own sake has been a supreme aspiration of schoolmen. Scholars have voiced long-standing doubts as to whether vocational training develops the whole person and encourages the full life (Petersen, 1975).

In the future, against the broader historical backcloth, the age of industrialisation, which required an emphasis on technical studies and encouraged a work-like approach, even when the content of education was non-vocational, may be judged an exceptional period. The greatest emphasis on technical subjects seems to occur early in the development of industrialism. Afterwards there are opportunities to reassert humanistic aims and studies. This is not because work itself becomes more humane. Entwistle (1970) has argued that in the future, and therefore for present generations in school, there need be no conflict between liberal and practical goals, education for work and leisure, since automation will eradicate boring routine jobs and employment itself and schooling in preparation can therefore become as exciting and stimulating as non-work activities.

There is not a shred of evidence of any trend towards work being organised to maximise intrinsic satisfactions rather than to minimise unit costs. If some people enjoy their work, this is an accidental by-product, not the prime purpose of business organisation. What happens as industrial societies mature is that it becomes financially possible, and maybe desirable, to offer mass not just élite education beyond what is technically essential to prepare individuals for their working lives. Hence our current problem, or opportunity: the economy has no need for young people as producers, and the young people do not genuinely need further education to render them employable. Even if governments are reluctant to bear the cost, many young people, supported by parents, will prefer to remain in education rather than withdraw to idleness and social marginality. We could elect to continue educating these young people as if they needed to amass qualifications and skills to ensure their eventual occupational success, but this use of education is no longer an economic imperative. There are alternatives, like reorganising education to reflect the growth of leisure.

Education could become less selective and competitive. Students could be encouraged to select subjects for their own sake, for the intrinsic satisfactions, whether literature, science, motor mechanics, art or sport. This would be less of a novel departure than a reassertion of traditional educational values that have survived, since before the Industrial Revolution, in privileged quarters, like universities. If more young people prolonged their education, this would help to balance the demand and supply of labour, and individuals would no longer face cut-throat competition for jobs with every CSE grade counting, maybe decisively. Orthodox leisure interests would find a natural place in this style of education. In addition, formerly minority academic subjects, like science and foreign languages, could be cultivated as mass leisure interests. If this sounds impracticable to experienced educators, maybe the relevance of their experience should be questioned. Are schools and colleges the best places for educating adolescents in an advanced industrial society? Or is school organisation inimical to learning for its own sake (Illich, 1971, 1978)? Do school walls and specialist teachers, accustomed to captive pupils, make education unnecessarily dull and divorced from real life (Goodman, 1971)?

If education is to become as geared to leisure as work, it will be as important to tailor the content to the recreational opportunities subsequently available as it was to relate courses to jobs in the previous era. One reason for the enormous drop in sports participation following school-leaving has been the absence of facilities to allow young people to retain their interests. When high-quality sports centres attached to schools are available for use by the wider community, the majority who participate at school continue to be active upon leaving (Grimshaw and Prescott-Clarke, 1978). Is this a case for attaching more leisure facilities to schools, and opening them for community use? Or is there a stronger case for building an educational function on to leisure facilities – youth clubs, arts, sports and community centres? Colin and Mog Ball (1979) have pressed the educational and vocational merits of basing the education of adolescents in community organisations. The case for community-based education for leisure is even more irresistible. There has been a (modest) trend towards appointing youth workers to school staffs, and attaching youth clubs to schools. Would it be more profitable to trade in the opposite direction, and attach educational programmes to community-based youth services?

Fortunately we do not need to answer these questions in either/or terms. Schools and colleges will survive in recognisable forms, and not only because teachers are sufficiently organised to protect their jobs. Young people will continue to seek qualifications; parents and the wider community will wish to retain child-care institutions; and it will remain necessary to accustom children to work-tasks in formal organisations. Formal education will retain a growing proportion of young people beyond the age of 16 if regimes become less selective and élitist, and if schools borrow youth-work styles and skills as well as recreation facilities. These developments will not be at the expense of work preparation: they will be exploiting our ability to offer more education than is vocationally necessary. However, it is likely that some young people will continue to leave at the earliest opportunity, and attend as spasmodically as possible in anticipation, not necessarily because they lack ability, but simply from a dislike of school. There is no reason why these young people must relinquish all opportunities to acquire work skills and qualifications. School functions can be grafted on to Youth Training Schemes, youth and community groups, and even leisure centres. Schooling can become leisurely, while other provisions for young people become educational.

Unemployment, Education and Leisure
This book is not building to a climax with an instant leisure solution to youth unemployment. The young people will not be impressed if we abolish joblessness by calling their condition leisure. Identifying the young people at risk, educating them for leisure rather than employment, then offering sports centres instead of jobs, will not work. An implication of the analysis in Chapter 9 is that it will be

difficult for official leisure services to engage, let alone solve, the young unemployed's problems. Unemployed youth's contra-cultural styles are likely to repel and resist officially promoted recreation. Existing projects designed and specifically aimed at jobless youth have not been swamped by customers. One study reports that 50 per cent of attenders become one-timers (Glyptis, 1982). A well-meaning local education authority whose further education college was invaded daily by unemployed youth seeking a sheltered environment to hang about in, designated a room for their use, whereupon the clientele disappeared. All young people enjoy creating their own space, and the young unemployed have an additional interest in 'fighting back'.

Unemployment spotlights the relevance and simultaneously increases the difficulty of delivering the leisure opportunities that working-class youth have always lacked. The wider society is unlikely to license leisure workers to support and maybe politicise out-of-work youth's contra-cultural styles, and the young unemployed are equally unlikely to co-operate in leisure projects designed to undermine their own cultures and reconcile them to their disadvantaged conditions.

There are two arguments which amount to an overpowering case against tackling youth unemployment by promoting recreation as a direct substitute for work. These do not include unemployment proving less devastating for some young people than demands for a leisure solution may imagine. Nor do they include the absence of strident grass-roots demands for leisure education and provision. Work-oriented schooling could be blinding young people destined for unemployment to their true interests. First, however, leisure simply cannot replace work. Occupations perform functions that leisure, as currently defined and serviced, is inherently incapable of fulfilling (Kelvin, 1981). Jobs structure time, then confer status and identity. Current leisure provisions cannot perform these roles. They can fill time, but cannot impose a structure upon days, weeks and years because, by definition, leisure activities are not obligatory. Also by definition, leisure activities are performed for intrinsic personal satisfactions rather than for their value to others, and cannot replace jobs as sources of equivalent esteemed identities.

Secondly, offering the young unemployed leisure skills and facilities would clearly be a second-best palliative. The social-control functions would be impossible to conceal (Basini, 1975). The real worry of many moral crusaders who hope to deliver recreational interests, skills and opportunities to out-of-work youth is that the latter's ways of structuring and using time are inconsistent with work habits, and law and order. They may well be right, but the intended beneficiaries are likely to be as impressed by education for leisure as with the now defunct secondary modern. This type of preparation for adulthood is obviously intended for other people's children. Are writers who advocate education for leisure rather than work experimenting with their own offspring? Or are the latter on academic courses that will transport them well clear of unemployment?

Leisure cannot play the role of employment, and there is no need to make it a poor substitute. The answers to joblessness are to provide occupations in employment, education and training that unemployed young people find more attractive than their existing predicaments. The case for expanding leisure provision and education stands on its own merits. When many of the jobs awaiting school-leavers are, at best, means to an end, sources of income or, worse still, disagreeable and stultifying, schools help to disable and alienate young people when education for work is the prime objective. These young people invest their selves and energies in their own youth cultures, despite the stream of evidence, from working-class youth in particular, of lacking the combinations of interests, skills and money to derive satisfaction from much of their leisure time.

It is not only unemployment that makes education for leisure a main challenge facing our comprehensive schools (Watts, 1978; Hargreaves, 1982). Targeting leisure education and provision primarily at the (potentially) young unemployed would stigmatise such schemes from their inception. All young people, not just those unable to obtain good O-levels, can now spend longer in education than is technically necessary to prepare for their working lives, and can anticipate more work-free time throughout the life-cycle than former generations. The entire process of education can become more leisurely. There is no need to cram additional school and college years with technically superfluous training, work experience or a scramble for credentials. Leisure can play a stronger role in a less competitive, non-selective comprehensive system of educational opportunities, many based outside schools, catering for all young people, some full-time, others part-time, until the age of 18 or 19, often beyond.

Leisure cannot replace, but it can complement and support work in roles that employment has never performed satisfactorily, especially for the unskilled. Most current recreations were devised following the Industrial Revolution, to be enjoyed at the end of the working day or week. Present-day leisure services and professions have grown from these foundations, offering immediate pleasures to clients and customers. It is not only young people who now possess more work-free time than during industrialism's early phases. Rather than more of the same, the best use of this time may require different types of leisure service, offering new varieties of leisure experience.

Contemporary youth and leisure workers need to be as innovative as their late-nineteenth-century predecessors. Can we develop forms

of recreation in which all individuals, not just the talented few who
become professional performers, can build careers rather than derive
instant gratifications? Such careers might offer more reliable life-span
structures than intermittent jobs. The retired, in addition to the
young, could be major beneficiaries. Can we design recreational
activities through which participants offer goods and services valued
by the wider community? Young people, like other citizens, have
human needs, and one is a need to be needed.

Modern sports are prime examples of leisure activities geared to the
rhythm of industrial life. They allow individuals to 'burn off' physical
and emotional energy, and simultaneously introduce possibilities of
character-training, at the end of the school day and working week.
School games periods usually mean sport. However, in terms of
building leisure careers, our major sports have in-built defects. Games
that require twenty-two or thirty people to gather at prearranged
times are difficult to sustain as individuals leave school, marry and
become parents. Furthermore, sports where peak performances
require peak fitness will not permit life-long improvements. Traditional arts including music, dance and drama offer better prospects for
long-term leisure careers, which could be given mass appeal if our
guardians of high culture were replaced or joined by educators, able
and willing to respond to young people's existing keen interests in
dance, music and 'acting' the latest styles. Forms of community work,
including the organisation and delivery of recreational opportunities
to their own and other age-groups, that currently engage volunteers
and some Youth Trainees, could be developed into life-long leisure
interests. This would be another example of blending skills and activities formerly compartmentalised as job substitutes, recreation and
voluntary social service.

Distributing Leisure Opportunities

This chapter is not attacking any institutions that deliver any
recreational opportunities to any young people. That would be a
perverse response to the continuing growth of work-free time.
Advanced industrial societies are still becoming increasingly prosperous, while the economic independence of certain groups, like young
people, is being undermined. The central problem facing societies
such as Britain is not production, but distribution, and an obvious
answer will be to strengthen public services for the non-working
population, maybe at the expense of that 'other welfare state' composed of mainly private provisions for persons in employment,
especially in better-paid and relatively secure jobs.

This chapter's argument is for developing the entire network of
leisure services, rather than concentrating resources on any specially

favoured agencies or programmes. The schools, youth and other leisure services, community and project-based training schemes, voluntary community work, politics, sport, countryside recreation and the traditional arts must be conserved, disseminated and sometimes blended into novel forms. As the opening chapter warned, this book has not been addressing practitioners' standard problems: how to fill youth clubs, how to defeat commercialised youth cultures or how to persuade all young people to continue sports participation after school-leaving.

The book has been rethinking and redrafting the entire youth and leisure issue, inviting all youth and leisure workers to regard themselves as specialists within a broader network of provisions, capable of modifying patterns rather than replacing other determinants of young people's leisure, unable to redeem the entire generation but capable of making substantial improvements in the leisure opportunities of specific groups. If all young people are to amass sufficient leisure interests and abilities – the cultural capital to enjoy the remainder of their leisure careers – in addition to work skills and qualifications, we will need to develop all the organisational structures that can contribute, often combining their styles and expertise. Young people as members, clients, participants, audiences and purchasers can learn from educational, leisure and other youth workers – teachers, coaches, counsellors and managers.

Many types of young people with diverse interests will be best served by an equally diverse network of leisure delivery systems, and the distribution of resources within this network must depend not on professional standing and political clout developed in previous years, but on institutions' ability to deliver, particularly to young people who are relatively disadvantaged. Instead of following other privileges, as at present, the delivery of public resources could positively discriminate in favour of young people whose recreational opportunities are otherwise limited – those from working-class backgrounds, the ethnic minorities and girls in all strata. Providers can be judged and rewarded, maybe with weighted subsidies, or even salary bonuses, not in terms of 'how many of any', but the numbers in priority groups that are attracted (Sports Council, 1982). Different organisations and staffs can be allowed to demonstrate their worth, but I suspect that voluntary organisations in the youth and community sectors will prove their ability and cost-effectiveness in engaging socially marginal groups, including ethnic-minority youth, and that organisations which market facilities, coaching and skill models will prove at least as effective as provisions which rely on self-directed young people who already know their own minds.

Even space to hang about costs money. 'More' is never 'enough', and it is impossible to place a precise figure on the required level of public spending. However, as a rough guideline, the facilities to practise sport and the arts, and the provisions for informal social intercourse, including private rooms, that are considered proper for young people in higher education, could be adopted as the norm for the age-group. Custom and practice aside, should young people's opportunities to live independently from their families, their access to independent accommodation, which widens opportunities throughout work-free time, remain dependent on becoming parents or higher-education students? Envisaging more generous support for young people at leisure does not require the construction of new, arbitrary, wishful standards. Is the current 16-plus in recreational opportunities defensible? Young people who terminate full-time education are no longer enjoying the limited affluence that was available in the 1950s and 1960s. Vested interests apart, are there any arguments against extending the opportunities and public subsidies already available for young people with educational, and usually additional advantages, to the whole generation?

Bibliography

Abbott, J. (1970), *Student Life in a Class Society* (Oxford: Pergamon).

Abrams, M. (1961), *The Teenage Consumer* (London: London Press Exchange).

Abrams, M. (1977), 'Quality of life studies', in *Leisure and the Urban Society*, ed. M. A. Smith (Manchester: Leisure Studies Association).

Abrams, M., *et al.* (1960), *Must Labour Lose?* (Harmondsworth: Penguin).

Albemarle Report (1960), *The Youth Service in England and Wales* (London: HMSO).

Anderson, N. (1967), *Work and Leisure* (London: Routledge & Kegan Paul).

Ashdown-Sharpe, P. (1972), 'The engagement pill', *Sunday Times*, 27 February.

Ball, C., and Ball, M. (1979), *Fit for Work?* (London: Writers and Readers Publishing Co-operative).

Banks, J. A. (1954), *Prosperity and Parenthood* (London: Routledge & Kegan Paul).

Barker, E. (1981), *Sect and Society*, D207, Tape 1 (Milton Keynes: Open University).

Barnett, L. A. (1981), 'Play and creativity: an investigation of preschool children', *Leisure Studies Association Quarterly, vol. 2, no. 4, pp. 5–7*.

Barthes, R. (1967), *Elements of Semiology* (London: Cape).

Basini, A. (1975), 'Education for leisure: a sociological critique', in *Work and Leisure*, ed. J. T. Haworth and M. A. Smith (London: Lepus Books).

Becker, H. S., and Carper, J. W. (1956a), 'The development of identification with an occupation', *American Journal of Sociology*, vol. 61, pp. 289–98.

Becker, H. S., and Carper, J. W. (1956b), 'The elements of identification with an occupation', *American Sociological Review*, vol. 21, pp. 341–8.

Becker, H. S., and Carper, J. W. (1957), 'Adjustments to conflicting expectations in the development of identification with an occupation', *Social Forces*, 36, pp. 51–6.

Bednarik, K. (1955), *The Young Worker of Today* (London: Faber).

Bell, C. (1968), *Middle Class Families* (London: Routledge & Kegan Paul).

Bell, C., and Healey, P. (1973), 'The family and leisure', in *Leisure and Society in Britain*, ed. M. A. Smith *et al.* (London: Allen Lane).

Bell, D. (1960), *The End of Ideology* (New York: The Free Press).

Beswick, W. A. (1976), 'The relationship of the ethnic background of secondary school boys and their participation in and attitudes towards physical activity', *Research Papers in Education*, No. 3.

Birksted, I. K. (1976), 'School performance viewed from the boys', *Sociological Review*, 24, pp. 63–77.

Blackstone, T., *et al.* (1970), *Students in Conflict: LSE in 1967* (London: Weidenfeld & Nicolson).

Blood, R. O., and Wolfe, D. M. (1960), *Husbands and Wives* (Glencoe, Ill.: The Free Press).

Blos, P. (1962), *On Adolescence* (Glencoe, Ill.: The Free Press).

Bocock, R. (1980), *Changes in Western Culture's Sexual Moralities*, D207, 1, 8 (Milton Keynes: Open University).

Bone, M. (1972), *The Youth Service and Similar Provision for Young People* (London: HMSO).

Boothby, J., Tungatt, M., Townsend, A. R., and Collins, M. F. (1981), *A Sporting Chance?*, Study 22 (London: Sports Council).

Bowles, S., and Gintis, H. (1976), *Schooling in Capitalist America* (London: Routledge & Kegan Paul).

Brake, M. (1980), *The Sociology of Youth Culture and Youth Sub-Cultures* (London: Routledge & Kegan Paul).

Brandon, D., *et al.* (1980), *The Survivors* (London: Routledge & Kegan Paul).

British Broadcasting Corporation (1978), *The People's Activities and the Use of Time* (London: BBC).

British Broadcasting Corporation Television (1974), *Children as Viewers* (London: BBC).

Brittain, C. V.(1963), 'Adolescent choices and parent–peer cross-pressures', *American Sociological Review*, vol. 28, pp. 385–91.

Broderick, C. B., and Rowe, G. P. (1968), 'A scale of preadolescent heterosexual development', *Journal of Marriage and the Family*, 30, pp. 97–101.

Butler, D., and Stokes, D. (1969), *Political Change in Britain* (London: Macmillan).

Carrington, B. (1982), 'Sport as a sidetrack', in *Class, Race and Gender in Education*, ed. L. Barton (London: Croom Helm).

Carter, M. P. (1962), *Home, School and Work* (Oxford: Pergamon).

Cashmore, E. (1979), *Rastman* (London: Allen & Unwin).

Cashmore, E. (1981), 'The black British sporting life', *New Society*, 6 August.

Casson, M. (1979), *Youth Unemployment* (London: Macmillan).

Central Advisory Council for Education (CACE) (1963), *Half Our Future*, the Newsom Report (London: HMSO).

Cherry, N. (1976), 'Persistent job-changing – is it a problem?', *Journal of Occupational Psychology*, 49, pp. 203–21.

Child, E. (1981), 'Play as a social product', *Leisure Studies Association Quarterly*, vol. 2, no. 4, pp. 2–4.

Clark, B. R. (1960), 'The cooling-out function in higher education', *American Journal of Sociology*, vol. 65, pp. 569–76.

Clarke, J. (1977), *Football Hooliganism and the Skinheads*, Occasional Paper No. 42 (Birmingham: Centre for Contemporary Cultural Studies).

Cloward, R., and Ohlin, L. E. (1960), *Delinquency and Opportunity* (Glencoe, Ill.: The Free Press).

Coalter, F. (1980), 'Leisure and ideology', *Leisure Studies Association Quarterly*, 1 (May), pp. 6–8.

Cohen, A. K. (1955), *Delinquent Boys* (London: Collier Macmillan).

Cohen, P. (1976), 'Subcultural conflicts and working class community', in *The Process of Schooling*, ed. M. Hammersley and P. Woods (London: Routledge & Kegan Paul).

Cohen, P. S. (1981), 'Sex, gender and equality', *British Journal of Sociology*, vol. 32, pp. 411–31.

Cohen, S. (1972), *Folk Devils and Moral Panics* (London: MacGibbon & Kee).

Coleman, J. S. (1961), *The Adolescent Society* (New York: The Free Press).

Colledge, M., Llewellyn, G., and Ward, V. (1977), *Young People at Work* (London: Manpower Services Commission).

Commission for Racial Equality (1978), *Looking for Work* (London: CRE).

Committee on Higher Education (1963), *Higher Education* (Robbins Report) (London: HMSO).

Conant, J. B. (1965), 'Social dynamite in our large cities', in *Schools and the Urban Crisis*, ed. A. Kerber and B. Bommarito (New York: Holt, Rinehart & Winston).

Corrigan, P. (1979), *Schooling and Smash Street Kids* (London: Macmillan).

Crane, A. R. (1958), 'Pre-adolescent gangs and the moral development of children', *British Journal of Educational Psychology*, vol. 28, pp. 201–8.

Crichton, A., James, E., and Wakeford, J. (1962), 'Youth and leisure in Cardiff', *Sociological Review*, 10, pp. 203–20.

Crowther Report (1959), *15–18*, Report of the Central Advisory Council for Education (London: HMSO).

Cunningham, H. (1980), *Leisure in the Industrial Revolution* (London: Croom Helm).

Damer, S. (1974), 'Wine Alley: the sociology of a dreadful enclosure', *Sociological Review*, vol. 22, pp. 221–48.

Daniel, S., and McGuire, P. (eds) (1972), *The Paint House* (Harmondsworth: Penguin).

Daniel, W. W., and Stilgoe, E. (1977), *Where Are They Now?* (London: Political and Economic Planning).

Davies, C. (1975), *Permissive Britain* (London: Pitman).

Davies, L. (1979), 'Deadlier than the male', in *Schools, Pupils and Deviance*, ed. L. Barton and R. Meighan (Driffield: Nafferton Books).

Deem, R. (1982a), 'Women, leisure and inequality', *Leisure Studies*, 1, pp. 29–46.

Deem, R. (1982b), 'Women's leisure: does it exist?', paper presented to British Sociological Association Conference, Manchester.

De Grazia, S. (1962), *Of Time, Work and Leisure* (New York: Twentieth Century Fund).

Derrick, E., *et al.* (1973), *School-Children and Leisure: Interim Report*, Working Paper No. 19 (Birmingham: Centre for Urban and Regional Studies, University of Birmingham).

Dolk, K., and Pink, W. (1971), 'Youth culture and the school: a replication', *British Journal of Sociology*, vol. 22, pp. 160–71.

Douglas, J. W. B. (1968), *All Our Future* (London: Peter Davies).

Douglas, J. W. B., *et al.* (1966), 'Delinquency and social class', *British Journal of Criminology*, 6, pp. 294–302.

Douvan, E. A., and Adelson, J. (1966), *The Adolescent Experience* (New York: Wiley).

Dower, M., Rapoport, R., Strelitz, A., and Kew, S. (1980), *Leisure Provision and People's Needs* (London: HMSO).

Downes, D. (1966), *The Delinquent Solution* (London: Routledge & Kegan Paul).

Downes, D. (1966), 'The gang myth', *The Listener*, 14 April.

Driver, G. (1980), 'How West Indians do better at school (especially the girls)', *New Society*, 17 January.

Dumazedier, J. (1974), *Sociology of Leisure* (Amsterdam: Elsevier).

Dunnell, K. (1979), *Family Formation 1976* (London: Office of Population, Censuses and Surveys, HMSO).

Dunning, E. G., *et al.* (1982), 'The social roots of football hooligan violence', *Leisure Studies*, 1, pp. 139–56.

Dunphy, D. C. (1963), 'Social structure of urban adolescent peer groups', *Sociometry*, vol. 26, pp. 230–46.

Edelstein, A. S. (1962), 'Since Bennington: evidence of change in student political behaviour', *Public Opinion Quarterly*, vol. 26, pp. 564–77.

Edgell, S. (1980), *Middle-Class Couples* (London: Allen & Unwin).

Edwards, H. (1973a), *Sociology of Sport* (St Louis:Mosby).

Edwards, H. (1973b, 'The black athlete: twentieth century gladiators for white America', *Psychology Today*, November.

Eggleston, J. (1976), *Adolescence and Community* (London: Edward Arnold).

Eggleston, J. (1979), 'The implications of school-to-work programmes for the development of vocational identities', Organisation for Economic Co-operation and Development, Paris, mimeo.

Eiferman, R. R. (1970), 'Co-operativeness and egalitarianism in Kibbutz children's games', *Human Relations*, vol. 23, pp. 579–87.

Eisenstadt, S. N. (1956), *From Generation to Generation* (Chicago: The Free Press).

Elder, G. H. (1974), *Children of the Great Depression* (Chicago: University of Chicago Press).

Elias, N., and Scotson, J. L. (1965), *The Established and the Outsiders* (London: Cass).

Elkin, F., and Westley, W. A. (1955), 'The myth of the adolescent culture', *American Sociological Review*, vol. 20, pp. 680–4.

Elkin, F., and Westley, W. A. (1967), 'Protective environment and adolescent socialisation', in *Middle Class Delinquency*, ed. E. W. Vaz (New York: Harper & Row).

Emmett, I. (1971), *Youth and Leisure in an Urban Sprawl* (Manchester: Manchester University Press).

English Tourist Board (1981), *Aspects of Leisure and Holiday Tourism* (London: ETB).

Entwistle, H. (1970), *Education, Work and Leisure* (London: Routledge & Kegan Paul).

Eppel, E. M., and Eppel, M. (1966), *Adolescents and Morality* (London: Routledge & Kegan Paul).

European Economic Commission (1979), *Chomage et recherche d'un emploi: attitudes et opinions des publics européens* (Brussels: EEC).

Evans, T. D. (1979), 'Creativity, sex-role socialisation and pupil–teacher interaction in early schooling', *Sociological Review*, 27, pp. 139–55.

Evans, W. M. (1965), *Young People in Society* (Oxford: Blackwell).

Eysenck, J. J., and Nias, D. K. B. (1978), *Sex, Violence and the Media* (London: Temple Smith).

Fendrick, J. M. (1977), 'Keeping the faith or pursuing the good life', *American Sociological Review*, vol. 42, pp. 144–57.

Feuer, L. S. (1969), *The Conflict of Generations* (London: Heinemann).

Field, D. (1978), 'Leisure provision by local authorities in areas of urban deprivation', in *Social and Economic Costs and Benefits of Leisure*, ed. M. A. Talbot and R. W. Vickerman (Leeds: Leisure Studies Association).

Firth, R. (1951), *Elements of Social Organisation* (London: Routledge & Kegan Paul).

Firth, R., Hubert, J., and Forge, A. (1970), *Families and their Relatives* (London: Routledge & Kegan Paul).

Flacks, R. (1971), *Youth and Social Change* (Chicago: Markham Press).

Fletcher, C. (1966), 'Beat and gangs on Merseyside', in *Youth in New Society*, ed. T. Raison (London: Hart-Davis).

Fogelman, K. (ed.) (1976), *Britain's Sixteen Year Olds* (London: National Children's Bureau).

Fowler, B., Littlewood, B., and Madigan, R. (1977), 'Immigrant school-leavers and the search for work', *Sociology*, 11, pp. 65–85.

Friedmann, G. (1961), *The Anatomy of Work* (London: Heinemann).

Friedenberg, E. Z. (1963), *Coming of Age in America* (New York: Vintage Books).

Frith, S. (1978), *The Sociology of Rock* (London: Constable).

Fuller, M. (1980), 'Black girls in a London comprehensive school', in *Schooling for Women's Work*, ed. R. Deem (London: Routledge & Kegan Paul).

Fyvel, T. R. (1963), *The Insecure Offenders* (Harmondsworth: Penguin).

Gagnon, J. H., and Simon, W. (1974), *Sexual Conduct* (London: Hutchinson).

Gallop, G., and Dolan, J. (1981), 'Perspectives on the participation in sporting recreation amongst ethnic minority youngsters', *Physical Education Review*, vol. 4, no. 1, pp. 61–4.

Gardner, J. (1966), 'The student reader', *New Society*, 14 April.

Garrison, L. (1979), *Black Youth, Rastafarianism and the Identity Crisis in Britain* (London: Acer Project).

Gaskell, G., and Smith, P. (1981), 'Alienated black youth: an investigation of conventional wisdom explanations', *New Community*, 9, pp. 182–93.

Gershuny, J. I., and Thomas, G. S. (1980), *Changing Patterns of Time Use: UK Activity Patterns in 1961 and 1975* (Falmer: University of Sussex, Science Policy Research Unit).

Gill, O. (1977), *Luke Street* (London: Macmillan).

Gittins, D. (1982), *Fair Sex* (London: Hutchinson).

Glasser, R. (1970), *Leisure: Penalty or Prize* (London: Macmillan).

Glyptis, S. (1982), 'Unemployment, sport and recreation: issues and initiatives in two midland cities', paper presented to Leisure Studies Association Conference, London.

Goetschius, G., and Tash, M. J. (1967), *Working with Unattached Youth* (London: Routledge & Kegan Paul).

Goldthorpe, J. H., Lockwood, D., Bechhofer, F., and Platt, J. (1969), *The Affluent Worker in the Class Structure* (Cambridge: Cambridge University Press).

Goldthorpe, J. H., Llewellyn, C., and Payne, C. (1980), *Social Mobility and Class Structure in Modern Britain* (Oxford: Clarendon Press).

Goodman, P. (1971), *Compulsory Miseducation* (Harmondsworth: Penguin).

Gorer, G. (1971), *Sex and Marriage in England Today* (London: Nelson).

Gregory, S. (1982), 'Women among others: another view', *Leisure Studies*, 1, pp. 47–52.

Grimshaw, P. N., and Prescott-Clarke, P. (1978), *Sport, School and the Community*, Research Working Paper No. 9 (London: Sports Council).

Gupta, Y. P. (1977), 'The educational and vocational aspirations of Asian immigrant and English school-leavers', *British Journal of Sociology*, 28, pp. 185–98.

Hall, G. S. (1916), *Adolescence* (New York: Appelton).

Hall, S., and Jefferson, T. (eds) (1976), *Resistance Through Rituals* (London: Hutchinson).

Hall, S., *et al.* (1978), *Policing the Crisis* (London: Macmillan).

Hall, S., *et al.* (1979), *Fads and Fashions* (London: Social Science Research Council/Sports Council).

Halsey, A. H., Heath, A. F., and Ridge, J. M. (1980), *Origins and Destinations* (Oxford: Clarendon Press).

Hamblett, C., and Deverson, J., (1964), *Generation X* (London: Tandem Books).

Hargreaves, D. (1967), *Social Relations in a Secondary School* (London: Routledge & Kegan Paul).

Hargreaves, D. H. (1982), *The Challenge for the Comprehensive School* (London: Routledge & Kegan Paul).

Harker, D. (1978), *One for the Money* (London: Hutchinson).

Haworth, J. T. (ed.) (1979), *Community Involvement and Leisure* (London: Lepus Books).

Hebdige, D. (1979), *Sub-Culture: The Meaning of Style* (London: Methuen).

Hechinger, G., and Hechinger, F. M. (1964), *Teenage Tyranny* (London: Duckworth).

Henderson, J. (1980), 'Leisure and social discipline', *Leisure Studies Association Quarterly*, 1 (May), pp. 9–13.

Hendry, L. B. (1978), *School, Sport and Leisure* (London: Lepus Books).

Hendry, L. B. (1979), *Adolescence and Leisure* (London: Social Science Research Council/Sports Council).

Hillman, M., and Whalley, A. (1977), *Fair Play for All* (London: Political and Economic Planning).

Himmelweit, H. T., Oppenheim, A. N., and Vince, P. (1958), *Television and the Child* (London: Oxford University Press).

Hiro, D. (1971), *Black British, White British* (London: Eyre & Spottiswoode).

Hite, S. (1977), *The Hite Report* (London: Talmy Franklin).

Hobson, D. (1979), 'Working class women, the family and leisure', in *Leisure and Family Diversity*, ed. Z. Strelitz (London: Leisure Studies Association).

Hoggart, R. (1957), *The Uses of Literacy* (London: Chatto & Windus).

Hopper, E., and Osborn, M. (1975), *Adult Students* (London: Frances Pinter).

Hornsby-Smith, M., and Lee, R. (1979), *Survey of Roman Catholic Attitudes* (Guildford: University of Surrey).

Housden, R. (1971), 'Youth's model force', *New Society*, 19 August.

Howkins, A., and Lowerson, J. (1979), *Trends in Leisure: 1919–1939* (London: Social Science Research Council/Sports Council).

Humphrey, R. E. (1978), *Children of Fantasy* (New York: Wiley).

Humphries, S. (1982), *Hooligans or Rebels?* (Oxford: Blackwell).

Illich, I. (1971), *Deschooling Society* (London: Calder & Boyars).

Illich, I. (1978), *The Right to Useful Unemployment* (London: Marion Boyars).

Ineichen, B. (1972), 'Home ownership and manual workers' life-styles', *Sociological Review*, vol. 20, pp. 391–412.

Ineichen, B. (1975), 'Teenage brides', *New Society*, 7 August.

Ineichen, B. (1981), 'The housing decisions of young people', *British Journal of Sociology*, vol. 32, pp. 252–8.

Ingham, R. (ed.) (1978), *Football Hood: The Wider Context* (London: Inter-Action Inprint).

Jahoda, M. (1979), 'The psychological meanings of unemployment', *New Society*, 6 September.

Jephcott, P. (1955), *Some Young People* (London: Allen & Unwin).

Jephcott, P. (1967), *Time of One's Own* (London: Oliver & Boyd).

Kandel, D. B., and Lesser, G. S. (1972), *Youth in Two Worlds* (San Francisco: Jossey-Bass).

Kaplan, M. (1975), *Leisure: Theory and Policy* (New York: Wiley).

Kelly, J. R. (1978), 'Situational and social factors in leisure decisions', *Pacific Sociological Review*, vol. 21, pp. 317–30.

Kelvin, P. (1981), 'Work as a source of identity: the implications of unemployment', *British Journal of Guidance and Counselling*, 9, pp. 2–11.

Keniston, K. (1972), *Youth and Dissent* (New York: Harcourt, Brace, Jovanovitch).

Kew, S. (1979), *Ethnic Groups and Leisure* (London: Social Science Research Council/Sports Council).

Kitwood, S. (1980), *Disclosures to a Stranger* (London: Routledge & Kegan Paul).

Klein, J. (1964), *Samples from English Cultures*, Vol. II (London: Routledge & Kegan Paul).

Lafitte, F. (1972), 'Abortion in Britain today', *New Society*, 14 December.

Larson, R. F., and Leslie, G. R. (1968), 'Prestige influences in serious dating relationships of university students', *Social Forces*, 47, pp. 195–202.

Latey Report (1967), *Report of the Committee on the Age of Majority*, Cmnd 3343 (London: HMSO).

Leigh, J. (1971), *Young People and Leisure* (London: Routledge & Kegan Paul).

Leonard, D. (1980), *Sex and Generation* (London: Tavistock).

Leslie, G. R. (1967), *The Family in Social Context* (New York: Oxford University Press).

Lewis, B., Chisnall, A., and Hall, A. (1974), *Unattached Youth* (London: Blond & Briggs).

Lewis, J. D., and Weigert, A. J. (1981), 'The structures and meanings of social time', *Social Forces*, no. 60, pp. 432–62.

Linder, S. (1970), *The Harried Leisure Class* (New York: Columbia University Press).

Lipset, S. M., and Altbach, P. G. (1967), 'Student politics and higher education in the United States', in *Student Politics*, ed. S. M. Lipset (New York: Basic Books).

Lipset, S. M., and Ladd, E. C. (1971), 'College generations and their politics', *New Society*, 7 October.

McFarland, R. A., and Moore, R. C. (1961), 'Youth and the automobile', in *Values and Ideals of American Youth*, ed. E. Ginzberg (New York: Columbia University Press).

McRobbie, A., and Garber, J. (1976), 'Girls and subcultures', in *Resistance Through Rituals*, ed. S. Hall and T. Jefferson (London: Hutchinson).

Makeham, P. (1980), *Youth Unemployment*, Research Paper No. 11 (London: Department of Employment).

Manpower Services Commission (1977), *Young People and Work* (London: MSC).

Marchant, H., and Smith, H. M. (1977), *Adolescent Girls at Risk* (Oxford: Pergamon).

Markall, G. (1979), 'Young workers and the crisis in employment', William Temple Foundation, Manchester, mimeo.

Marsh, P., et al. (1978a), *The Rules of Disorder* (London: Routledge & Kegan Paul).

Marsh, P., et al. (1978b), *Aggro: The Illusion of Violence* (London: Dent).

Mays, J. B. (1965), *The Young Pretenders* (London: Michael Joseph).

Mead, M. (1935), *Sex and Temperament in Three Primitive Societies* (London: Routledge & Kegan Paul).

Mead, M. (1962), *Male and Female* (Harmondsworth: Penguin).

Melody, W. (1973), *Children's TV* (New Haven, Conn.: Yale University Press).

Merton, R. K. (1938), 'Social structure and anomie', *American Sociological Review*, vol. 3, pp. 672–82.

Merton, R. K., Reader, G. G., and Kendall, P. L. (eds) (1957), *The Student Physician* (Cambridge, Mass.: Harvard University Press).

Michaelson, M. (1979), 'The moral dimension of leisure', in *Leisure and Family Diversity*, ed. Z. Strelitz (London: Leisure Studies Association).

Miller, D. (1969), *The Age Between* (London: Cornmarket/Hutchinson).

Mills, R. (1973), *Young Outsiders* (London: Routledge & Kegan Paul).

Millward, N. (1968), 'Family status and behaviour at work', *Sociological Review*, 16, pp. 149–64.

Morley-Bunker, N. (1982), 'Preceptions of unemployment', paper presented to British Psychological Society, Sussex.

Morse, M. (1965), *The Unattached* (Harmondsworth: Penguin).

Mungham, G., and Pearson, G. (eds) (1976), *Working Class Youth Culture* (London: Routledge & Kegan Paul).

Munn, J. M. (1978), 'Relationships of recreation provision and delinquency', in *Social and Economic Costs and Benefits of Leisure*, ed. M. A. Talbot and R. W. Vickerman (Leeds: Leisure Studies Association).

Murdock, G. (1975), 'Education, culture and the myth of classlessness', in *Work and Leisure*, ed. J. T. Haworth and M. A. Smith (London: Lepus Books).

Murdock, G. (1977), 'Class stratification and cultural consumption', in *Leisure and the Urban Society*, ed. M. A. Smith (Manchester: Leisure Studies Association).

Musgrove, F. (1963), *The Migratory Elite* (London: Heinemann).

Musgrove, F. (1964), *Youth and the Social Order* (London: Routledge & Kegan Paul).

Musgrove, F. (1971), *Patterns of Power and Authority in English Education* (London: Methuen).

Musgrove, F. (1974), *Ecstasy and Holiness* (London: Methuen).

Neulinger, J. (1982), 'Leisure lack and the quality of life', *Leisure Studies*, 1, pp. 53–63.

Newson, J., and Newson, E. (1963), *Infant Care in an Urban Community* (London: Allen & Unwin).

Newson, J., and Newson, E. (1968), *Four Years Old in an Urban Community* (London: Allen & Unwin).

Newson, J., and Newson, E. (1976), *Seven Years On in the Home Environment* (London: Allen & Unwin).

Noble, G. (1975), *Children in Front of Small Screen* (London: Constable).

Norris, G. M. (1978), 'Unemployment, subemployment and personal characteristics', *Sociological Review*, 26, pp. 89–108, 327–47.

O'Connor, J. (1978), *The Young Drinkers* (London: Tavistock).

Oakley, A. (1972), *Sex, Gender and Society* (London: Temple Smith).

Oakley, A. (1981), *Subject Women* (Oxford: Martin Robertson).

Open University (1980), *Changes in Western Culture's Sexual Moralities*, D207, study section 8 (Milton Keynes: Open University).

Organisation for Economic Co-operation and Development (1980), *Youth Unemployment: The Causes and Consequences* (Paris: OECD).

Pahl, R. E. (1978), 'Living without a job: how school-leavers see the future', *New Society*, 2 November.

Pahl, R. E., and Wallace, C. (1980), *17–19 and Unemployed on the Isle of Sheppey* (Canterbury: University of Kent).

Paloczi-Horvath, G. (1971), *Youth up in Arms* (London: Weidenfeld & Nicolson).

Parker, H. (1974), *View from the Boys* (Newton Abbot: David & Charles).

Parker, S. (1971), *The Future of Work and Leisure* (London: MacGibbon & Kee).

Parkin, F. (1968), *Middle Class Radicalism* (Manchester: Manchester University Press).

Parry, S. J. (1980), 'Leisure and unemployment in an industrial society', B.Ed. dissertation, St Katherine's College, Liverpool.

Parsons, T. (1954), 'Age and sex in the social structure of the United States', in *Essays in Sociological Theory* (Chicago: The Free Press).

Parsons, T. (1962), 'Youth in the context of American society', *Daedalus*, vol. XCI, pp. 97–123.

Partridge, W. L. (1977), *The Hippie Ghetto* (New York: Holt, Rinehart & Winston).

Patterson, O. (1969), 'The cricket ritual in the West Indies', *New Society*, 26 June.

Petersen, A. D. C. (1975), 'Education for work and for leisure', in *Work and Leisure*, ed. J. T. Haworth and M. A. Smith (London: Lepus Books).

Phillips, D. (1973), 'Young and unemployed in a northern city', in *Men and Work in Modern Britain*, ed. D. Weir (London: Fontana).

Plant, M. (1975), *Drugtakers in an English Town* (London: Tavistock).

Popil, A. (1982), 'Background perceptions of Asian textile workers', unpublished paper, Department of Sociology, Liverpool University.

Prosser, R. (1981), 'The leisure systems of advantaged adolescents', Ph.D. thesis, University of Birmingham.

Pryce, K. (1979), *Endless Pressure* (Harmondsworth: Penguin).

Quine, W., and Quine, L. (1966), 'Boys, girls and leisure', *New Society*, 18 August.

Rapoport, R., and Rapoport, R. N. (1975), *Leisure and the Family Life-Cycle* (London: Routledge & Kegan Paul).

Reed, B. H. (1950), *Eighty Thousand Adolescents* (London: Allen & Unwin).

Rehberg, R. A., and Schafer, W. E. (1968), 'Participation in interscholastic athletics and college aspirations', *American Journal of Sociology*, vol. 73, pp. 732–40.

Reich, C. A. (1972), *The Greening of America* (Harmondsworth: Penguin).

Remmers, H. E., and Radler, D. H. (1957), *The American Teenager* (Indianapolis, Ind.: Bobbs-Merrill).

Reuter, E. B. (1937), 'The sociology of adolescence', *American Journal of Sociology*, vol. 43, pp. 414–27.

Rex, J., and Tomlinson, S. (1979), *Colonial Immigrants in a British City* (London: Routledge & Kegan Paul).

Roberts, K. (1979), *Contemporary Society and the Growth of Leisure* (London: Longman).

Roberts, K. (1981), *Leisure* (London: Longman).

Roberts, K., Duggan, J., and Noble, M. (1981), *Unregistered Youth Unemployment and Outreach Careers Work, Part I, Non-Registration*, Research Paper No. 31 (London: Department of Employment).

Roberts, K., Noble, M., and Duggan, J. (1982a), *Unregistered Youth Unemployment and Outreach Careers Work*, Research Paper No. 32 (London: Department of Employment).

Roberts, K., Noble, M., and Duggan, J. (1982b), 'Youth unemployment: an old problem or a new life-style?', *Leisure Studies*, 1, pp. 171–82.

Roberts, K., White, G. E., and Parker, H. J. (1974), *The Character Training Industry* (Newton Abbot: David & Charles).

Robins, D., and Cohen, P. (1978), *Knuckle Sandwich* (Harmondsworth: Penguin).

Rock, P., and Cohen, S. (1970), 'The teddy boy', in *The Age of Affluence, 1951–61*, ed. V. Bognador and V. Skodalsky (London: Macmillan).

Rosenberg, M. (1965), *Society and the Adolescent Self-Image* (Princeton, NJ: Princeton University Press).

Roszak, T. (1970), *The Making of a Counter-Culture* (London: Faber).

Rowntree, G., and Pierce, R. M. (1961), 'Birth control in Britain', *Population Studies*, 15, pp. 3–31.

Salter, B. (1973), 'Explanations of student unrest: an exercise in devaluation', *British Journal of Sociology*, vol. 24, pp. 329–40.

Sargeant, A. J. (1972), 'Participation of West Indian boys in English school sports teams', *Education Research*, 14, pp. 225–30.

Sawdon, A., and Taylor, D. (1980), *Youth Unemployment* (London: Youthaid).

Schofield, M. (1965), *The Sexual Behaviour of Young People* (London: Longman).

Schofield, M. (1973), *The Sexual Behaviour of Young Adults* (London: Allen Lane).

Schools Council (1968), *Young School-Leavers*, Vol. I (London: HMSO).

Schwartz, G., and Merten, D. (1967), 'The language of adolescence', *American Journal of Sociology*, vol. 72, pp. 453–68.

Seeley, J. R., Sim, R. A., and Loosley, E. W. (1956), *Crestwood Heights* (London: Constable).

Sennett, R. (1977), 'Destructive gemeinschaft', in *Beyond the Crisis*, ed. N. Birnbaum (New York: Oxford University Press).

Sharpe, S. (1977), *Just Like a Girl* (Harmondsworth: Penguin).

Simmons, R. G., and Rosenberg, F. (1973), 'Disturbance in the self-image at adolescence', *American Sociological Review*, vol. 78, pp. 553–68.

Sinfield, A. (1981), *What Unemployment Means* (Oxford: Martin Robertson).

Smith, C. S., Farrant, M. R., and Marchant, H. J. (1972), *The Wincroft Youth Project* (London: Tavistock).

Smith, D. J. (1977), *Racial Disadvantage in Britain* (Harmondsworth: Penguin).

Smith, D. M. (1981), 'New movements in the sociology of youth: a critique', *British Journal of Sociology*, vol. 32, pp. 239–51.

Smith, E. A. (1962), *American Youth Culture* (New York: The Free Press).

Smith, M. A. (1982), *Brewing Industry Policy: The Public House and Alcohol Consumption Patterns in the UK* (Salford: University of Salford, Centre for Leisure Studies).

Social Science Research Council/Sports Council (1978a), *Report of the Joint Working Party on Recreation Research* (London: SSRC/SC).

Social Science Research Council/Sports Council (1978b), *Public Disorder at Sporting Events* (London: SSRC/SC).

Speck, R. V. (1972), *The New Families* (London: Tavistock).

Sports Council (1982), *Sport in the Community: The Next Ten Years* (London: SC).

Stanley, L. (1977), 'Sex, gender and the sociology of leisure', in *Leisure and the Urban Society*, ed. M. A. Smith (Manchester: Leisure Studies Association).

Start, K. B. (1966), 'Substitution of games performance for academic achievement as a means of achieving status among secondary school children,' *British Journal of Sociology*, vol. 17, pp. 300–5.

Stone, M. (1981), *The Education of the Black Child in Britain* (London: Fontana).

Sugarman, B. (1967), 'Involvement in youth culture, academic achievement and conformity in school', *British Journal of Sociology*, vol. 18, pp. 151–64.

Swann Report (1981), Committee of Inquiry into the Education of Children from Ethnic Minority Groups, *West Indian Children in our Schools*, Cmnd 8273 (London: HMSO).

Talbot, M. (1979), *Women and Leisure* (London: Social Science Research Council/Sports Council).

Taylor, I. R. (1971), 'Soccer consciousness and soccer hooliganism', in *Images of Deviance*, ed. S. Cohen (Harmondsworth: Penguin).

Thomas, G., and Shannon, C. Z. (1982), 'Technology and household labour: are times a-changing?', paper presented to British Sociological Association conference, Manchester.

Thompson, E. P. (1967), 'Time, work discipline and industrial capitalism', *Past and Present*, 38, p. 60.

Thornes, B., and Collard, J. (1979), *Who Divorces?* (London: Routledge & Kegan Paul).

Toffler, A. (1970), *Future Shock* (New York: Random House).

Tumber, H. (1982), *A Report on the Television Coverage of the July 1981 Riots in Inner-City Areas* (London: Broadcasting Research Unit).

Turner, G. (1963), *The Car-Makers* (London: Eyre & Spottiswoode).

Turner, R. H. (1960), 'Sponsored and contest mobility in the school system', *American Sociological Review*, vol. 25, pp. 855–67.

Turner, R. H. (1964), *The Social Context of Ambition* (San Francisco: Chandler).

Tylor, E. B. (1871), *Primitive Culture* (London: John Murray).

Vener, A. M., and Snyder, C. A. (1966), 'The pre-school child's awareness and anticipation of adult sex-roles', *Sociometry*, 29, pp. 159–68.

Wallace, C. (1980), 'Adapting to unemployment', *Youth in Society*, 40, pp. 6–8.

Waller, W. (1937), 'The rating and dating complex', *American Sociological Review*, vol. 2, pp. 727–34.

Ward, J. (1948), *Children out of School* (London: Central Advisory Council for Education).

Watts, A. G. (1978), 'The implications of school-leaver unemployment for careers education in schools', *Journal of Curriculum Studies*, 10, pp. 233–50.

West, J. (1945), *Plainville USA* (New York: Columbia University Press).

White, D. (1972), 'Spending on sport', *New Society*, 28 December.

Wilkins, L. T. (1955), *The Adolescent in Britain* (London: Central Office of Information).

Willis, M. (1979), 'Youth unemployment and leisure opportunities', Department of Education and Science, London, mimeo.

Willis, P. (1977), *Learning to Labour* (Farnborough: Saxon House).

Willis, P. (1978), *Profane Culture* (London: Routledge & Kegan Paul).

Willmott, P. (1966), *Adolescent Boys of East London* (London: Routledge & Kegan Paul).

Wilson, B. R. (1970), *The Youth Culture and the Universities* (London: Faber).

Yablonsky, L. (1967), *The Violent Gang* (Harmondsworth: Penguin).

Young, J. (1971), *The Drugtakers* (London: MacGibbon & Kee).

Young, L. R. (1954), *Out of Wedlock* (New York: McGraw-Hill).

Young, M., and Willmott, P. (1973), *The Symmetrical Family* (London: Routledge & Kegan Paul).

Youth Service Development Council (1969), *Youth and Community Work in the 70s* (London: HMSO).

Youthaid (1979), *Study of the Transition from School to Working Life* (London: Youthaid).

Zweig, F. (1961), *The Worker in an Affluent Society* (London: Heinemann).

Index

Abbott J. 162
Abrams M. 16, 103, 106
Adelson J. 76
adventure training 179
Agnew S. 36
Albemarle Report 21, 176
alcohol 29–30
Altbach P. G. 168
Anderson N. 54
Ashdown-Sharpe P. 66

Ball C. and M. 187
Banks J. A. 63
Barker E. 82
Barnett L. A. 74, 184
Barthes R. 43
Basini A. 188
Becker H. S. 162, 163
Bednarik K. 36
Bell C. 68, 161
Bell D. 106
Beswick W. A. 153
Birksted I. K. 113
Blackstone T. 165, 167
Blood R. O. 68
Blos P. 32
Bone M. 22, 180
Boothby J. 58
Bowles S. 74
Brake M. 40, 116, 119, 158
Brandon D. 182
British Broadcasting Corporation 20, 28
Brittain C. V. 38
Broderick C. B. 85
Butler D. 34

Carper J. W. 162, 163
Carrington B. 153, 154, 155
Carter M. P. 20
Cashmore E. 153, 156
Central Advisory Council for Education 97
Cherry N. 133
Child E. 74
children's play 74–5
Clarke J. 29
Coalter F. 51

Cohen P. 17, 18, 41, 81, 90, 120, 122, 182
Cohen P. S. 71, 96
Cohen S. 27, 124
Coleman J. S. 80, 111
Collard J. 87
Colledge M. 113
community education 187
community service 182
community schools 183
Conant J. B. 143
contraception 63–4
Corrigan P. 120
courtship 82–5
Crane A. R. 76
Crichton A. 18, 20, 28
Crowther Report 18, 97
culture 5–7
Cunningham H. 47

Daniel S. 182
Daniel W. W. 133
dating 79–82
Davies C. 54
Davies L. 93
Deem R. 70, 76, 100
De Grazia S. 183
delinquency 21, 111–12, 143
Derrick E. 30
detached youth work 182
Deverson J. 22, 36
divorce 64, 87
Dolan J. 153
Dolk K. 111
Douglas, J. W. B. 16, 22, 128
Douvan E. A. 76
Dower M. 53
Downes D. 77, 114
drugs 23, 30, 170
Dumazedier J. 50
Dunnell K. 63
Dunning E. G. 29
Dunphy D. C. 83

Edelstein A. S. 163, 168
Edgell S. 70

education 93, 98–9, 108–9, 110–11,
    113–14, 131, 153–6, 158–75, 183–90
Edwards H. 153
Eggleston J. 135, 181
Eiferman R. R. 184
Eisenstadt S. N. 39
Elder G. H. 134
Elias N. 155
Elkin F. 37, 38
Emmett I. 184
English Tourist Board 181
Entwistle H. 185
Eppel E. M. and M. 40, 80
ethnic groups 2–3, 83, 145–57
Evans T. D. 92
Evans W. M. 181
Eysenck H. J. 19

fads 27
feminism 2, 68–71, 73, 99
Fendrick J. M. 174
Feuer L. S. 36
Field D. 176
Firth R. 5, 68
Flacks R. 168, 169
Fletcher C. 21
Fogelman K. 28, 30, 37, 38
football hooliganism 29, 42
Fowler B. 148
Friedenberg E. Z. 37
Friedmann G. 112
Fuller M. 155
functionalism 37–40, 72–3, 96, 105–7
Fyvel T. R. 21

Gagnon J. H. 91
Gallop G. 153
gangs 77
Garber J. 63, 81
Gardner J. 110
Garrison L. 156
Gaskell G. 148
Gender 2, 60–101, 140
Gershuny J. I. 48, 52
Gill O. 155
Gintis H. 74
Gittins D. 63
Glasser R. 54
Glyptis S. 188
Goetschius G. 182
Goldthorpe J. H. 162
Goodman P. 186
Gorer G. 66, 100
Gregory S. 52, 69
Grimshaw P. N. 187

Hall G. S. 32
Hall S. 25, 40, 116, 121, 124, 158
Halsey A. H. 13
Hamblett C. 22, 36
Hargreaves D. 111, 189
Harker D. 17
Haworth J. T. 182
Healey P. 68
Heath A. F. 13
Hebdige D. 43, 122, 150
Hechinger G. and F. M. 18, 37
Hegemony 122
Henderson J. 51
Hendry L. B. 80, 108, 110, 161, 183, 184
Hillman M. 176
Himmelweit H. T. 20
Hiro D. 146
Hite S. 67
Hobson D. 79, 83
Hoggart R. 21
homosexuality 65–6, 91, 98
Hopper E. 162
Hornsby-Smith M. 64
Howkins A. 12
hours of work 48
Housden R. 182
housework 70
housing 85–6, 150
illegitimacy 66, 150
Illich I. 186
income 108–10, 140–1, 161
Ineichen B. 86

Jahoda M. 135
Jefferson T. 25, 42, 116
Jephcott P. 21, 78, 109

Kandel D. B. 38
Kelly J. R. 50
Kelvin P. 188
Keniston K. 25, 164
Kitwood S. 39
Klein J. 64, 85

Ladd E. C. 174
Lafitte F. 66
Latey Report 35
Lee R. 64
Leigh J. 18–21, 181
leisure centres 176
Leonard D. 66, 76, 80, 82, 83, 84, 85
Leslie G. R. 69, 82, 85
Lesser G. S. 38
Lewis B. 182

Lewis J. D. 71
Linder S. 108
Lipset S. M. 168, 174
Lowerson J. 12

McFarland R. A. 19
McGuire P. 182
McRobbie A. 63, 81
Marchant H. 182
Markall G. 136
marriage 64–5, 84–5
Marsh P. 29, 42
Marxism 40–2, 116
Mays J. B. 112
Mead M. 33
Merten D. 42
Merton R. K. 111, 163
Michaelson M. 149
Mills R. 167, 174
Moore R. C. 19
Morley-Bunker N. 142
mugging 124
Mungham G. 40, 116
Munn J. M. 176, 182
Murdock G. 121, 158
Musgrove F. 26, 36, 37, 108, 163, 165,
   166, 167, 184
music 17

Neulinger J. 47
Newson J. and E. 69, 74, 76
Nias D. K. B. 19
Noble G. 20
Noble T. 62
Norris G. M. 133

O'Connor J. 30
Oakley A. 63, 90, 91
Osborn M. 162
outward bound 179

Pahl R. E. 135
Paloczi-Horvath G. 36
Parker S. 112
Parkin F. 23
Parry S. J. 139, 141
Parsons T. 39
Partridge W. L. 170
Patterson O. 155
Pearson G. 40, 116
Peer groups 75–9, 88–9
Peterson A. D. C. 185
Phillips D. 137
Pierce R. M. 63

Pink W. 111
Plant M. 30, 123
play 46, 74–5
politics 104, 124–6, 136, 163, 164–9, 171,
   174, 175
Popil A. 150
Prescott-Clarke P. 187
Prosser R. 16, 109
Pryce K. 138, 148, 152, 157
puberty 32, 64

Quine W. and L. 81

race, see ethnic groups
racial discrimination 147–9
Radler D. H. 38, 80
Rastafarians 155–6
Rehberg R. A. 111
Reich C. A. 36, 166
Remmers H. E. 38, 80
Reuter E. B. 33, 37
Rex J. 146
Ridge J. M. 13
riots 136, 165
Roberts K. 49, 52, 56, 132, 133, 134, 138,
   143, 148, 179, 182
Robins D. 81, 90, 120, 182
Rock P. 17
Rosenberg F. 35
Rosenberg M. 75
Roszak T. 36, 166
Rowe G. P. 85
Rowntree G. 63

Salter B. 166
Sargeant A. J. 153
Schafer W. E. 111
Schofield M. 37, 39, 66, 81, 83, 107
Schools Council 40
Schwartz G. 42
Scotson J. L. 155
Seeley J. R. 77, 81, 86
semiotics 43, 122
Sennett R. 54
sex 61–71, 80–2, 90–5, 100, 140
sex education 65
Shannon C. Z. 70
Sharpe S. 92, 150
Simmons R. G. 35
Simon W. 91
Sinfield A. 135
Smith D. J. 147
Smith D. M. 40, 116, 127, 129
Smith E. A. 79, 83

Smith H. M. 182
Smith M. A. 30
Smith P. 148
Snyder C. A. 93
social mobility 162, 168
Social Science Research Council 29, 44
Soviet Union 179–80
sport 28–9, 110–11, 153–6, 183–4
Sports Council 29, 44, 191
Start K. B. 110
Stilgoe E. 133
Stokes D. 34
Stone M. 154
students 23–6, 58, 99, 105, 108, 158–75,
    184
Sugarman B. 111
Swann Report 148, 154
symmetrical families 68

Tash J. M. 182
Taylor E. 5
Taylor I. R. 29
television 19–20, 178
Thomas G. 48, 52, 70
Thompson E. P. 47, 74
Thornes B. 87
Toffler A. 34
Tomlinson S. 146
Transport 18–19
Tumber H. 165
Turner G. 106
Turner R. H. 38, 107, 162

unemployment 100, 101, 131, 144,
    187–90

Vener A. M. 93

Wallace C. 135
Waller W. 80
Ward J. 14, 108
Watts A. G. 189
West J. 33
Westley W. A. 37, 38
Whalley A. 176
White D. 184
Wigert A. J. 71
Wilkins L. T. 14
Willis M. 141
Willis P. 41, 114, 119, 120, 158
Willmott P. 18, 22, 68, 78
Wilson B. R. 23, 24, 36, 168
Wolfe D. M. 68
women's liberation 68–71, 159
work 112–13, 117, 119, 134, 137, 162–3,
    169, 185–6

Yablonsky L. 77
Young J. 123
Young M. 68
Young Workers' Scheme, 139
Youthaid 113, 136, 138
youth clubs 10, 11, 14–15, 21–2, 58–9,
    111, 176–92
Youth Service Development Council 22,
    181

Zweig F. 106